A Preacher's Guide to
Lectionary Sermon Series

VOLUME 2

A Preacher's Guide to Lectionary Sermon Series

VOLUME 2

THEMATIC PLANS FOR YEARS A, B, AND C

Compiled by Jessica Miller Kelley

WESTMINSTER
JOHN KNOX PRESS
LOUISVILLE · KENTUCKY

© 2019 Westminster John Knox Press

First edition
Published by Westminster John Knox Press
Louisville, Kentucky

19 20 21 22 23 24 25 26 27 28—10 9 8 7 6 5 4 3 2 1

Book design by Drew Stevens
Cover design by Lisa Buckley Design

Library of Congress Cataloging-in-Publication Data
Names: Kelley, Jessica Miller, editor.
Title: The preacher's guide to lectionary sermon series : thematic plans for
    Years A, B, and C / [edited by] Jessica Miller Kelley.
Description: First edition. | Louisville, Kentucky : Westminster John Knox
    Press, 2016.
Identifiers: LCCN 2015051049 (print) | LCCN 2016005048 (ebook) | ISBN
    9780664261191 (alk. paper) | ISBN 9781611646658 ()
Subjects: LCSH: Lectionary preaching.
Classification: LCC BV4235.L43 P74 2016 (print) | LCC BV4235.L43 (ebook) |
    DDC 251/.6—dc23
LC record available at http://lccn.loc.gov/2015051049

The Preacher's Guide to Lectionary Sermon Series, Volume 2
ISBN: 9780664264635 (paperback)
ISBN: 9781611649499 (ebook)

PRINTED IN THE UNITED STATES OF AMERICA

♾ The paper used in this publication meets the minimum requirements of the American National Standard for Information Sciences—Permanence of Paper for Printed Library Materials, ANSI Z39.48-1992.

Most Westminster John Knox Press books are available at special quantity discounts when purchased in bulk by corporations, organizations, and special-interest groups. For more information, please e-mail SpecialSales@wjkbooks.com.

Contents

YEAR B

Using This Resource

I've heard colleagues explain why they prefer to avoid the lectionary: people respond better to thematic preaching, sermon series on a particular topic. . . . They have to surrender the rich experience of preaching the lectionary, they argue, in order to give people what they want.

This reasoning is problematic for me, fundamentally because of the dangerous theological assumption that church is about giving people what they want. It's not. But this argument also assumes that lectionary preaching and series preaching are incompatible. And that's just not true, either.

—Amy K. Butler, in the Foreword to the first volume of
A Preacher's Guide to Lectionary Sermon Series

Some church leaders love the Revised Common Lectionary for the consistency it brings to proclamation and education across congregations and denominations. Others consider lectionary preaching boring and limiting.

Some church leaders prefer to preach in topical series, crafting sermons that explore a book of the Bible, a meaty section of Scripture, or a significant theme in Christian living, over a period of weeks or even months. Others say series preaching is hokey or contrived, and that choosing one's own texts biases a preachers toward their favorite passages.

A Preacher's Guide to Lectionary Sermon Series is designed to offer the best of both worlds with this comprehensive manual of sermon series ideas designed to frame consecutive weeks of lectionary texts into seasonal and short-term series. Taking into consideration both the liturgical calendar and the secular calendar, this resource includes plans for twenty-eight thematic sermon series using the Revised Common Lectionary, series that both celebrate holy days and seasons *and* respond to typical patterns of church attendance, maximizing visitor retention and member engagement.

Twelve experienced preachers from seven denominations—some dedicated lectionary preachers, others accustomed to topical series—accepted the creative challenge of developing these thematic series plans using the assigned readings of the lectionary. You will find among their work series exploring specific books of the Bible and significant biblical figures as well as lessons for discipleship from across the Bible's sections and genres. You may wish to use these outlines as they are, adapt them for your congregation's needs, or get inspired to design your own thematic series from the lectionary.

What's Included   Each of the twenty-eight series plans includes:

- A series overview, introducing the overall message of the series
- A chart outlining the sermon titles and focus Scriptures for each week of the series, along with a very brief description of each sermon's theme
- Tips and ideas for the series, with suggestions for worship elements, visuals, fellowship activities, and outreach efforts that enhance the congregation's engagement with the series topic
- Sermon starters for each Sunday to summarize the week's message, prompt your research and writing process, and offer sermon illustrations to enhance your preaching

In the back of this volume, you will find a calendar listing the Sundays for Years A, B, and C for three lectionary cycles, from the 2019–20 liturgical year (Year A) all the way to 2027–28 (Year C). This nine-year calendar enables you to plan your preaching schedule to make use of all the series plans this book has to offer, regardless of when you begin to use it.

While this resource respects the liturgical calendar, and the lections designed to accompany them, a few exceptions are made for floating holy days like Trinity Sunday and special days that may fall on weekdays but be observed on a Sunday (Epiphany and All Saints' Day, for example). In those cases, the assigned lections for the special day may be substituted for the regularly scheduled lections, or vice versa. You will also find that not every Sunday is included in a series. There are breaks between some series, allowing for quirks in the liturgical calendar and for weeks you may wish to have a guest preacher, special service, or other stand-alone sermon.

Making the Most of a Series   Exploring a theme or book of the Bible across several weeks (as short as three weeks and as long as eleven in this resource) gives congregants and visitors a memorable handle to latch onto from week to week. Knowing what is being preached on the following week keeps people engaged, coming back, and telling friends. Like a television show or miniseries, preaching in series can create a "don't want to miss it" desire to be there for each week of worship.

Maximize the impact of each series with the following tips:

Use consistent visuals. Even without a dedicated graphic design person in your church, you can create one image or typographic treatment for the series that can be used on your printed materials (bulletins, flyers, etc.) and digital media (website, Facebook page, or worship screen if you use one). Some of the "tips and ideas" sections of series plans include ideas for altar displays and other visual elements to enhance the worship space.

Go beyond the sermon. We all know that worship and spiritual growth do not hinge entirely on the sermon. Incorporate the theme when planning music and special moments in the service like testimonies or dramas. Plan special events at which congregants can discuss or put into practice the ideas being preached on in the series. Many "tips and ideas" sections have suggestions for such events.

Spread the word. Visitors may be more likely to give your church a try if they know an upcoming service will be addressing a topic or question they have wondered about. Promotion of the series can be done through church newsletters, posters, special mailings, and social media. The week before the series begins, send a special email about the series to all members, encouraging them to attend and asking them to forward the email to family, friends, neighbors, and coworkers.

Get your congregation excited about the opportunity to explore biblical stories and themes in depth across a number of Sundays, and watch their engagement grow.

Year A

Advent Series: Waiting Well

Five Parts: First Sunday of Advent through Fourth Sunday of Advent, plus Christmas Eve

Advent gives us a lesson in waiting—and knowing when to act.

BRUCE REYES-CHOW

Series Overview Waiting is generally something that the world does not like to do. Waiting is inconvenient and, depending on the source of the waiting, can be seen as some kind of affront to our personhood or perceived as the result of incompetence or malice. Sure, there are times when the frustration of waiting is justified and worthy of challenge. But I believe that learning to wait well, no matter the reason or the season, is a spiritual discipline that contributes to emotional health, spiritual

	Sermon Title	Focus Scripture	Theme
Advent 1	Quick, Look Busy!	Matt. 24:36–44	How do we challenge the narrative of faith being just about what we do?
Advent 2	Not All Actions Are Created Equal	Matt. 3:1–12	How do we determine what actions are worthy of God and bear good fruit in our world?
Advent 3	That's OK, I'll Wait	Matt. 11:2–11	Sometimes, waiting is wise; but sometimes we'd rather keep waiting than make a daring move.
Advent 4	Don't Drop the Baby	Matt. 1:18–25	How do we prepare for and handle what comes to us during the immediacy of waiting for an impending moment?
Christmas Eve	The Gift of Fragility	Luke 2:1–14 (15–20)	What is our calling in response to God's embodiment in such powerful fragility?

vitality, and actions that are grounded in faith. This series will look at ways in which we can wait well, challenging the negative assumptions that waiting means inaction, apathy, or a lack of passion, and moving toward waiting that is deliberate, disciplined, and just.

Tips and Ideas for This Series

The theme of "waiting" invites a number of poignant sermon illustrations. To introduce the theme, awkward worship moments always work well. You might make people wait in silence for something and name the uncomfortable reactions to waiting even for a minute or two. Later in the series, demonstrate the importance of waiting with a story about something being sent out before it is ready. I think about any kind of food that simply needs time before it is ready, such as bread and baked goods. Please avoid the possibility of a salmonella outbreak, but an undercooked cupcake would be a very simple opening illustration.

Advent 1: Quick, Look Busy!
Matthew 24:36–44

"Keep awake therefore, for you do not know on what day your Lord is coming."
(Matthew 24:42)

When I read this passage, all that pops into my head is the bumper sticker that says, "Jesus is coming. Hurry up and look busy." As if Jesus would not be able to tell that we are faking it. That said, in a society that (over)values productivity, deliverables, and always being busy, too often it is easy to see how individuals, institutions, and communities fall into the trap of measuring faithfulness by what gets checked off on the to-do list.

There is value in waiting, in being still and remaining watchful, instead of filling those awkward spaces in life with action for the sake of action—that is, busy-ness. We are reminded of this time and again during Advent, when Scriptures focus our minds on some future event. We cannot rush God's coming through any particular action.

At the same time, we cannot just let folks pretend that what we *do* has no impact on the world and God's hopes for it and for us. As today's Scripture suggests, we carry on with life—raising families and working at our jobs—but with the awareness and anticipation of Christ's coming. Leaning on the belief that we have already been reconciled to God, that we can wait with faithful and hopeful hearts, our urgency to *do* must be born from the idea that God so loves us that we can do nothing else but act in the world every day as if that love matters.

How can a community find that space where what it *does* is a faithful response to God's calling upon its life, while guarding against the danger of actions morphing into an exercise of busywork? This is the challenge: to find and name those places in the world where God is calling us to be and act . . . and to be there, not with an expectation of instant solutions but of relationship that lasts. At the same time, we must find ways to determine what actions, while seemingly productive, actually take energy, time, and passion away from those things that we need to do.

I encourage the preacher to be specific about the kinds of things that draw us away from doing what God would hope, while also naming those actions that God is probably pleased with. This way, doing in itself is not our faith, but what we do is a manifestation of that faith.

Advent 2: Not All Actions Are Created Equal
Matthew 3:1–12

"Bear fruit worthy of repentance. . . . Even now the ax is lying at the root of the trees; every tree therefore that does not bear good fruit is cut down and thrown into the fire." (Matthew 3:8, 10)

After last week's challenge of productivity and busyness, Matthew comes back with this challenge to "bear fruit"—not just any fruit, but fruit "worthy of repentance." During this season of waiting, we are reminded that waiting is not about inaction, but discerning the action that has meaning and actually changes the world.

I am loathe to try and make a list of those actions that would qualify as repentance worthy. Yet this is what we are being challenged to do: both to determine the repentance-worthiness of what we do and to decide what actions we are called to take in the first place.

Repentance and faithful living are about much more than sin-avoidance. There are sins of omission when we fail to act in ways that God is calling us to. Talk about these different types of sin, but of course also about forgiveness and the idea of unconditional grace. There are "slippery slopes" with any argument, but when it comes to sin and grace, who gets it and why, the preacher should aim to set the record straight. A good example of this would be to take on the idea of ranking sin and help people to differentiate between secular and spiritual repercussions and responses to sin in the world. For instance, pride is often considered an invisible sin; it doesn't do as much harm as, say, murder. A court of law would certainly see those offenses very differently, but our need for spiritual repentance goes beyond any criminal code.

We have to unpack the idea of "repentance worthy" or the idea that our actions and faith are truly about turning away from sin and narrowing the space between our actions and God's hopes. Does the living of my faith result in my moving closer to God? Am I resting on the laurels of past successes, or am I engaging in acts that result in widening the division between God and humanity? Are there things going on in the world where the need for human unity (comfort, not rocking the boat) is working against what may bring us closer to God?

Be bold here. Dive deep on this and land in some places where people will be forced to examine core understandings of their faith. Name some things. Call out situations that demand our response and reactions. For even in this season of waiting, if we fail to acknowledge that our faith must actually impact the world, then we only further contribute to the brokenness and divide between us and God that we claim we want to heal and narrow.

Advent 3: That's OK, I'll Wait
Matthew 11:2–11

When John heard in prison what the Messiah was doing, he sent word by his disciples and said to him, "Are you the one who is to come, or are we to wait for another?" Jesus answered them, "Go and tell John what you hear and see." (Matthew 11:2–4)

One of the best parts of waiting can be the opportunity to rest: rest our hearts, rest our minds, rest our spirits. This time is definitely needed, but sometimes that's not what God has determined we need.

I can imagine that Jesus' command to the disciples to tell what they have seen, while exciting, also made it very real that this whole "following Jesus" thing is no joke. They might have preferred to keep waiting for another messiah—maybe one that wouldn't challenge them quite so much. It would have been much easier if soft robes, physical security, and comforts of the institutions of power were the vehicles for Christ to come into the world; but nope, that was actually *not* what Jesus was about.

The disciples and we are being invited into a new reality. They and we have waited long enough, and now our waiting has revealed new ways of seeing and navigating the world! So now we must make a choice: do we follow Christ into this new reality?

As I think about these things for myself, I wonder if sometimes my "self-care" can turn into an idolization of that which is easy and comfortable. Self-care is vital, but we must take care that we do not put so much stock in comfortable things that we fail to see the disruptive nature of Christ's acts in the world. Again, this is not a call to burn out or overfunctioning, but rather a challenge to find ways to remain open to the ways that Jesus walks into our lives, lets us know about ways that God is active in the world, and calls us to follow in faith.

Ponder together what you or your community have been waiting for, spiritually. Recall the last time you waited on God for something and God surprisingly revealed something life-changing. How might we all be more open and ready to hear the ways Christ may be calling us to follow?

Advent 4: Don't Drop the Baby
Matthew 1:18–25

Now the birth of Jesus the Messiah took place in this way. When his mother Mary had been engaged to Joseph, but before they lived together, she was found to be with child from the Holy Spirit. (Matthew 1:18)

There are plenty of themes gifted to us in this text: unpacking "virgin," thinking about God speaking through dreams, and the patriarchal focus on Joseph's role in it all. The awesome responsibility of child-rearing is one that many will relate to, though we should approach parenting examples with caution, out of sensitivity to those who have struggled with infertility or the loss of a child. Knowing that by choice or circumstance not everyone will raise children of their own, we can ask questions like what it means for the church to welcome children into the world today. How might your congregation better raise the children and support families that live in the surrounding community?

Many congregants may identify with the terror one may feel when suddenly handed a tiny, fragile newborn to hold even for a minute.

When my second child was born, a friend came to visit. He clearly had never held a baby . . . or he had, and no one had the heart to tell him that he was doing it wrong. In any case, we could sense his reluctance to take this newborn in his arms. Did that stop me from placing my child in his hands? Nope. You see, this was the world that he stepped into, and by choice or circumstance, he too was now responsible for raising up our child.

We may not be ready for it, we may not seek it, and we may not even really want it, but here we are. The baby Jesus is coming into the world, and now we have to decide how we respond. What are the responsibilities we take on when we claim faith in the coming of the Christ child?

Before you get too caught up in the broader theological or social issues that are brought up in this passage and that question, be sure to acknowledge the very human feelings surrounding the impending birth. We have anxieties, expectations, and fears that may be stirred up by the prospect of meeting God in the flesh. We may have lived our whole lives waiting for such an experience of the Divine. Can we ever adequately prepare ourselves for a life-altering moment? How can we try?

While you should hold some Baby Jesus sermon brilliance back for Christmas Eve, it is OK to name that it is this moment, as the end of the waiting comes into view, that we are prompted to think about what the birth will mean for us.

Christmas Eve: The Gift of Fragility
Luke 2:1–14 (15–20)

And she gave birth to her firstborn son and wrapped him in bands of cloth, and laid him in a manger, because there was no place for them in the inn. (Luke 2:7)

Too often church people make a big deal about people coming to church only on Christmas Eve and Easter. While this may be a reality for many, the preacher must hold in tension being honest about this reality of faith life today while avoiding coming off as shaming or judgmental.

That said, there are few days when preachers will have the ears of those who may not often attend church services. These are also the folks who may someday recall "that church where that preacher said [insert profound idea about life and faith here]." Seeds of faith are planted every day and, no matter the longevity of the person's presence, we can inspire movement with words of love, hope, joy, and peace.

Visitors and members alike are interested in the basic "So what?" of Jesus' birth, and this is a great chance to do some teaching on why this event is crucial to the church's understanding of Christ in the world. We don't know exactly what will be going on in the world on any given day, but we do know that whatever the political, social, or cultural turmoil, there will always be suffering, pain, and brokenness that need to be addressed.

The birth story is rich with moments of grace, so the preaching will have to determine the most compelling aspect of the passage. Some people will challenge the sanitization of an inherently "messy" narrative, while others will focus on political parallels between then and now, and yet others will speak to the radical nature of God being "with us."

More than those other approaches to a Christmas sermon, however, I am often drawn to the absurdity of the Christ arriving as a baby. While baby humans are resilient to most parental gaffes, at the end of the day they would not survive if left on their own. How could God trust humanity with such a fragile presence in the world? This culmination of so many years of God's people waiting for Messiah—this "long-expected Jesus" on whom so much depends—is placed in the hands of mere mortals. Yet we are entrusted with this gift and must take it seriously.

At the end of the day, the incarnation is about our coconspiracy with God to bring about the promises promised in the birth of Christ into the world: love, hope, peace, and joy. We have a job to do, and the world is waiting.

Epiphany Series: Gifts That Keep on Giving

Eight Parts: Epiphany through Transfiguration Sunday

Discovering the gifts God offers—and the challenge to accept them.

BRUCE REYES-CHOW

Series Overview

Due to the beautiful complexities of culture, ethnicity, family, and society, participating in the giving and receiving of gifts is fraught with potential conflicts, confusions, and perhaps outright *bad* surprises. Accepting gifts graciously can sometimes be a challenge. With the commercialized "gift-giving season" behind us, let's focus on some of God's unexpected gifts that we can enjoy long after the Christmas tree has been hauled away—gifts that reveal themselves in new ways as time goes on. This Gospel-based series is about recognizing the often-surprising gifts that are extended to humanity and are ours to receive if we are bold and loving enough to accept them.

	Sermon Title	Focus Scripture	Theme
Epiphany[1]	The Gift of Unexpected Gifts	Matthew 2:1–12	What does it mean for us to see and accept unexpected gifts?
First Sunday after Epiphany	The Gift of Committed Community	Matt. 3:13–17	How do communities embody the vows offered in the event of baptism?
Second Sunday after Epiphany	The Gift of Unbridled Curiosity	John 1:29–42	Encouragement to keep searching for God and God's intentions for our lives.
Third Sunday after Epiphany	The Gift of Bold Action	Matt. 4:12–23	Taking on bold challenges to live differently in the world—individually and together.

1. The congregation can observe Epiphany on the Second Sunday of Christmas if January 6 does not fall on a Sunday.

	Sermon Title	Focus Scripture	Theme
Fourth Sunday after Epiphany	The Gift of Poetic Challenge	Matt. 5:1–12	How creative means of expression can provoke meaningful and faithful action in the world.
Fifth Sunday after Epiphany	The Gift of Public Witness	Matt. 5:13–20	Learning how to faithfully and respectfully give public witness to our faith.
Sixth Sunday after Epiphany	The Gift of Outrageous Grace	Matt. 5:21–37	Seeing and honoring the God-created humanity in those with whom we disagree.
Transfiguration Sunday	The Gift of the Unpredictable Jesus.	Matt. 17:1–9	Staying focused on our goals while also being open to the ways God may surprise us.

Tips and Ideas for This Series

Using wrapped packages (perhaps in white, silver, and "ordinary time" green to mark the change in liturgical season) in graphics and around the worship space offers a good segue out of the cultural Christmas season and into the faith we live as a result of the incarnation. Depending on your level of comfort with cheesiness and props, the first week might begin with images or actual gifts as a lead-in to help people explore and expand their understanding of "gifts" today. With the unexpected, surprising, and unpredictable nature of God's gifts explored in this series, take the opportunity to try new things in worship to start a fresh new year.

Epiphany: The Gift of Unexpected Gifts
Matthew 2:1–12

When they had heard the king, they set out; and there, ahead of them, went the star that they had seen at its rising, until it stopped over the place where the child was. When they saw that the star had stopped, they were overwhelmed with joy. (Matthew 2:9–10)

Not all gifts are freely given.

Far too many gifts come with emotional or expectational strings attached—some spoken, some unspoken. Some gifts are given with the expectation of some kind of reciprocation; others are given as a way to purchase forgiveness. Sometimes these gifts are genuine expressions of one person's gratitude for the other; at other times gift-giving only perpetuates the commodification of unhealthy relationships.

We've all experienced some type of gift-giving awkwardness: the inappropriate gift, the obvious regift, or a stark difference in the size or significance of the gifts two people exchange. Giving or receiving a gift when none is offered in return can be awkward, depending on the circumstances, but it can also be an occasion of deep sincerity, generosity, and gratitude.

The gifts brought by the magi were completely unexpected by the household of Jesus. The gifts given were not self-centered in any way. The magi weren't obligated to give gifts to this family (they didn't even know them!), and certainly they weren't given out of guilt or the expectation of anything in return. No, these gifts were completely born out of a genuine realization of the reality of Christ—an epiphany.

Gifts that are offered freely and out of a deep sense of joy, generosity, and gratitude are powerful both for the one who gives and for the one who receives.

In our world today, we so often give in to cynicism and distrust that we become unable to recognize and receive the offerings of others. This inability to receive gifts is not just about material things, but about other ways that we are able to receive the gifts of love and affirmation as well. Too often if someone affirms something about our personhood, we too quickly want to deflect and deny the gift that has just been given. We can't accept a simple compliment. No, we do not want to become arrogant in our assessment of ourselves, but at the same time, when someone gifts us with a gesture meant to acknowledge the holy, beautiful, and just that we embody, we must be able to simply receive it as offered.

What keeps us from graciously accepting the unexpected gifts we are offered? What holds us back from *offering* a gift that is born out of joy, generosity, and gratitude? How can today's Scripture show us how to give and receive more faithfully?

First Sunday after Epiphany: The Gift of Committed Community
Matthew 3:13–17

And when Jesus had been baptized, just as he came up from the water, suddenly the heavens were opened to him and he saw the Spirit of God descending like a dove and alighting on him. And a voice from heaven said, "This is my Son, the Beloved, with whom I am well pleased." (Matthew 3:16–17)

If I was forced to choose a favorite Sunday in the church year, it would be this one, Baptism of the Lord Sunday. I say this because my own life has been so shaped and formed by the promises made at my baptism: a community that vowed to care for me and the knowledge of a God who loves and forgives more that I could ever imagine. The committed community of Christ's family is one of the greatest gifts God offers us.

Throughout my life there have been moments when individuals have failed to fulfill promises. Some disappointments have been cursory events, while others have left places of still-discovered pain. I have also been on the side of letting others down, breaking promises to loved ones, and not valuing my own createdness in God.

Throughout all these events, one thing has remained: my church community has loved me. They are not always perfect, but there has always been someone to remind me to whom I belong. From food being placed in front of me that soothed much more than my hunger, to the challenge to take seriously the idea that I was to always seek God's intentions for my life, this church raised me. And for this I will always be grateful.

Make no mistake. My church would have this approach with anyone, baptismal vows or not, but in the act of affirming these vows, they were also reminding me that I was not marked for myself, but for the well-being of the entire body.

People often wonder, as John himself did in the text, why Jesus—sinless Son of God—would need to be baptized. This question itself reveals our bias toward the individual, focusing only on questions of sin and salvation. The culmination of this story, in which God claims Jesus as beloved son, demonstrates the too-often-overlooked significance of our own baptism. We too are being claimed as children of God, joining a family with all our siblings in Christ.

In this day and age, when people may not know the nitty-gritty of church life, this Sunday offers a great chance to do some actual teaching about baptisms, the hows and whys of our theological and denominational traditions. Examine what baptism means, not just for the individual being baptized, but for the whole church community, who often make vows to help nurture each baptized individual in their faith.

Think about what our baptismal vows mean even beyond the congregation or Christian faith. On this day, we remember the commitment that people of faith have to all members of the community, baptized or not. In fact, in the commitment to these vows of baptism taken toward anyone means that we, in all ways, are called to care for, raise, and love all.

Second Sunday after Epiphany: The Gift of Unbridled Curiosity
John 1:29–42

When Jesus turned and saw them following, he said to them, "What are you looking for?" They said to him, "Rabbi" (which translated means Teacher), "where are you staying?" He said to them, "Come and see." They came and saw where he was staying, and they remained with him that day. (John 1:38–39a)

I have had the privilege of raising three human children, and I *love* them with all my heart, body, mind, and soul.

Yet from infancy to adulthood they could also be annoying to no end. I am sure they would say the same things about their parental units, but in our house it was common to say about a frustrating characteristic, "Wow, that will sure serve them later in life, . . . but right now it's a pain in the butt." The annoyance was not usually about a particular action or habit, but rather about one of those burgeoning personality traits: claiming agency, oppositional behavior, unbridled curiosity.

It's hard to get from point A to point B when your four-year-old wants to stop and examine every tree or ask questions about every building.

Curiosity is a gift.

Curiosity is a gift.

Curiosity is a gift.

Repeat that phrase however many times you need to—until you truly believe it.

In my experience, curiosity is often more of a theoretically awesome idea than a settling and secure practical act. What I have found is that curiosity, this yearning to see what may be just ahead or to understand why something is the way it is, can be disruptive to the surrounding community.

If you think about this moment in the disciples' journey, they could have simply walked on, but no . . . they kept answering the internal prodding to see what was next: who was this Jesus and what did it all mean? There was a nagging curiosity that kept them moving despite the fact that they were at the seminal stages of a life transformation beyond their own imagination and, at times, even beyond their ability to truly follow Christ.

This curiosity was also not just about them. With every person who chooses to follow Jesus, from the first moments to today, there are larger communities that look upon this curiosity as a disruptive annoyance. Be it family, friends, or faith community, our default choice is comfort and stability; so anytime anyone begins to question the status quo and explore ways that we may be called out of that space, there is going to be disruption and resistance. Some people handle these moments with grace and openness, while others become more calcified and belligerent.

No matter how people respond, curiosity changes us and changes the world. How does our community handle curiosity and the possibility of change? How have we seen curiosity lead to meaningful transformation in our selves or our community? How do we discern whether or not the path down which our curiosity is leading us is a good path?

The end of this passage sees the disciples brought fully into the community where new names are given and lives are committed to being in the world differently. Not every path must be traveled, but being open to new paths at all times is a must if we are to grow in faith.

Third Sunday after Epiphany: The Gift of Bold Action
Matthew 4:12–23

As he walked by the Sea of Galilee, he saw two brothers, Simon, who is called Peter, and Andrew his brother, casting a net into the sea—for they were fishermen. And he said to them, "Follow me, and I will make you fish for people." Immediately they left their nets and followed him. (Matthew 4:18–20)

There will come a time in everyone's life when bold choices need to be made. From deeply personal actions like publicly calling out sexism, racism, or ableism in our daily conversations, to more global actions like how we engage in our political systems, there will be a time when we need to answer the words "Follow me."

Following Christ is complex. We have made many aspects accessible, built structures to support, and collectively agreed that certain ways of people are just and right. And yet . . . there are still times when we will have to step out and away from what we have been, in order to discover what God hopes for us to become.

A difficult aspect of following Christ out into the unknown is that so many others may be dismissive, confused, or downright oppositional. There will always be rational reasons not to follow Christ: our own safety, the security of our families, and the burden of communal judgment. That said, our faith demands us always to discern where God is leading. Not only do we have always to be alert for the ways in which God's path is being revealed before us. We then have continually to decide if we are going to walk it.

What ordinary people have you seen make bold choices despite the risk or opposition they faced? It is easy to hold up as heroes people who have chosen bold actions, but we should be wary of encouraging the idea that one has to be some kind of larger-than-life figure to follow Christ in bold ways. Often real, lasting change is made when many ordinary people make a bold choice as a group—the Montgomery bus boycott, for example. How might we as a community discern what it means to follow as a group of people?

As difficult as discerning God's calling can be, I have always found that what seems bold or risky to others seems quite normal and natural to those who genuinely trust that they are following where God is leading. Holding this tension between the unstable and unknown and a clarity of calling is a gift that allows us to be bold in how we live our faith and gives us the courage and calm to follow.

Fourth Sunday after Epiphany: The Gift of Poetic Challenge
Matthew 5:1–12

"Blessed are the poor in spirit, for theirs is the kingdom of heaven. Blessed are those who mourn, for they will be comforted. Blessed are the meek, for they will inherit the earth." (Matthew 5:3–5)

I am one of those people who loves musicals. Musicals move me, not just because of the stories, but because I am in awe of people who have excelled at the craft. Being able to sing well and dance with joy are gifts in themselves, but when exercised at the same time, they are mind-blowing! The ways in which my heart, mind, and soul are beckoned forth by an individual's command of a vocal movement, a communicative facial expression, and the well-timed delivery of a line are truly holy.

I feel the same way about the craft of the spoken word. The way in which individuals can craft word and tone in order to challenge and comfort an audience is also holy and awe-inspiring. Some inspire with soaring oration, while others captivate listeners through their calm and careful speech. Like many others for whom using words well is part of our calling, I too often allow myself to be confined to a narrow understanding of how the gospel can be shared, usually defaulting to *too many words*. It takes discipline and discernment to preach or write with brevity. As some have quipped, "I didn't have time to write a thousand words, so I wrote two thousand." Twitter has its faults, but sometimes we need some encouragement to rethink the verbosity we too often rely on.

I believe that the Beatitudes are the best of Christ's poetic expressions of faith, not only a challenge to what we do in our faith, but a challenge for me to express myself in different ways. Jesus is still using words, but this captivating portion of the Sermon on the Mount is a challenge to think about not only *what* we share but also *how* we share. In this passage, not only are we given insight into the kinds of things we need to be attuned to in the world; we are also being challenged to hear and express those profound challenges in different and more creative ways than we have been in the past.

The simplicity and nakedness with which Jesus talks about who is blessed is brilliant. This is a radical message, made clear and memorable for his hearers because of its poetic power. This should be held as a reminder that in order to share the challenges and calling of faith we must be creative in our expressions. More words, fewer words, better crafted words, no words—expressions of faith must take many forms in order to speak to the many ways in which people take in information.

If you have the space and ability, try to do some more creative things in worship today to demonstrate how different ways of expressing an idea—story, poetry, a painting or sculpture, dance, for example—affect people in different ways. Be wise in gauging how much creativity a community can take in one dose without rebelling, but because there is built-in permission given by the focus, don't pass up the opportunity.

Fifth Sunday after Epiphany: The Gift of Public Witness
Matthew 5:13–20

"You are the light of the world. A city on a hill cannot be hid. No one after lighting a lamp puts it under the bushel basket, but on the lampstand, and it gives light to all in the house. In the same way, let your light shine before others, so that they may see your good works and give glory to your Father in heaven." (Matthew 5:14–16)

Scripture is filled with apparent contradictions, especially when it comes to what we do in private and what we do in public. Jesus himself often tells people to go and tell no one of miracles that they have witnessed; at other times, the mandate is clear: go out and heal people, free people, feed people . . . all very public acts of faith.

One of the greatest challenges of being people of faith in an increasingly secular world is knowing the whens, hows, and wheres of expressing one's faith. When is the right time? How should we do this? Where is the right place to be public? Of course there is no one answer to the methods of our faith, no one way to express faith, and

[Handwritten top margin: "A gebeuchter can not do aull + / Franz Jägerstätter"]

[Handwritten left margin: "sometimes salt sometimes light ..."]

[Handwritten left margin: "The spirit will tell us ... I think we know ... (I still remember a comment ...)"]

[Handwritten left margin: "look @ the worder of this cong:"]

no one time to act on our faith. Some might say to avoid talking "religion" or values altogether because you're bound to offend someone. Given the diversity and complexity of theological expressions in our world and even just within Christianity, there may be a risk of being misunderstood or having your message contorted.

Yet it is clear that there *are* times when we are called out into the world to bear a public and powerful witness to Christ. If we do not, then we pay lip service to a faith that so clearly calls us to both private and public expressions of faith. Without public actions and expressions of faith, we risk becoming that bland, tasteless faith that draws fewer and fewer people *and* stands directly in contradiction to the ways Christ "took on" many people he had known for quite a while.

What are some of the ways in which you or your community has boldly lived or expressed faith in public? What are the biggest obstacles to living faith out in public? What is at stake if you don't?

Public expressions of faith can be difficult and anxiety laden, but barring any odd circumstances, talking with family, friends, mentors, and others will help you better to talk about and share the ways in which God has called you into and onto this journey of faith.

[Handwritten: "season a conv in questions + openness; more light less heat ..."]

Sixth Sunday after Epiphany: The Gift of Outrageous Grace
Matthew 5:21–37

"So when you are offering your gift at the altar, if you remember that your brother or sister has something against you, leave your gift there before the altar and go; first be reconciled to your brother or sister, and then come and offer your gift." (Matthew 5:23–24)

Every day whenever I check my phone for the latest political or social kerfuffle, my blood pressure rises and metaphorical steam comes shooting out of my ears. I assume that I am not the only one who has this reaction, as there are plenty of events for us all to become angry about. When I see someone do something horrible, I usually react in a couple of ways. At my best I see each person, no matter what they have done or said, as a created and complex child of God. At my worst, I question the very humanity of my enemy, wondering if they are not really an evil alien in disguise, sent from another planet with a mission to prove why human beings should not have nice things.

Then I realize that, just as I am judging them over there, the odds are pretty good that I am someone else's "them" and I am being judged right here. Yes, humanity's capacity for goodness is vast, but our proclivity to chip away at the dignity and humanity of the other is also strong. Throughout the political and social history in the United

States, a tactic used to "win" in struggles big and small is to dehumanize and other our enemy. This tactic knows no ideological bounds, as all people fall into this trap of creating distance between themselves and others with drastically different opinions and perspectives.

But no matter what we do as human beings, God somehow still loves us as God's own. This love does not mean acceptance or approval of acts or thoughts that dehumanize, but it is a love that is grounded in grace that goes far beyond anything that my heart or head could ever imagine. Jesus knows we are nowhere nearly as gracious with one another, but he calls us to repentance and reconciliation, with his command to repair the breaches in relationship that we have created, before we make our offerings to God.

The teachings in today's Gospel reading may seem like mere rules (a stricter standard than the Law of Moses, in fact) but at their core are a call to see the humanity in one another first and foremost, treating one another with the grace we would want for ourselves. This does not mean glossing over differences for the sake of "unity," or accepting abusing behavior. We can maintain healthy boundaries of behavior and belief while still acknowledging that all human beings are God's.

Like so many elements of the magnitude of God's presence, we humans often only hear whispers or feel glancing touches. This loving presence is extended to *all* of us: the people we feel are "deserving" of it, as well as those whom we may feel have lost the right to God's love.

Transfiguration Sunday: The Gift of the Unpredictable Jesus
Matthew 17:1–9

And he was transfigured before them, and his face shone like the sun, and his clothes became dazzling white. Suddenly there appeared to them Moses and Elijah, talking with him. . . . And when they looked up, they saw no one except Jesus himself alone. (Matthew 17:2–3, 8)

I often wonder if the disciples ever just looked at Jesus and said, "Seriously, Jesus, one more thing we have to try and understand?"

In this passage, everything that makes total sense to do, the disciples do, and then Jesus shifts. The disciples must have been so frustrated. Why not build a home for three prophets? Seems like the hospitable and welcoming thing to do. Why not tell everyone what they have just seen? This seems like a pretty good example of why they were following Christ in the first place.

Yes, there is a holy moment in the appearance of Moses and Elijah with Jesus. Again, this was *proof* of the divine nature of Jesus, but the fact that Jesus challenges reactions that seem perfectly understandable should not be overlooked. Too often we act simply because it's what we are "supposed" to do. But what if there are things that we have been doing for generations or for a few days that are simply not what we should be doing?

This moment points to the need for us to be discerning and open to the ways that Jesus may want us to be a presence of unexpectedness in the world. We may instinctually move toward an action, but having the discipline and commitment to think, pray, and discern individually and communally may sometimes point us toward new responses that are beautifully surprising.

This goes far beyond simply challenging the idea that we too often do things a certain way because we have always done certain things in a certain way. Sure, many things do need to change, but how unexpected would it be to discern that not *all* things need to change? And for the things that we do believe need to change, what are the unexpected places toward which Jesus is directing us? We need to plan and discern while always being open to the surprises that our faith may introduce.

While we may sometimes react in fear like the disciples, if we remain open to the ways that Christ surprises us, maybe we can join in on the unexpected ways that Christ shows himself to the world.

Now *that* would be unexpected.

Lenten Series: Heart-to-Heart Talks

Seven Parts: First Sunday in Lent through Easter Sunday

Conversations in the Gospels prompt questions about our own relationship with Jesus.

MARTHA K. SPONG

Series Overview

We remember the important heart-to-heart talks in our lives, whether a dashboard confessional between parent and child, a wee-hours dialogue with a friend, or a life-changing FaceTime with the one we love. For seven Sundays, from the first week in Lent through Easter Sunday, we will explore conversations with Jesus depicted in the Gospels. As people come seeking answers to their deepest questions, or making claims about their faith, or wondering who he is, Jesus engages, challenges, and exhorts. What would we ask Jesus, if we could meet him at night or at noon, in the wilderness or in the garden? And how might he answer us?

	Sermon Title	Focus Scripture	Theme
Lent 1	Not Today, Satan	Matt. 4:1–11	Jesus' temptation in the desert prompts us to ask: What tempts us?
Lent 2	Hush-Hush	John 3:1–17	Nicodemus leads us to consider: What will we risk to be close to Jesus?
Lent 3	Well, Actually . . .	John 4:5–42	The Samaritan woman makes us wonder: Does Jesus know us?
Lent 4	So Many Questions	John 9:1–41	The healing of a blind man sparks difficult questions, most poignantly: Do we know Jesus?

	Sermon Title	Focus Scripture	Theme
Lent 5	Too Little, Too Late?	John 11:1–45	Lazarus's death raises the question: Where is Jesus when things go wrong?
Palm/Passion Sunday	The Truth Hurts	Matt. 26:14–35	The disciples' denial makes us ask: What happens when we fail Jesus?
Easter Sunday	Spread the Word	John 20:1–8	Mary Magdalene inspires our daily mission: What does Jesus want from us today?

Tips and Ideas for This Series

Consider using informal photos of members of the church family in different combinations, engaged in conversation. Some can be serious, some lighthearted, some one-on-one, and some a small group. Choose a range of ages and physical types to illustrate the range of people Jesus talks to in these stories. When reading the texts in worship, divide the parts such that the voices are distinct, choosing one reader to narrate while others read the dialogue, emphasizing the conversational nature of these Gospel stories.

Lent 1: Not Today, Satan
Matthew 4:1–11

Then Jesus was led up by the Spirit into the wilderness to be tempted by the devil. He fasted forty days and forty nights, and afterwards he was famished. The tempter came and said to him, "If you are the Son of God, command these stones to become loaves of bread." But he answered, "It is written, 'One does not live by bread alone, but by every word that comes from the mouth of God.'" (Matthew 4:1–4)

Jesus had forty days to get ready for the devil. Led up by the Spirit into the wilderness, he spent almost six weeks fasting. The symptoms of physical hunger start with an empty feeling in the stomach, which might include growling sounds. When the average person goes a long time without eating, he may develop a headache, or she may grow shaky and light-headed. Hungry people can be grumpy, or "hangry" as the Snickers® wrapper calls it. A person suffering from extreme hunger will grow weak. To be sure, we don't think Jesus might be above such struggles, Scripture tells us he was famished. Before he can find a town and ask for something to eat, he meets the tempter.

Before he can prove his divinity, he shows us his humanity. The man is hungry.

Initiating this dialogue, the tempter's first move was an attempt to take advantage of that hunger, inviting Jesus to show his supernatural power by turning stones into bread.

Temptation comes to us in the same way. We are empty, or shaky. Our heads ache, or our hearts. Ready to lash out, weak in spirit, we find it hard to resist the temporary high of the bottle, the online purchase, or the text message we know better than to send. When we feel hollow enough, we may not have the impulse control to avoid the fried food, the lottery ticket, or the office flirtation.

It may seem that Jesus came to the encounter weakened because he inhabited a human body. For forty days he had lived without shelter, companionship, and sustenance. Exposure, loneliness, starvation should combine in detrimental fashion. The tempter might seem to have the advantage. But Jesus did not wander in a wilderness vacuum. Each day he prepared for the inevitable challenge to his purpose.

We sometimes meet individuals who would willingly lead us into temptation, but more often than not we find ourselves most vulnerable to going astray when we are leading ourselves, the proverbial angel and devil on our shoulders, debating the cost of wrongdoing.

"Why not try it? No one will know." "Why shouldn't I cheat?" "Everybody does it."

What can we find in Jesus' heart-to-heart talk with Satan to prepare and strengthen ourselves? In response to each temptation, Jesus put God first. He reminded us not to test God and to worship God alone. And while our own very real human bodies may resist the first of his answers, Jesus was not making a case that it's noble to starve for God's sake. Jesus turned down an easy fix and took up his call to live as one of us.

Our battles will not be as cosmic; we will not find ourselves tempted to rule all the kingdoms of the world, or to survive a life-threatening risk by depending on angels. Those are temptations scaled to the power and potential of the Son of God. Yet we will feel empty; we will face challenges. Jesus showed us how to take them one at a time and say, "Not today, Satan."

Lent 2: Hush-Hush
John 3:1–17

Nicodemus said to him, "How can these things be?" Jesus answered him, "Are you a teacher of Israel, and yet you do not understand these things?" (John 3:9–10)

Have you ever wanted to go somewhere but been a little afraid of who might see you arriving or departing? Maybe you would like to hear a speaker on a topic of interest you would rather keep secret, or listen to a band or see a play or go to a movie that you fear might reveal something about you. Perhaps you live in an area where local team loyalties are strong; you still root for your home(town) team and would never put out a yard sign or wear a jersey around the neighborhood.

Sometimes we keep our loyalties, our interests, and our questions hush-hush.

Nicodemus makes three appearances in John, to go along with the three occasions Jesus visits Jerusalem in this Gospel. The first follows a story most of us associate with Holy Week. Jesus upends the tables in the temple, crying out against its use as a marketplace. It's important to note that in John's Gospel, unlike the other three, this happens early in Jesus' ministry rather than in the days before his arrest and crucifixion. It is the opening round of Jesus' conflict with those in authority.

No wonder Nicodemus comes to Jesus by night. Surely his colleagues among the religious leaders would not be happy to know he is consorting with a radical. He goes to find Jesus at night, a time of literal darkness, when he can move through the city without being seen. He has a public reputation to protect, the status that goes along with his power and authority. At the same time he takes a risk, coming to Jesus to make an important claim in verse 2: "Rabbi, we know that you are a teacher who has come from God; for no one can do these signs that you do apart from the presence of God."

Nicodemus tries to establish himself as a friend, although a secretive one, by saying he knows Jesus is godly. He puts himself out there, showing he thinks differently than his cohorts, perhaps thinking he has gone as far as he needs to go, but he does not fully understand. Jesus is more than a teacher.

In the rest of the passage, Jesus points to Nicodemus's limited grasp of whom he is talking to; it comes as no surprise to those who have read ahead. We know Jesus is the Messiah. Nicodemus learns in real time. He returns in 7:50–51, during Jesus' second visit to Jerusalem, listening at the temple and reminding his colleagues to give Jesus a full hearing. In chapter 19, he is seen bringing spices for Jesus' burial. His understanding grows and changes his life.

If we had the chance for a hush-hush heart-to-heart with Jesus, what would we say to show we know who he is? Would we stay with him after we find out how much more there is to learn? What would we risk to know him better?

Lent 3: Well, Actually . . .
John 4:5–42

The woman said to him, "Sir, I see that you are a prophet." (John 4:19)

When we cross paths with strangers, most of the time the interactions are casual. We hope our seatmates will ignore us on the airplane and equip ourselves with the earbuds or reading material that show we are busy. We thank the person who holds a door open or the bagger at the grocery store. We smile at the winsome toddler on the playground or at the library; at most we make eye contact with the parent standing watch. When the casual encounter comes with someone visibly different from us, we may ignore, or we may overcompensate. The particularly outgoing among us may compliment the color someone is wearing or ask how old a child is, but mostly we keep moving.

Occasionally, though, we make an unexpected connection.

The woman who came to draw water at noon could see a man sitting there as she approached. She may have wondered how or if he would speak to her at this well, where famous matches had been made. Would he be flirtatious, or rude, or would he simply ignore her? Coming closer, she could see from his clothing that he was Jewish. When he asked for a drink, she expressed surprise that he would be willing to take water from a Samaritan woman.

Suddenly they went deep into the well of living water.

Why did Jesus ask her to go and call her husband? The unfortunate result of this moment in the narrative has been centuries of preaching that dismisses her as a loose woman, even a prostitute. Perhaps we miss the point when we try to chase down the implications of her marital history.

Jesus knew her.

This story has no parallels in the other Gospels, although Jesus did have a brief and contentious interaction with another foreign woman, a mother seeking healing for her daughter, in Mark and Matthew. The difference here is that Jesus taught her. He knew not only her history but her capacity for faith. There was no secret-keeping here. She knew the Messiah was coming, and Jesus revealed himself to her. He knew she was a woman of strength, one who would talk back and not let other people's opinions keep her from speaking up. He knew she was a person who could spread the word.

Jesus knows us too.

There may be things we wish we could hide from God, pieces of our stories we hope will not have to be confessed. The good news for all of us is that God knows us and has work for all of us, no matter who we are or where we have been or what has happened in our lives. If Jesus appeared at noon today, sitting in the town square or the church garden or at the brew pub down the road, he would actually know us, just as he knew the woman.

Is it daunting to think of being known so intimately? Or is it a relief?

There is living water for all.

Lent 4: So Many Questions
John 9:1–41

Jesus answered, "Neither this man nor his parents sinned; he was born blind so that God's works might be revealed in him." (John 9:3)

In John 9, we start with a question, based on an assumption, which leads to other questions. "Whose sin caused this man to be born blind?" the disciples ask. Whose sin meant that he would live life begging on the side of the road? Jesus' answer points in another direction. The man was born blind so that we might see God's works through him. This may raise more questions for us about cause and effect. Did God cause or allow a child to be born blind so that he could later make a cameo appearance in the Gospel to illustrate a point about a lack of spiritual vision?

Such a literal reading of Jesus and the situation gets in the way of appreciating an extended metaphor about the capacity of human beings to deny what is right in front of us. In this story, the local religious leaders in particular hold on to their principles instead of opening their hearts and minds to the Messiah in their midst. Their questions start to feel like swats taken at a piñata, intended to break the people they question and to get the answers they want. What would it mean for them to accept the testimony of the man born blind?

In a congregation I served as interim, members complained about communication that went beyond poor to pathological. People in leadership seemed determined to misunderstand each other. I began to ask questions. The church had a history of shameful actions by a pastor and secret-keeping for the sake of saving face in the community. Despite their collective effort to preserve the church's reputation, the leaders felt suspicious of each other. They grew accustomed to their unhappiness. I came to see that the problem was exacerbated by the unusual number of people in leadership who lived with significant hearing loss. They literally could not hear each other.

On the Fourth Sunday of Lent, we read this story together in worship, printed with parts for the congregation. A man who had been born deaf read the part of the man born blind. The leaders of the church took the parts of the Pharisees. That day, they began to listen more closely. In the weeks and months that followed, they began to work harder at hearing each other, although communicating better disturbed the status quo.

It is not an easy choice to change. The religious leaders in John 9 could not see who Jesus was, although he stood right in front of them. They did not want to know him. They had questions, but they did not want his answers.

We might want to ask ourselves these questions: Whom do we not want to hear? Whom would we rather not see and know? What does that say about how we understand Jesus? Why was he born? He was born Jesus, Christ, that God's works might be revealed in him, for all of us to see. He was born Christ, Jesus, that God's work of love might be known in him.

Lent 5: Too Little, Too Late?
John 11:1–45

"Could not he who opened the eyes of the blind man have kept this man from dying?"
John 11:37

Some of the hardest times in our lives raise the question Mary and Martha asked of Jesus. Their family had a level of special intimacy with him, yet they knew him to be more than friend. His public title might have been the Teacher (John 11:28), but they addressed him as Lord. They called him Lord even as they confronted him, calling his absence into question. They believed in him wholeheartedly and believed he could have healed their brother and prevented his death.

In every Gospel, Jesus brings someone back to life, prefiguring the power of God that will be shown in his resurrection. Death is not the final word, and we can take some comfort in that ultimate truth. But how do we reconcile that belief—as Martha did in her confession that Jesus is the Messiah—with our grief and disappointment when things go terribly wrong, when we suffer crushing and seemingly unnecessary losses?

On a summer Sunday morning, a young family arrived for worship at a Congregational church in a country town in New England. The mother, thin and pale, wore a scarf over her head. The two children had never been to church, but they seemed happy to come up front for the children's message with friends they knew from school.

Their mom was a beloved volunteer at that local elementary school. She remained determined to do the things she loved with the children she adored despite the stage-four cancer threatening to kill her. Bringing her family to church might have been the only way she came close to admitting the situation was beyond her control. It was her husband who reached out to the pastor for support; even as the end came, she fought against death.

Her funeral filled the little church. People stood in the back of the sanctuary and along the sides. Many families brought their children, classmates of her second grader and kindergartener. Knowing this would happen, the pastor arranged the service to include a message for the children. In it she told the story of Jesus and the time he cried with his friends. She encouraged the children to share stories about their friends' mom with each other, and with their parents. She explained that some of those stories might make them cry, and some would make them smile, and both those things were fine. She told them that it was OK to be mad, and it was even OK to be mad at God.

Lazarus came out of the tomb, called by Jesus, and the Gospel story moved on, with new believers won and religious authorities provoked. What remains for us are the potent images of Martha's challenging Jesus on the road, of Mary's kneeling at his feet, of Jesus' weeping over his friend. Why didn't God prevent this? Why did someone down the street get a miracle but we didn't? Where is Jesus, for us, when we are grieving? This story lets us know that it is OK to ask.

Palm/Passion Sunday: The Truth Hurts
Matthew 26:14–35

Peter said to him, "Even though I must die with you, I will not deny you." And so said all the disciples. (Matthew 26:35)

Lucy went to church for her first Holy Week service when she was nine years old. As the child of the pastor, she had only the supervision of her twelve–year-old brother during the Tenebrae service. At the end of each passage of Scripture telling the passion story, a reader extinguished candles and walked away into the congregation, disappearing like the friends who fled after Jesus' arrest. When the last reader spoke the words, "he breathed his last," Lucy's mother carried the last candle, the Christ candle, out of the chancel and into a back hallway. The congregation departed in silence. When the choir came quietly through the same doorway from the chancel, Lucy followed, weeping, and found her way in the near darkness to her mother's arms. Choking back sobs, she whispered, "Mommy, there are lots of sad things in the Bible, but this is the saddest."

When we move too readily from the excitement of the palm parade to the joy of Easter morning, we miss that emotion, the commingled grief and regret felt by the disciples as they watched their teacher and friend marched off by the Roman soldiers, to be tried by the religious authorities. We miss the moments of helplessness and fear they experienced hiding in an upper room. We miss the ways the truth hurts.

After supper on their last night together, Jesus told the disciples they would desert him, not at some unpredictable time in the future, but that very night. Peter spoke up, and claimed that even if everyone else ran away, he would never desert Jesus. Imagine the rustle of their voices, all of them saying, "Jesus, dear Jesus, not me. I would never."

This is part of our faith story. We do what we do not want to do. We deny what matters to us. We behave in ways that do not represent what we believe. And all the time we say with Peter, "Even though I must die with you, I will not deny you."

This is part of our story. It is true, and the truth hurts.

It's not surprising, then, that we fill our sanctuaries with shouted hosannas and alleluias but see less of a turnout for the services in between.

When we avoid the pain, we also avoid the intimacy of those final conversations with Jesus, the passionate expressions of love and loyalty and the understated response from the one who knows what will happen. He does not sugarcoat it for them. He trusts them with the truth.

If you were to ask Lucy, who is now in her twenties, she would tell you that Tenebrae is her favorite service of the church year. Whether she participates as a reader or sits in the congregation, the stories of the passion move her and have formed her. We will all make mistakes and fall short, despite our best intentions to do otherwise. Jesus knows it, yet still loves us. This is the truth that heals.

Easter Sunday: Spread the Word
John 20:1–18

Early on the first day of the week, while it was still dark, Mary Magdalene came to the tomb and saw that the stone had been removed from the tomb. (John 20:1)

Early on the first Easter morning, when Mary Magdalene awoke, she felt the terrible shock we do when the death of someone close is so fresh that we have to realize it again, to tell ourselves the bad news and make ourselves believe it.

Some people respond to grief this way, determined to keep going. Do the tasks of daily life. Fold the towels. Load the dishwasher. Weed the flower bed. Take a walk. Go and visit the cemetery. We get up and move because we must, because we fear that if we do not, we may never move again. We get up and do something, anything, because anything is better than nothing.

Mary Magdalene got up and went to the tomb. She went there because she was a disciple. She may not appear on lists of the twelve—all men—but she appears in each of the four Gospels, in combination with various other women, and in John's Gospel, all alone. Every version of the story tells us that Mary Magdalene came to the tomb, early on the first day of the week. In John's Gospel, she is the first witness that Jesus' body is not there. She carried the message to the disciples, convincing them that they needed to come and see what had happened.

When they left the tomb, Mary stayed and wept, and then she saw angels—again, the number and description vary among the Gospels, but she always meets the transcendent delegation. Then she saw a man and spoke to him, "supposing him to be the gardener." He spoke to her, asking why she wept, but he had to do more than speak for her to recognize him. When he said her name, she knew her Lord.

Do we wonder why Jesus chose to speak to Mary Magdalene? He knew her faithful heart and trusted her above the other disciples to believe the impossible and to understand his meaning. She reached out to him, but when he told her, "Do not hold onto me," she did not argue.

They met at a liminal moment, when night touched day. He was between two states, and so was she. The Jesus of Friday had died, and the Christ of heaven had not yet ascended. Mary Magdalene, the grieving follower, had only a moment to kneel before him, a moment to be transformed into Mary Magdalene, the first evangelist. He knew how well-equipped she was to spread the word, determined and convincing and faithful.

"I have seen the Lord," she told the disciples, and they told others, and they told others, and so on until one day someone told us. It may be good news we have always known, told so long ago we cannot remember when, or it may have come as a gift when we needed it desperately, a word of hope at the end of a long night. It is our work now, to let the world know. Christ is risen. Spread the word.

Easter Series: Building Blocks

Seven Parts: Second Sunday of Easter
through Pentecost Sunday

Stories of the early church teach us the fundamentals of faith.

MARTHA K. SPONG

Series Overview During the Great Fifty Days, the texts include both stories we expect ("doubting" Thomas) and stories we may overlook (Paul preaching in the Areopagus). Some take place chronologically after Pentecost, although the season builds toward that event. These passages teach valuable fundamentals for a life of faith. What commitments are foundational to our Christian identity? We believe in what we cannot see, experience the resurrected Christ, learn to share in community, ask questions as we grow in faith, draw connections for those with other beliefs, draw strength from shared prayer, and value all who are part of the body of Christ.

	Sermon Title	Focus Scripture	Theme
Easter 2	Becoming a Believer	John 20:19–31	Everyone doubts; Jesus understands.
Easter 3	Recognizing Jesus	Luke 24:13–35	Look! See! Jesus is with us!
Easter 4	Living in Community	Acts 2:42–47	How can we share what we hold in common?
Easter 5	Asking Questions	John 14:1–14	In anxious times, seek help from others.
Easter 6	Sharing Our Faith	Acts 17:22–31	As we all grope in the dark, help others connect with God.
Easter 7	Seeking Guidance Together	Acts 1:6–14	We need each other for guidance and encouragement.
Pentecost Sunday	Being Moved	Acts 2:1–21	Keep watch together—the Spirit is coming!

Tips and Ideas for This Series

This series begins on a traditionally low-attendance Sunday and runs through the weeks that often mark the final events of the school year, and yet families who rarely attend church may be compelled to return after Easter for this series outlining basic, positive principles of faith. Use building-block imagery in your graphics and altar design, adding a block each week to symbolize growth. Consider having tables of toy blocks or Legos® in a common area so people can be creative together before or after worship.

Easter 2: Becoming a Believer
John 20:19–31

Jesus said to him, "Have you believed because you have seen me? Blessed are those who have not seen and yet come to believe." (John 20:29)

"Blessed are those who have faith but have *not* seen." Those are hard words. The lectionary includes this story every year, and over time we may begin to feel sympathetic to Thomas. His other appearances in the Gospel show a person who asked questions for clarification (John 14) even though he was ready to die beside Jesus (John 11).

People understand things differently. Some of us get faith with our minds and others with our hearts. Thomas wanted to see for himself. He stood in for other people who wanted to see the marks too, who were not there when Jesus came right through the locked doors. John's Gospel assures us it's true, all true, and John persists in offering evidence precisely because people—not just Thomas—doubted. The story grew stale. Others denied it. At least sixty years had gone by after Jesus' death before this Gospel appeared. The early church looked for Jesus to return, but he had not come back to them. The faithful needed to find a new way to understand his life and his death and his resurrection.

They could find it in this story of the disciples in the days after the resurrection. Ten of them—and some of the women, uncounted—saw the risen Christ. Then a week went by. They must have begun to wonder whether they were reliable witnesses to their own experiences. Did they hear his words about peace and calm down? Did they grieve again, realizing that the risen Lord could not remain with them forever? Did they question each other, retelling the stories of Mary in the garden and Jesus in the upper room, asking, "Do you remember exactly what he said next?"

Thomas lived through that time in a different kind of tension, understanding that they must have seen something, but feeling hurt to be the only one who saw no sign.

Then Jesus appeared again.

"Have you believed because you have seen me? Blessed are those who have not seen and yet have come to believe."

We may default to reading Jesus' encounter with Thomas as a scolding. How dare he demand to see and touch the marks of the nails! So much of how we understand these stories, especially the more famous ones, depends on the tone in which we hear them. Maybe Christ is not dismissing Thomas, or us, when we want some proof that we matter to him. Consider the words this way, spoken kindly:

"Better to be one who doesn't need proof. But Thomas, if you need to, put your hand here."

In that moment, Thomas believes.

It is better to be the one who doesn't need proof, cleaner and easier. But here is Thomas, in the Gospel, representing us in our moments of doubt. Jesus does not cast him out, does not dismiss us. He meets us where we are. He comes back so Thomas can see him. He comes back to Thomas and shows the marks of love.

Easter 3: Recognizing Jesus
Luke 24:13–35

When he was at the table with them, he took bread, blessed and broke it, and gave it to them. Then their eyes were opened, and they recognized him; and he vanished from their sight. (Luke 24:30–31)

After Hurricane Katrina, I traveled from Maine to Mississippi on a mission of pastoral relief to a Methodist minister whose house had been devastated by flooding during the storm. My presence for two Sundays allowed the pastor to take some much-needed time off to work on plans for rebuilding her home.

On the second Sunday, we celebrated Communion. As a United Church of Christ pastor, I asked a lot of questions in advance about the liturgy and logistics the congregation would expect. The differences in phrasing and practice were small, yet I knew it mattered to get them right in a traumatized community. It was my role to keep things going for them as best I could. I worried a bit about being coordinated enough to hold the plate and tear the bread and hand it to each person as their pastor would do while remembering to say precisely the familiar words: "The body of Christ, broken for you."

When the first person in line came to me, and I tore the bread, I experienced a moment of intense surprise, as if the bread itself were saying to me, "Look! See! I am here."

The two people who walked the road to Emmaus on the first Easter knew Jesus by sight. Scholars now say they may have been a married couple, and Cleopas is a name so close to another Gospel character's that we may wonder if the unnamed person was the "wife of Clopas" whom John's Gospel (19:25) places at the foot of the cross.

They knew Jesus, but they could not see he was right there with them. They didn't recognize his voice, or his turns of phrase.

Then they invited him in for supper.

Look! See! Their eyes were opened, and they recognized him! It happened in the breaking of the bread, the first time that people who knew Jesus made the connection to him through the bread that represented his body. They would go on to recognize him, to perceive his presence, each time the bread was broken.

Look! See! As I tore those pieces of bread at a Methodist church far from my home, Christ's presence became apparent and took away all my worries about getting Communion right that day. Sometimes we have to experience something anew to remember what we were doing in the first place. A whole loaf feeds no one. Bread is meant to be broken and shared.

Like Mr. and Mrs. Cleopas, we sometimes like to tell the story of how disappointing the world is, how things aren't fair or didn't turn out the way we planned. On the road, Jesus patiently explained it all to them, his place in history and all the teachings that seemed so confusing at the time. When they talked about it later, they realized their hearts were burning all along.

Look! See! The good news is this: death could not take away our Jesus, and resurrection brought us Christ, who is with us in every time and place.

Easter 4: Living in Community
Acts 2:42–47

All who believed were together and had all things in common. (Acts 2:44)

This gentle passage of Scripture, the conclusion of the second chapter of Acts, sounds almost like the end of a fairy tale. The thousands of people baptized on the day of Pentecost were devoted to one another, "wonders and signs" were being done, and they all lived happily ever after, under the teaching of the apostles, sharing everything they had with each other, praying and breaking bread.

In modern times, preachers may unpack these verses by trying to find a way out of them. That was a different time, we might say, and the believers thought Jesus was coming back soon. They did not need to plan for retirement by adding to a 401(k) or pay for expensive prescription medications or save for outrageous college tuition. We fear that asking for more from church members will move them to give less, or simply to move elsewhere. Yet there are church essentials in this passage we would not want to overlook. Can we find the middle ground on which we honor God's call to the early church in a way that stretches our listeners without alienating them?

These early Christians devoted themselves to learning more about Jesus and being in fellowship together. They broke bread, which might mean having meals as well as sharing the sacrament. They prayed together. Perhaps we can go along with verse 44 and the idea that they had all things in common; this could be interpreted to refer to the church itself, cared for and held in trust by the congregation.

Up to this point we have no problem navigating the text, but in verse 45, we hit the rough water of a more radical notion: "they would sell their possessions and goods and distribute the proceeds to all, as any had need." We don't need to be proponents of the prosperity gospel to find this idea uncomfortable. The believers gathered in Jerusalem expected Christ's imminent return. Almost two thousand years after Jesus, we have built systems that almost equally rely on his indefinite absence, centered on constructed gathering spaces intended to last for decades, if not centuries.

Meanwhile, the world changes around us, and the church as an institution is in a season of reformation, whether we like it or not. For many congregations, the buildings we have constructed are underused or impossible to maintain as our human numbers dwindle. Some churches have responded to this new era proactively. Consider the story of Arlington Presbyterian Church (APC) in Arlington, Virginia.[1] Members of the church assessed their situation, their location, and the needs of the wider community for affordable housing. After considering several possibilities, they sold their land at below market value to the Arlington Partnership for Affordable Housing. The church building was razed, making the way for 173 affordable apartments. What they held in common, they sold and distributed for the good of all. Now sharing space with a Methodist congregation, APC continues to advocate for the rest of the neighborhood.

1. Patricia Sullivan, "The Church Is Not the Building. It Is Our Faith and Our People," *Washington Post*, Dec. 26, 2015.

Easter 5: Asking Questions
John 14:1–14

Thomas said to him, "Lord, we do not know where you are going. How can we know the way?" (John 14:5)

In John 14, Jesus delivers a speech we often hear at funerals, intended to comfort those left behind, both about the fate of our loved ones and about our own future after death. Jesus is giving an assurance that he will expand later on, saying that even though they won't see him for a while, they will see him again. He is going ahead to prepare a place for them. In his Father's house there are many dwelling places, many mansions, many antique farmhouses, and homespun cottages, and solar-powered contemporaries, and converted lofts in old knitting factories—there is enough room for everyone.

You know the way, he tells them, you know the way to the place that I am going. He is rhapsodizing, painting a picture of another realm, but the disciples bring the words back to earth. God bless Thomas, because he is willing to say what everyone else must be thinking. "I have no idea what you are talking about!" Thank God for Philip, asking for the proof everyone wants, "Show us this Father you're always talking about!"

What will we do when you leave us behind, Lord? You have not told us specifically how to get to where you are going. You have not even proved your connection to God. That is what they are saying to him.

Despite Jesus' consoling words, the disciples will be left behind to deal with drama up to and including the stoning of visionaries like Stephen, as described in the Acts passage for today, and arrests and crucifixions of their own. They sense they are in trouble. They may not know exactly what's going to happen later in the evening, but they do know Jesus has been at the temple raising, well, heaven, and the authorities have tried, more than once, to get their hands on him. The disciples are naturally anxious about the future, particularly their immediate future.

What works does Jesus mean? Soon they would know: the work of God in the resurrection.

We live in anxious times too, in which political and cultural debates are fueled by interpretations of Scripture. What did Jesus really mean? Who is telling the truth about it? Will we ever know for sure? How can we find the way to follow him when we cannot watch him walking down an earthly road, when we cannot hurry to catch up and match our pace to his?

When we do not know the way, the interpretation, the truth, it is better to ask a question than to keep it to ourselves. We can ask the pastor, or a teacher, or a person whose faith we find admirable. We can ask someone who looks just as baffled as we feel. We have a strong example in the disciples, who asked for clarity when they did not understand, and who continued to work it out among themselves, centered on Jesus Christ, who is the way, and the truth, and the life.

Easter 6: Sharing Our Faith
Acts 17:22–31

"From one ancestor [God] made all nations to inhabit the whole earth, and he allotted the times of their existence and the boundaries of the places where they would live, so that they would search for God and perhaps grope for him and find him—though indeed he is not far from each one of us." (Acts 17:26–27)

At a retreat for clergy at a church unfamiliar to many of the group, the host pastor made the first announcement of the day. "I need to tell you the light switches are on the outside of the bathroom doors, so you won't be groping in the dark."

If only life were always so uncomplicated and instructions always so clear! If only God would always tell us clearly where to turn on the light. Yet it's the way of things that we put our hands out into the dark and run them up and down the wall, trying our best to find what is not in the place we are looking for it. We grope.

The world doesn't seem to know us in the church; sometimes it cannot even say where in town to find our buildings. We have so many audiences to reach, and we engage in this groping struggle not only for God but for our purpose in our particular contexts. It is the truth of our time and place that the God we love and seek may be largely unknown to the people we meet on the Mars Hills of our lives, at the town meeting, or the presidential caucus, or the big-box store, or the coffee shop, or the diner. And people find their way to us, when they come, for different reasons now, not to be part of a thriving, mainstream institution, but questioning, seeking, groping for a sense of purpose and meaning.

When they do come, when death, loss, dissatisfaction, or a joyful event bring people through our doors who don't know us well already, how do we welcome them? It's one thing to be friendly; please be friendly!

But we have to recognize that the things we do and the ways we do them can look very strange and unaccustomed. Presbyterian Church (USA) pastor Jan Edmiston tells a story about the time her college-age son brought his girlfriend to a worship service. When the choir came in wearing robes, the young woman asked, "Are all the singers in the National Honor Society?"

If our practices are mysterious, our stories may sound quaint and arcane. That brings us to Paul at the Areopagus. Our hero—because he really is our hero in the Acts of the Apostles—takes what is in front of him, the worship of an unknown God by the Athenians, and forms an argument to sway them to believing in his God. He shows some knowledge of their context and develops his argument organically.

All ministry takes place in a particular time and place, among people with stories and places with a past. How would you describe the nature of your community? Do the people who work close by live close by? Do the people who worship together resemble the people who drive or walk by without stopping? Paul points us toward finding the connections between the ways we are all groping for God.

Easter 7: Seeking Guidance Together
Acts 1:6–14

Then they returned to Jerusalem from the mount called Olivet, which is near Jerusalem, a sabbath day's journey away. When they had entered the city, they went to the room upstairs where they were staying, Peter, and John, and James, and Andrew, Philip and Thomas, Bartholomew and Matthew, James son of Alphaeus, and Simon the Zealot, and Judas son of James. All these were constantly devoting themselves to prayer, together with certain women, including Mary the mother of Jesus, as well as his brother. (Acts 1:12–14)

For Jesus' closest followers, the ascension marked another turning point.

After the crucifixion they held together and retreated to the upper room. Their time of grieving was short, one Sabbath and the night that followed. By Sunday morning grief gave way to shock and then amazement when Jesus appeared, first to the women and then to the disciples gathered in the upper room. For forty days they lived in a liminal time, still expecting to see Christ again.

Now he was really, truly gone. The men in white said so. What would become of those who had given up everything to follow Jesus? What might happen next?

Still pondering the last words the risen Lord shared with them, they returned to the upper room, where they prayed together. There we find the remaining eleven disciples—Judas Iscariot has fled and died—the mother and brothers of Jesus, and "certain women," who apparently the author prefers to remain anonymous. We can imagine them: Mary

Magdalene, perhaps the sisters from Bethany, and other women who went to the cross and the tomb. This is the crowd that won't go home, the faithful remnant, waiting for whatever would come, probably a bit stunned by the supernatural event they witnessed.

The men and women "constantly devoting themselves to prayer" could not predict what was coming next or what exactly they would be called to do, only that they would be witnesses to the world on behalf of Jesus Christ.

When we experience a major transition in our lives, or in the life of the church, we find ourselves similarly situated. Change can be exciting or unsettling, welcome or resisted, joyous or anxiety provoking.

Some years ago, in a season of discernment about my ministry, I attended the Festival of Homiletics in Atlanta. One of the preachers, the Rev. Dr. James Forbes of the Riverside Church in New York City, asked us to pair off with someone we didn't know and pray for him or for her. He gave us a list of what he called "anointings of the Spirit" that we might feel we needed in our lives. Dr. Forbes said, "You'll know when I describe the one you need. It will cause a burning in your heart."

The people seated around me paired off with one another, and I looked across the aisle, there in the balcony of the enormous Peachtree Road United Methodist Church. I caught the eye of a man on the other side, and we met at the brass banister dividing the stairs. He asked me what I needed, and I told him I felt that burning when Dr. Forbes spoke of asking for willingness. My prayer partner, a Presbyterian minister from Virginia, told me a bit about his situation and he said, at the moment I was thinking it, that we were in much the same position. Yet he asked me to pray on his behalf not for willingness, but for obedience.

We needed different anointings, but we needed prayer, and we needed each other.

Pentecost Sunday: Being Moved
Acts 2:1–21

And suddenly from heaven there came a sound like the rush of a violent wind, and it filled the entire house where they were sitting. (Acts 2:2)

The demanding tone on our smart phones meant our whole family paid attention to the tornado warning. We did not wait to hear the rush of violent winds roaring like a freight train; we hurried down to our basement.

Sometimes the Spirit of God falls on us like a late spring breeze, encouraging us gently in a new direction. Other times the movement of the Holy Spirit looks and feels and sounds more like a tornado that pulled water right up out of the Connecticut River at the same time it spat debris into the sky like birds in frantic flight.

The difference between a tornado watch and a tornado warning is this: a watch occurs when the atmospheric conditions are right, a warning when a tornado has been identified. We keep watch so we'll be ready to move.

Seven weeks have passed since the resurrection, and the men and women who loved Jesus and tried their best to understand what he wanted for them remain huddled in a rented room, attentive as they pray and ponder and puzzle about what has befallen them and what may come next. The conditions are right, and suddenly a severe spiritual event occurs, moving beyond the "watch" phase into a full-on "warning." The wind blows and tongues of fire appear, and suddenly people who do not know each other's languages understand what is being said.

We call it the birthday of the church, as if the tongues of flame were as benign as little birthday candles. But imagine the faithful friends of Jesus: shocked, terrified, transfixed, and amazed. Imagine thousands more in the neighborhood, caught up in a storm of God's power, a manifestation of the Spirit of God promised by Jesus.

We want a soft hand, a gentle breeze, a kindly prompt about our spiritual gifts and how to use them; and sometimes we get that. We prefer the peace of the predictable. We don't want to lose what we are accustomed to. We prefer to stay put, even when we know things are less than satisfactory. Moving into the unknown is risky. Even as the wind swirls around us, sounding like a freight train, the vibrations shaking the building, we hang on to what we know. We hope the storm will go by and leave us huddled safely in the basement.

But when the conditions are right, when we give ourselves over to God and pray sincerely to be guided and to be put to use, we need to watch out for the tornado that is coming. The Holy Spirit will change a person. The Holy Spirit will change a church. When the Spirit shows up, we will be moved! Wind-whipped, we cannot go back to our lives as if nothing has happened. When our inward lives have been illuminated by God's flame, blown open by God's wind, our outward lives have to respond.

Is there a significant risk that the Holy Spirit will blow into this church like the rush of a violent wind? Are the conditions right?

Summer Series: Family Reunion

Eleven Parts: Trinity Sunday through Proper 15

In the trials of one family, we find hope for our own.

CAROL CAVIN-DILLON

Series Overview

Summer is a time for family reunions. For some of us, family reunions are fun and fulfilling. For others of us, they are uncomfortable or even painful. We all have some dysfunction in our families. We all have stories that we'd rather not tell. In the stories of Genesis, we discover God's chosen family—those first generations of Israel—had struggles, secrets, sibling rivalries, and even threats of murder. As we explore these rich and ancient stories, we see how God works through and in spite of family dysfunction to bring about God's purposes for the world, and we find hope for God's presence and movement in our own families.

	Sermon Title	Focus Scripture	Theme
Trinity Sunday	God's Perfect Family	Gen. 1:1–2:4a	The Trinity is perfect relationship.
Proper 6	God Chooses an Imperfect Family	Gen. 18:1–15 (21:1–7)	God's purpose is to bless all families through one family.
Proper 7	A Painful Shortcut	Gen. 21:8–21	We get impatient, but God redeems our mistakes.
Proper 8	An Unthinkable Trial	Gen. 22:1–14	Even in the deepest trials, God makes a way.
Proper 9	A Biblical Romance?	Gen. 24:34–38, 42–49, 58–67	Romance makes a good story, but it's a small part of God's greater story.
Proper 10	Sibling Rivalry, Part I	Gen. 25:19–34	When we are all at fault, God is all-faithful.

	Sermon Title	Focus Scripture	Theme
Proper 11	Works in Progress	Gen. 28:10–19a	Every family has difficult people, but there is always hope for change.
Proper 12	Sibling Rivalry, Part II	Gen. 29:15–28	We seek power, but God seeks our good.
Proper 13	Holy Wrestling	Gen. 32:22–31	When we wrestle with doubt and fear, God comes to us and blesses us.
Proper 14	Sibling Rivalry, Part III	Gen. 37:1–4, 12–28	No more playing favorites—we're all longing for love.
Proper 15	Forgiveness in the Family	Gen. 45:1–15	God empowers us to forgive.

Tips and Ideas for This Series

This series runs through the summer, from early June to mid-August, and it gives us an opportunity to talk about family in all its many dimensions and forms. Of course, it is important not to talk about family in a way that excludes those who are single, divorced, or in families that don't conform to the "Mom, Dad, two kids, and a dog" model. Graphics might depict a variety of different images of families both happy and unhappy, or simply a gingham tablecloth pattern like one you might see at a big family picnic. Consider offering a special summer class for those who want to read the whole book of Genesis together. Or schedule an evening for people to gather and tell old family stories, looking for evidence of God's presence through our forebears. You might offer some parenting workshops, divorce recovery sessions, or marriage enrichment retreats. You might also talk about the congregation as a family and either kick off or end the summer with a "God's Family Reunion" picnic gathering.

Trinity Sunday[1]: God's Perfect Family
Genesis 1:1–2:4a

In the beginning when God created the heavens and the earth, the earth was a formless void and darkness covered the face of the deep, while the spirit of God swept over the face of the waters. (Genesis 1:1–2)

1. Trinity Sunday is observed the Sunday following Pentecost, and takes the place of the Proper that would fall on that Sunday (which could be Proper 3, 4, 5, or 6). In 2020, this is Proper 5, as reflected in this resource. In 2023 and 2026, Trinity Sunday will take the place of Proper 4 and require some adjustment to this series plan.

When I was fresh out of seminary serving in my first church, I was invited to talk with the first grade Sunday school class about worship. We met in the sanctuary, and I showed them the pulpit, the baptismal font, the altar table, and the paraments. When I asked for questions, one little girl raised her hand and said, "What is that picture on the tablecloth?" "It's the symbol of the Trinity," I replied. "What's the Trinity?" another child asked. Five minutes later I found myself still yammering on and trying to explain, while six confused faces looked up at me. With all that seminary education, I was still unable to explain the Trinity to first-graders!

The doctrine of the Trinity is a beautiful gift to the church, but let's be honest: we are often so baffled by its mystery, so paralyzed by our inability to explain it, that we avoid the subject altogether. Nevertheless, the liturgical calendar gives us a yearly invitation to celebrate Trinity Sunday and explore what it means to worship the Three-in-One. Why not dive in headfirst this year? As we begin a sermon series on family, the Trinity is quite literally the perfect place to start.

In Genesis 1, we get a glimpse of the eternal Trinity: The Spirit sweeps over the face of the waters as God the Creator calls forth light. From the prologue to John's Gospel we also know "in the beginning was the Word," which became flesh in Jesus of Nazareth. To put it another way, in the beginning was the Divine Family. The perfect family!

The three persons of the Trinity are in perfect communion with one another. There is uniqueness and unity. The love that flows from one to the other is pure, complete, eternal, and unconditional. They always have shared and always will share in mutual joy and peace. For one glorious chapter of the Bible, all creation is in harmony and God's will is perfectly fulfilled.

Let's pause to enjoy it for a moment, because in the next chapter, things go downhill. God creates the first human family, and within a few verses they mess up. They start blaming each other, and they hide in shame from God. They exile themselves from the loving community of the Trinity. And for the rest of human history, God has worked, is working, and will be working to bring God's children back into the family.

What follows in the book of Genesis is a series of stories about human families. We'll spend the next ten weeks hearing about sibling rivalry, adultery, trickery, and betrayal. And yet, through all the messiness of these human families, God continues the work of reconciling the world to Godself. The whole story gives us hope that in the midst of our imperfect families and messy lives, God is moving nevertheless to reunite us and all people into one divine family.

Proper 6: God Chooses an Imperfect Family
Genesis 18:1–15 (21:1–7)

Now Abraham and Sarah were old, advanced in age. . . . The Lord *said to Abraham, "Why did Sarah laugh, and say, 'Shall I indeed bear a child, now that I am old?' Is anything too wonderful for the* Lord*? At the set time I will return to you, in due season, and Sarah shall have a son." (Genesis 18:11a, 13–14)*

God has a funny way of doing things. If you were going to pick one family out of all the families of the earth to be "God's chosen family," wouldn't you choose two beautiful, young, wealthy and strong people living in the most powerful nation in the world? Well, that's not what God does at all. God chooses instead two elderly nomads who are beyond childbearing years. They are nobodies, living in a tent, not sure of their future.

Not only are they old and rootless, they are also finding it hard to trust God's promises. It was way back in chapter 12 that God first called Abraham—or Abram, as he was called then—and promised him offspring. But years have gone by, and there is still no baby. (The couple gets so impatient, in fact, that in chapter 16 they take matters into their own hands and really mess things up. More on that next week!)

Finally, in spite of their impatience, in spite of their age, in spite of their tent living, God shows up to reiterate the promise. The story describes three strangers, who are mysteriously and wonderfully also referred to as "the Lord" (a nice connection with last week's sermon on the Trinity) and who come to bring a message to the aging couple.

Abraham and Sarah show these guests great hospitality. They're awfully cute together as they fuss over their guests. Reading how Abraham "mansplains" to Sarah how to make cakes reminded me of my own parents. When my father retired, my mother called me on the phone in frustration one afternoon and said, "He stands over me in the kitchen and tells me what to do. You'd think I'd never made a sandwich before!" Abraham is just so eager to welcome these guests properly that he can't help hovering in the kitchen.

Once the guests have eaten, they relay their very specific message: "This time next year, Sarah will have a son." The message makes Sarah laugh with both joy and disbelief. The exchange between her and the messenger is quirky and takes us to a place of laughter. We end the story smiling at the goodness of God, who brings life and joy to a family that seems to have lost hope.

Special Note: Be sensitive to the fact that this story could be painful for those who struggle with infertility. The story gives us an opportunity to name that reality and also to point to God's love and provision.

God made a way where there seemed to be no way. God can enter into our families, into our griefs, into our hopelessness, and surprise us in unexpected ways with laughter and joy. We may not get easy answers or all that we wish for, but God comes to us nonetheless. May we do all we can to welcome God into our lives, as Abraham and Sarah welcomed the strangers, that we too might receive an unexpected blessing.

Proper 7: A Painful Shortcut
Genesis 21:8–21

And God heard the voice of the boy; and the angel of God called to Hagar from heaven, and said to her, "What troubles you, Hagar? Do not be afraid; for God has heard the voice of the boy where he is. Come, lift up the boy and hold him fast with your hand, for I will make a great nation of him." (Genesis 21:17–18)

When our story opens this week, we find God's family in the middle of a mess. In order to untangle some of the mess, we need to go back a few chapters.

Way back in Genesis 12, God had told Abraham that he would be the father of a great nation. God had promised him offspring. However, time goes by and nothing happens. Chapters, years go by, and still no baby for Sarah. So, in Genesis 16, Sarah takes matters into her own hands. In an act of impatience and power that should disturb us, Sarah "gives" her slave-girl Hagar to Abraham in order that she might bear a child for them. Sarah's plan works, and Hagar gives birth to Ishmael.

It is after the birth of Ishmael that God sends messengers to Abraham saying that he *and Sarah* will have a son. (Remember last week's story.) God reiterates and clarifies God's promise, and Sarah indeed gives birth to Isaac at the beginning of chapter 21.

But here's where it gets messy and even ugly. Hagar and her son Ishmael have been part of the family for fourteen years now, but Sarah suddenly grows jealous and fearful of them. Even though she was the one who mistrusted God's promise, tried to take a shortcut, and dragged Hagar into her schemes, she now demands that Hagar and Ishmael be cast out.

This story casts a dark shadow over the history of God's family. Abraham and Sarah are supposed to be our heroes, and yet they not only own Hagar as a slave but abuse and mistreat her and her son. Hearing this story about our spiritual ancestors is not unlike a contemporary Southerner learning that her ancestors owned slaves. The story can also be painful for those who are descended from slaves and see in Hagar the abuse of their ancestors.

It is possible and even powerful for a preacher to name these truths in the story, to help us name the sins or struggles of our ancestors, to recognize that history is messy and human beings are sinful. Even the patriarchs and matriarchs of the faith acted in ways that broke God's heart.

But the good news in this story is that God does not agree with Sarah and Abraham's rejection of Hagar and Ishmael. Even though they cast her into the wilderness, God goes looking for the young woman and her son. God speaks directly to Hagar, gives her water to drink, and promises to make a great nation of *her* son.

This is a deeply reassuring story. Although we at times fail to trust God, take matters into our own hands, and cause a lot of harm in our wake, God intervenes to redeem and to save. God can use our shortcuts and mistakes to bring about something new.

Proper 8: An Unthinkable Trial
Genesis 22:1–14

But the angel of the LORD called to him from heaven, and said, "Abraham, Abraham!" And he said, "Here I am." He said, "Do not lay your hand on the boy or do anything to him; for now I know that you fear God, since you have not withheld your son, your only son, from me." (Genesis 22:11–12)

I know, I know. Why in the world would a preacher choose this text? When the lectionary offers us "a cup of cold water" in Matthew, why would we enter into the horror, confusion, and theological conundrum of the binding of Isaac?

God's actions in this story are simply unfathomable. If verse 1 is true, God is choosing to put Abraham to the test. And, for most of us, the test is cruel. Why, after the years Abraham and Sarah have spent waiting and wandering, would God pretend to demand that they give up the one gift that God had promised them?

The truth is, there are no easy answers. This is a story that invites us to wrestle. It drives us to explore what other scholars, rabbis, and readers across the centuries have said about it. It's far too easy for us in the church today to choose the easier text or to jump to the quickest solutions. We just can't do that with this story, and that is a good thing.

As you prepare your sermon for this Sunday, be honest with yourself and with your congregation about your struggle with the text. If you find it hard to accept that God would test Abraham in this way, say so! If you think that Abraham was wrong to lift the knife and threaten his son, then express that! Your listeners will likely appreciate your honesty.

One way to usher your listeners into this story is to consider how Abraham was willing to give up the great gift he had received from God. His trust was in God, not in the gifts of God. You might invite your listeners to ask themselves, "Do we love the Giver more than we love the gift?" In other words, "Do we trust God for God's sake, or are we more interested in what God can do for us?"

Leonard Sweet suggests that God actually wanted Abraham to push back and resist the order. Abraham had defended the citizens of Sodom and Gomorrah, bargaining with God to save as many as he could. In the case of his own son, however, Abraham did not engage but simply put his head down and walked up the mountain. After the trauma was over, God never spoke directly with Abraham again.

As difficult as this story is, the truth is that God ultimately does not want Abraham to harm Isaac. We know in our hearts that God's desire is to protect the innocent. Perhaps this story was handed down to us to make it clear that the God of Israel does not tolerate the sacrifice of the innocent. How many ways do we sacrifice the innocent in our culture today? How might God "stay our hand"?

Proper 9: A Biblical Romance?
Genesis 24:34–38, 42–49, 58–67

Then Isaac brought her into his mother Sarah's tent. He took Rebekah, and she became his wife; and he loved her. (Genesis 24:67)

Our culture is obsessed with romance. From the novels of Danielle Steele to the "romcoms" playing in movie theaters everywhere, we like to see two people discover each other, fall in love, overcome obstacles, and end up "happily ever after."

Unfortunately, when it comes to romance, the Bible is seriously lacking. If we set aside the Song of Songs, which plenty of people would like to do, we're not left with many good love stories. Yes, there are marriages. There is sex and adultery and jealousy. But rarely do we hear about two people falling in love and getting married.

The closest we get is probably Isaac and Rebekah. Granted, theirs is basically an arranged marriage. Abraham wants his son Isaac to marry someone "in the family," so he sends a servant to Nahor to find the right girl. It is the servant who first sees Rebekah, talks with her, and asks her to marry Isaac. It is Rebekah's father and uncle who make the deal, although Rebekah is given some freedom to choose. Isaac and Rebekah don't even see each other until the deal is done.

But the "romantic" moment comes when Rebekah arrives in the Negeb, where Isaac has settled. She sees Isaac, "slips off her camel," and puts on her veil. When Isaac sees her, he takes her as his wife, and he loves her. Not quite as riveting as *Sleepless in Seattle*, but still sort of sweet.

Clearly God's purposes are at work in this story. Although God is not directly managing the action, God's will seems to be that Rebekah marry Isaac. God is working to bring these two together. Their love story might invite us to consider how God is involved in our own "love lives." Do we invite God into our dating relationships, our marriages? Do we believe that God can guide us toward the right partner?

While this story gives us an opportunity to preach about romantic love and even about marriage, the truth is that the romance is not that important to the narrative. It's a nice detail, that Rebekah and Isaac seem to have loved each other, but romantic love is not really at the heart of what God is doing in Genesis—or in our world.

We spend a lot of time and energy in our culture pursuing, discussing, obsessing over, and celebrating romantic love. To be sure, romantic love is a wonderful gift that brings us joy. But it is just a small part of what it means to be married and an even smaller part of what it means to love. The love story between two people is only a glimpse of the much greater love story of God and the world. The love that begins at home, within our marriages and our families, is both an anchor and a springboard, empowering us to go out and love the world in God's name.

Proper 10: Sibling Rivalry, Part I
Genesis 25:19–34

When the boys grew up, Esau was a skillful hunter, a man of the field, while Jacob was a quiet man, living in tents. Isaac loved Esau . . . but Rebekah loved Jacob." (Genesis 25:27–28)

This sermon series gives us three opportunities to explore sibling rivalries: Jacob and Esau, Leah and Rachel, and the sons of Jacob. Many of us know what sibling rivalry is like. We have struggles with our own siblings, or we are raising children who bicker and compete with each other on a daily basis. Knowing and even recounting our own experiences can help bring these Scriptures to life.

In this first story of sibling rivalry, we see the "romantic couple" from last week at odds with each other. They are playing favorites with their twin boys, which is a recipe for conflict. Granted, the boys were already at odds with each other in their mother's womb, but the favoritism of their parents only feeds the rivalry.

Ultimately, Rebekah and son Jacob outsmart Isaac and son Esau. It is Jacob who, through deceit and trickery, ends up with the blessing of Isaac and the covenant promise of God. God's role in the whole thing is not straightforward. Did God choose Jacob all along? When God told Rebekah that "the elder shall serve the younger," was God stating a preference or simply recognizing the inevitable? Did Rebekah scheme for Jacob because she thought God had chosen him, or simply because she loved him more? None of the answers is clear. We must read for ourselves and come to our own conclusions.

One thing is clear in the story: neither son is a great hero. Esau is strong and likable, but he is foolish. He chooses to satisfy his bodily hunger rather than hold on to God's promise. Jacob is conniving and grasping, but he longs for the birthright and blessing of his father.

In spite of the faults on all sides of the family, God works anyway. God sees that Jacob has prevailed in his efforts to gain the birthright, and God chooses to work with him. This family is totally dysfunctional, but God works through them anyway!

God moves forward with the covenant with Jacob, but God does not abandon Esau. While Jacob eventually becomes Israel, God also blesses Esau with land and offspring. And as time passes, the two brothers are able to reconcile in their own way and stand together to bury their father (Gen. 35). There is hope, even in our dysfunctional families, for reconciliation.

Proper 11: Works in Progress
Genesis 28:10–19a

"Know that I am with you and will keep you wherever you go, and will bring you back to this land; for I will not leave you until I have done what I have promised you." (Genesis 28:15)

We find ourselves in the middle of the Jacob saga in Genesis. At this point in the story, we know a lot about Jacob's past, and we may have decided that we don't like him very much. Let's face it, he's not a very nice guy. He is grasping and scheming. His very name means "Grabber"; he is so named because he came out of the womb grabbing onto the heel of his twin brother Esau. He and his mother tricked his father into giving him the blessing of the family, and when his brother Esau found out about it, Jacob ran in fear. If anything, we may find ourselves wishing that the birthright had gone to the foolish but more likable Esau.

When we find him in chapter 28, Jacob is on the run, sleeping outdoors with a stone for a pillow. At this point in the story, we are hoping that something will change within Jacob. Perhaps he will begin to feel remorse for how he tricked his brother Esau. Maybe he will turn to God and ask for forgiveness and help.

Instead, what we find in this story is that God reaches out to Jacob first. Before Jacob seeks God, God finds Jacob. In the night Jacob has a dream of angels ascending and descending a ladder. God speaks to him and reiterates the promise God had made to Jacob's grandfather Abraham. In spite of the tricky ways that Jacob had come to inherit the promise, God accepts him as a partner in the covenant. God is ready to do God's part.

Jacob is overwhelmed with awe and realizes that the Lord has been with him, even in this runaway wilderness. God has proven to Jacob that God is with him, God is faithful, God is constant. God will uphold God's side of the bargain because that's who God is.

You would think that this kind of grace and faithfulness would change Jacob. You would hope that he could now rest in the assurance of God's presence with him. But that's not quite the case. Although the lectionary reading stops after Jacob praises God, the very next verse shows Jacob continuing to scheme and negotiate. He doesn't seem quite sure that he trusts God, and he tries to throw "bread to eat and clothing to wear" into the bargain. Jacob has not fully changed. He is still a work in progress.

Nevertheless, God is faithful. This story is a powerful reminder of God's steadfast love. Regardless of Jacob's scheming and trickery, God is present with him. Despite his lack of trust, God is patient with him. Although Jacob is totally unlikable, God loves him anyway and will continue to work with him.

The truth of the gospel lies beneath this story: God's grace is not contingent on our deserving. God's love is not conditional. God's covenant does not have any fine print. God loves us and will never stop working on us to become more faithful and loving members of God's family.

When morning came, it was Leah! And Jacob said to Laban, "What is this you have done to me? Did I not serve with you for Rachel? Why then have you deceived me?" (Genesis 29:25)

In Genesis 29 the family soap opera continues. We see more deception, more tangles and more family rivalry. For the first time we meet someone who can out trick the trickster Jacob. Uncle Laban seems to be a more cunning schemer than Jacob.

The chapter begins with another love story at the side of a well. Jacob sees Rachel at the well and decides she is "the one" for him. Whether it's really love at first sight is hard to tell. Jacob makes quite a scene when he first sees Rachel—and the sheep of Laban—at the well (Gen. 29:10). Is this story less about romantic love and more about a business transaction between two men? The sisters seem to be the bargaining chips, passed from one household to another with no power to choose.

As our lectionary text opens, Jacob is making a deal with Rachel's father, his uncle Laban: he will work seven years for his uncle in order to marry Rachel. At the end of those seven years, Laban hosts a wedding feast but ends up substituting his older daughter Leah for Rachel. He's tricking the trickster! We might wonder how Laban managed this deceitful power play. How did Jacob not know? Or did he know? Are he and Laban playing some elaborate game? For centuries rabbis and readers have asked these questions. Either way, Jacob wakes up in the morning claiming that Laban has treated him unfairly, and we, as readers, have to agree.

When Laban tries to explain to Jacob, he says, "This is not done in our country—giving the younger before the firstborn." We cannot help but hear the irony here, for the pattern of the story so far has shown that God's covenant is with the younger sibling. God's ways seem to counter the ways of the world. But Laban is a man of the world and finds a way to stick with convention. In the end, Jacob accepts what has happened and works another seven years for Rachel.

Sadly, the transaction between Laban and Jacob sets up a rivalry between the two sisters. Jacob has clearly preferred Rachel all along, and Leah feels unloved. Rachel is jealous because Leah bears Jacob children before Rachel does. As their ancestor-in-law Sarah (and others in that culture, to be sure) did before them, the sisters volunteer their servant girls to bear children on their behalf, struggling for power and favor in the only way available to women at the time. Leah gloats, and Rachel herself remains barren. Once again, we see dysfunction and rivalry passed from one generation to the next.

But once again we see God at work in spite of human brokenness. As we look at the whole "Jacob-Leah-Rachel" saga, we recognize God's compassion and goodness: God sees Leah's sadness. God sees that Rachel is barren. Both of them bear children, and the tribe of Jacob multiplies. From this family soap opera come the twelve tribes of Israel.

And the promise of God continues.

Proper 13: Holy Wrestling
Genesis 32:22–31

Jacob was left alone; and a man wrestled with him until daybreak. (Genesis 32:24)

Jacob is in trouble. We have traveled with him for several chapters now, and we have seen him win out over his adversaries again and again. At a young age he tricked his father Isaac and his brother Esau into giving him the birthright and the blessing of the covenant. As an adult he tricked his father-in-law, Uncle Laban, and managed to grow for himself a large family and a large estate.

At this point in Jacob's saga, he is leaving the land of his Uncle Laban and heading back home. Responding to the instructions of God, he is traveling back to the land where he grew up and where his brother Esau still resides. It's time for Jacob to face his brother and to own up to what he has done to him.

Jacob is not looking forward to this family reunion; so he sends word to his brother that he is on the way home. Fearful that his brother's hatred has festered and that Esau will try to destroy him, he sends an advance party with gifts. In his cunning way he is trying to butter up his brother and to save his own skin.

On the night before the final confrontation, Jacob spends the night alone. There is so much that can be read into this story of the wrestling match, because so many questions remain unanswered. Is Jacob's nocturnal opponent a man? Esau himself? An angel? God?

And who exactly "wins" the match? Jacob is wounded and walks away limping. His opponent declares that Jacob has "striven with God and with humans, and [has] prevailed." Does that mean that Jacob is the winner? Perhaps this is a match where there is no winner and no loser.

Here's what we know: by the end of the night, Jacob believes he has been wrestling with Yahweh. Jacob does not die in the wrestling match but holds on for dear life. In the end he is blessed and given a new name.

The story invites us to acknowledge our own wrestling matches—with family members, friends, and even within ourselves. Perhaps we wrestle with our own past. We remember those we have hurt, and we struggle to come to terms with our own sin. We wrestle with God when life gets hard. We want to get our own way and for our life to be easier than it is. We long for God's blessing and approval, yet there are things within us that keep us from yielding to God's will.

the presence of God in each of these wrestlings: in diff ways—

This story of Jacob's wrestling reminds us that God welcomes our struggle. God will meet us where we are, and though we will never conquer God, God will stay with us and bless us in the struggle. We may end up with a limp or a new way of naming ourselves, but we will know God's love that never lets us go.

Proper 14: Sibling Rivalry, Part III
Genesis 37:1–4, 12–28

Now Israel loved Joseph more than any other of his children, because he was the son of his old age. . . . But when his brothers saw that their father loved him more than all his brothers, they hated him, and could not speak peaceably to him. (Genesis 37:3–4)

Once again, the family of God is in turmoil because somebody played favorites. Jacob has now settled with his large family in the land of Canaan, and all seems to be going well. He has many children, and his crops and cattle are flourishing. He is now enjoying the fulfillment of God's promises to his ancestors. All should be well.

But it's not. Like his parents before him, Jacob, who is now called Israel, is playing favorites with his children. He loves his son Joseph most of all, and he does not hesitate to show it. The elaborate robe he gives to Joseph sets him apart from and above all his brothers. It is an outward sign of Israel's favoritism.

Joseph did not ask for this special attention, but he certainly seems to capitalize on it. He wears the robe with pride, he is a tattletale, and he's not shy about sharing with his family the dreams he has about his ascendancy over them.

This story gives us another opportunity to reflect on our own families. Have we seen parents who blatantly show favoritism to some of their children? Have we been singled out as the favorite? Have we felt the hurt of the other brothers in the story, knowing that we are less favored by our parents?

Taking this story beyond the realm of families, do we see favoritism in our culture? Are we among the privileged to whom society has given a colorful robe? Or do we watch as others receive special treatment while we are overlooked and undervalued? What kind of strife arises in the family of God because some are lifted above others?

Although the story of Joseph and his colorful coat is the subject of musicals and vacation Bible school curricula, there is much about the story that is tragic. Today's text ends in a horrifying way. Most of Joseph's brothers hate him enough to kill him, and in the end they sell him into slavery. They are content never to lay eyes on him again.

A deeper tragedy of the story is that, underneath their behavior, what all the characters want is to be loved. Joseph's brothers are hurt and angry because their father does not love them as much as Joseph. And in his own way Joseph longs for the love of his brothers. We see him wandering in the fields of Shechem and telling a stranger, "I am seeking my brothers."

What if we looked at one another—in our nuclear families and throughout the family of God—and recognized that deep longing for love? What if we remembered that God, unlike Jacob or Isaac or Rebekah or many of our own parents, does not play favorites but loves each one of us completely? How might that affect how we treat our brothers and sisters in the family of God?

Proper 15: Forgiveness in the Family
Genesis 45:1–15

"I am your brother Joseph, whom you sold into Egypt. And now do not be distressed, or angry with yourselves, because you sold me here; for God sent me before you to preserve life." (Genesis 45:4b–5)

We come now to the final installment in this series. We have traveled through the book of Genesis and watched our spiritual ancestors navigate their family troubles. We have seen abuse, favoritism, deceit, and sibling rivalry in many forms, and now we come to the emotional climax of the saga: Joseph forgives his brothers.

At the end of last week's Scripture lesson, the legacy of favoritism and rivalry had ended tragically. The hatred and jealousy of Joseph's brothers led them to sell him into slavery. In our text for today, years have passed, and Joseph has prospered. He is now the second-most-powerful man in Egypt, and his brothers have come to him begging for help.

The drama of the scene is heightened by the fact that the brothers do not recognize Joseph. They think that he is an Egyptian, and they approach him with fear and deference. Joseph plays with this power dynamic for a while, but eventually his emotions get the best of him. We see him, a powerful official of Egypt who has every right to be angry with his brothers, break down and weep because he is overcome with love. Love and forgiveness win out over anger and retribution.

After spending these past thirteen weeks watching parents, children, and siblings misbehaving and treating each other badly, we finally see someone acting with grace and mercy. We see Joseph acting as God would have him (and us) act. We see reconciliation!

The truth is, when we look back on these Genesis stories, most of them actually end with some form of reconciliation. Isaac and Ishmael stand together to bury their father Abraham (Gen. 25:9). Leah and Rachel speak with one voice as they pledge their loyalty to Jacob (31:14). Esau forgives Jacob (33:4) and together they bury Isaac (35:29).

The arc of God's story moves toward reconciliation and peace. Although our human nature pulls us toward rivalry and favoritism, God is always at work within us and beyond us to deepen our love and forgiveness. The question for us is: Will we participate in the reconciling work of God? Will we choose to play favorites and to deepen the rivalries within our families and within the family of God? Or will we join in the work that God is doing to create one human family grounded in love and peace?

Fall Series 1: Learning to Love Our Enemies

Four Parts: Proper 18 through Proper 21

Though it often seems more easily said than done, loving the unlovable is possible with guidance from our Scriptures.

ANTHONY J. TANG

Series Overview The capacity for love to overcome all obstacles is easier to believe when talking about two people who want to be together, but can be especially challenging when thinking of ourselves and someone we don't want to be with, especially someone who has hurt or betrayed us. Yet our ability to overcome conflict within ourselves and find peace (despite what others may do) is an incredible opportunity to reflect the unconditional love of Jesus Christ, who loves us despite the ways we have failed. This four-week series offers practical guidance (largely from the Old Testament) to equip our members to practice the kind of enemy love Jesus preached.

	Sermon Title	Focus Scripture[1]	Theme
Proper 18	Love through Due Process	Ezek. 33:7–11; Matt. 18:15–20	People may not like us for being honest, but it is truly the pathway of love.
Proper 19	When God Transforms Evil into Good	Gen. 50:15–21	Others may intend evil, but God can make all things work toward good.
Proper 20	Mercy and God's Higher Calling	Jonah 3:10–4:11	Clarifying God's goals can help us see better options than punishment.
Proper 21	Loving the Enemy Within	Ezek. 18:1–4, 25–32	God's desire is that we have life, not punishment.

1. This series uses the complementary Old Testament texts rather than semicontinuous.

Martin Luther King Jr. has marvelous quotes about loving enemies. The sixth chapter of *Stride toward Freedom* reflects on winning the friendship and understanding of one's opponents. For an image, consider the 1996 photo of eighteen-year-old Keshia Thomas—a black woman—who threw herself on top of KKK-sympathizer Albert McKeel Jr. to protect him from a violent mob.

When speaking about violent situations, take care to avoid suggesting that victims are responsible for their abusers. Often the most loving act victims can offer abusers is to let them face the appropriate consequences for their actions, like jail or loss of relationship.

Proper 18: Love through Due Process
Ezekiel 33:7–11; Matthew 18:15–20

Say to them, As I live, says the Lord God, I have no pleasure in the death of the wicked, but that the wicked turn from their ways and live. (Ezekiel 33:11a)

"If another member of the church sins against you, go and point out the fault when the two of you are alone." (Matthew 18:15a)

The goal of this sermon is to communicate that God uses conflict and confrontations as ways to help us and others grow in healthy, vital ways. Consider examples in which confrontations led to new insights and personal growth for all parties. If the preacher is willing, an appropriate personal example of when the preacher was lovingly corrected after a mistake may humanize and humble the sermon, making it more accessible and relatable to the congregation.

Many people don't believe that God can use conflict and confrontation to our mutual benefit, because they have seen too much bad conflict—conflict handled poorly.

Bad conflict avoids. We don't want others to feel bad, but allowing someone to unknowingly walk in dangerous ways is not loving. If others are hurtful or offensive, it is not enough to assume they should know better. This is the primary focus of Ezekiel 33:8: if we do not warn others of bad behavior, their repeated mistakes and suffering will be on our hands.

Bad conflict tries to make us into someone else's savior. Proselytizing creates resistance and resentment and makes ourselves into a false idol of self-righteousness. In a worst-case scenario, "the most serious symptoms in family life, e.g., anorexia, schizophrenia, suicide, always show up in families in which people make intense efforts to bend one another to their will.[2] Ultimately, we are not the savior, and if others don't heed our warning, we must trust the Holy Spirit. Our Scripture passages for today in no way suggest we are responsible for other people's choices, only that we are responsible for warning them.

A healthier pathway is *due process*.

Bad managers ignore due process, do not tell employees of mistakes, overreact emotionally, and then fire employees at will. Responsible managers clearly communicate warnings in writing, name problem behaviors, explain consequences for repeated infractions, and identify actions for future success. If the local church has an employee handbook and/or a policy on due process, share it.

Granted, it is not helpful to treat others like employees, but the concept is consistent. If someone is hurtful, offensive, or harmful, we should assume the behavior will be repeated unless or until we have followed our Scriptures in Ezekiel and Matthew by pulling that person aside and clearly, lovingly communicating our feelings. If that does not communicate, then Matthew suggests we bring along another mediator or appropriate body in the church.

If all else fails, then treat them as Gentiles or tax collectors—remembering that Jesus treated even those maligned parties with forgiveness and shared meals (Matt. 9:9–13).

While conflict is unavoidable, the good news is that God uses it to help us learn from our mistakes and the mistakes of others. Jesus Christ loves us and will give us the strength and courage we need to confront conflicts with love and grace.

Proper 19: When God Transforms Evil into Good
Genesis 50:15–21

"Even though you intended to do harm to me, God intended it for good, in order to preserve a numerous people, as he is doing today." (Genesis 50:20)

Last week's sermon addressed the question, "When someone does something bad or wrong, how does God want *us* to respond?" This sermon addresses, "When someone does something bad or evil, how does *God* respond?"

Warning: this sermon addresses theodicy. When a parishioner has been traumatized and not yet healed, this sermon can create a

---

2. Edwin H. Friedman, "How to Succeed in Therapy without Really Trying," in *The Myth of the Shiksa and Other Essays* (New York: Church Publishing, 2008), 51.

temptation to believe God abusively inflicts or punishes for some "higher plan." If one does not reject this fallacy, one can lose their faith in Christ due to insensitivity. There is a vast difference between "God causes terrible things for a reason" (which presents God as selfish, unloving) and "God takes terrible events and transforms them into good" (which presents God as creative and healing). Addressing this issue later in the sermon can be pastoral for people who suffer silently.

In preparation, consider calling parishioners to ask, "Would you share a story of the greatest challenge or difficulty you overcame as a child and how it impacted your life?" People like answering this question with remarkable levels of disclosure because it was in the past and because it often makes them feel good. Time helps them take a "10,000-foot view" of how the crisis contributed in positive ways to who they are today. These stories personalize the sermon to be relatable. Parishioners believe, "If it could happen to them, it could happen to me too."

Most engaging stories include a crisis moment that propels main characters into their futures. In Disney's 2007 movie *Enchanted*, the evil queen throws Giselle down a well and out of paradise, but this also begins the adventure to introduce her to true love. Or consider the real-life story of Malala Yousafzai, the Pakistani activist for female education who survived an attempted assassination in 2012 when a gunman shot her in the head. That assassination attempt rallied leading Muslim clerics in Pakistan against the Taliban and gave her cause an international spotlight.

Of course, the main focus of this sermon is Joseph and his brothers, who sold him into slavery. In overcoming this betrayal and the suffering he endured, Joseph not only forgave, but also saw how God transformed his brothers' evil intents so that Joseph could eventually protect his family and others from famine.

The good news is that if God has the creative and healing power to transform the evil done against Joseph for good, then God has the creative and healing power to transform evil in our lives for good. Being a witness to God's creative and healing power gives grace for ourselves and our enemies and brings forgiveness, releasing the resentments and bitterness of our past, enabling us to fully embrace where God is leading tomorrow.

Finally, if this sermon helps parishioners see God's creative and healing powers in their own lives, it can also help them see how God made them to be heroes (as opposed to being helpless victims). And if they can believe they are the heroes of their own stories, what can they not accomplish with God's help?

Proper 20: Mercy and God's Higher Calling
Jonah 3:10–4:11

"And should I not be concerned about Nineveh, that great city, in which there are more than a hundred and twenty thousand persons who do not know their right hand from their left, and also many animals?" (Jonah 4:11)

As the first two sermons of this series explored how to respond and how God responds when others do wrong, this sermon shifts direction to ask, "What does God intend or desire for those who do wrong?" Of course, the answer is that God wants them to turn from evil and live.

In this Scripture's conversation, God is trying to help Jonah shift his perspective. Revenge, just deserts, and comeuppance are the failed goals of Jonah. As Jonah 3:10–4:2 reveals, Jonah was running from God because he did not want the Ninevites to be spared. He wanted them to be punished for their sins and destroyed. Perhaps that gave Jonah a false sense of superiority, schadenfreude, or self-righteousness, but it accomplished nothing.

The challenge of this topic is that the desire to punish others can drive someone into a self-destructive fury, or in this case, rejecting this sermon on loving our enemies. Therefore, a wise preacher will not attack this topic head on, but will first help parishioners connect to God's higher plans for redemption. Seeing and celebrating the possibility of redemption for all people makes it easier then to consider God's higher plans of redemption for our enemies.

To make these connections, start with a story or two about people or characters who experience a change of heart. In 1983's *Star Wars: Return of the Jedi*, Darth Vader redeems himself to save his son, Luke. In 1942's *Casablanca*, Rick Blaine gives up on his own cynicism and selfish interests to let Ilsa join her husband, Victor, in their escape to support the resistance, and Captain Louis Renault (the corrupt official and Nazi sympathizer) changes heart, ends up helping Rick in the end, and even ponders joining the resistance himself.

Or consider the story of Walt Everett and Michael Carlucci. Everett was a United Methodist pastor when, in 1987, Carlucci murdered Everett's son, Scott. The event almost destroyed Everett's life until he forgave Carlucci, eventually helping to secure Carlucci's early release, officiating at Carlucci's wedding, and working with Carlucci to speak to schools and churches about how decisions affect lives.[3]

---

3. Everett and Carlucci's story can be found on various web pages, including a July 2004 *Rolling Stone Magazine* article.

Once the congregation can see the power of redemption and second chances and how it connects with personal values of hope and devotion, the Scripture can be integrated with the concept that God does not desire punishment or death but that people be redeemed, turn from their evil ways, and live.

The good news is that God actively works to lead everyone, including us, from self-destructive and harmful paths back to righteousness and vitality. Our God is a God of second and third chances and will do whatever it takes to touch our hearts and make us whole. We too can trust in God's love for us, all of us, and even our enemies.

Proper 21: Loving the Enemy Within
Ezekiel 18:1–4, 25–32

Cast away from you all the transgressions that you have committed against me, and get yourselves a new heart and a new spirit! Why will you die, O house of Israel? For I have no pleasure in the death of anyone, says the Lord GOD. Turn, then, and live. (Ezekiel 18:31–32)

Having addressed the godly response to people we consider enemies, we now turn inward to explore the times when we are our own worst enemy. It is hard enough to make peace with those who have wronged us; sometimes making peace with ourselves is even harder. Perhaps no one else is trying to punish us for the things we regret, but we punish ourselves ten times over and hurt others in the process. Internalized shame and guilt can manifest themselves in self-harm, attempts to control one's surroundings and other people, and even smoldering rage. That guilt prevents peace, even if others are brought to justice, because it is a spiritual struggle.

In *Manchester by the Sea*, Lee Chandler has violent outbursts and can hardly care for his nephew because of the guilt he carries from a tragedy. Nobody blames Chandler, but he blames himself.

In *Three Billboards outside Ebbing, Missouri*, Mildred fights with cops to find her daughter's killer, yet replays their last argument and the hurtful words exchanged. Mildred did not cause her daughter's death, but she carries that guilt and it erupts violently as she hurts others.

The same internal struggle happens in nightmares. Ever dream you are running from a monster or trying to escape an unfamiliar place? Nightmares are mental expressions of subconscious fears. It is impossible to kill thoughts or run from ourselves, so fears trap us in nightmares until we wake or replace fear with love and laughter.

Ezekiel 18 argues against transgenerational punishment. God refuses to impose punishments from one generation onto another. There are consequences for sin, but repentance and redemption negate the need for punishment. Thank God, because punishment is not effective.

In *Positive Discipline*, the classic guide for parents and teachers to help children develop self-discipline, responsibility, cooperation, and problem-solving skills, Jane Nelsen says, "Children do not develop responsibility when parents and teachers are too strict and controlling, nor do they develop responsibility when parents and teachers are permissive. Children learn responsibility when they have opportunities to learn in an atmosphere of kindness, firmness, dignity, and respect."[4]

We are the same. People are consumed with punishment. Instead, Ezekiel declares that (1) we are not punished for others' sins and (2) we can change our ways and live.

If we let go of punishments, there will always be natural consequences. With a "new heart and new spirit" like what Ezekiel describes, we may live by kindness, firmness, dignity, and respect. Then forgiveness, love, and laughter can heal and open new possibilities in ways that punishment never could.

What do a new heart and new spirit look like? In *Harry Potter and the Prisoner of Azkaban*, "boggarts" are shape-shifters that look like our worst fears. Professor Lupin teaches students a spell that changes boggarts into amusing or ridiculous shapes. In *The Sixth Sense*, Cole is terrified of ghosts until he learns to help them. In *Monsters, Inc.*, bedroom monsters and children are frightened until they all realize there is power in laughter.

The good news is that God does not want punishment, but a new heart and new spirit for life. We make mistakes, or maybe we just feel bad, but when we accept Christ's forgiveness to cleanse our souls and love the enemy within, we live freely in the grace of God.

4. Jane Nelson, *Positive Discipline* (New York: Ballantine Books, 1996), 5.

Fall Series 2: Thriving

Four Parts: Proper 22 through Proper 25

A stewardship series that guides our congregations in generosity while honoring and respecting their rationality, personhood, and value.

ANTHONY J. TANG

Series Overview

How can church members be charitable, but also balance burdensome debt, lifestyle maintenance, and limited retirement savings? How do churches balance their budgets without harming members who struggle financially? The two struggles are not as different as they seem.

Step away from false dilemmas and consider how our church, our relationship with Christ, and we personally benefit from faithful stewardship. Sacrificial givers experience this when giving becomes disciplined and life balance is achieved and maintained. The more we have grace, lead by example, and speak to the joy of giving, the more new givers will thrive.

	Sermon Title	Focus Scripture	Theme
Proper 22	When the Church Accounts for Its Harvest	Matt. 21:33–46	Good stewardship begins with an organization that is trustworthy.
Proper 23	Building Faithfulness on the Way to the Promised Land	Exod. 32:1–14; Ps. 106:1–6, 19–23	Good stewardship builds upon a mission that is clear and forward-moving.
Proper 24	God's Imprint on Our Lives	Matt. 22:15–22; Gen. 1:26	Stewardship is less about what we give than it is about who and whose we are.
Proper 25	Committed to the Win-Win-Win	Matt. 22:34–46	Giving should not reduce our lives as much as complete our lives.

Many find value having church members testify on stewardship. Avoid asking church members who already tithe 10 percent or more, are very wealthy, or are the biggest givers in the church, because those testimonies demotivate. Their words are emotionally discarded for being impossible or unintentionally shaming to the average person. Instead, ask anyone who has increased their pledge to speak about why and how they are inspired to give more. Not everyone will be able to give 10 percent this year or a considerable sum, but everyone can do a little better than last year, and that is inspiring.

Proper 22: When the Church Accounts for Its Harvest
Matthew 21:33–46

When the chief priests and the Pharisees heard his parables, they realized that he was speaking about them. (Matthew 21:45)

In the book *Not Your Parents' Offering Plate: A New Vision for Financial Stewardship*, Clif Christopher explains three reasons why people give: "Number one is a belief in the mission. Number two is a regard for staff leadership, and number three is fiscal responsibility."[1] How can pastors cultivate an environment that will allow church members and ministry to thrive?

The purpose of this sermon is to focus on the leadership and fiscal responsibility aspects of that formula. The church does this by being transparent about financial leadership and presenting the church honestly and vulnerably as being worthy of every dollar donated.

Transparency builds trust. In the book *Originals: How Non-Conformists Move the World*, Adam Grant describes what happened when an employee wrote a scathingly critical email of Ray Dalio, CEO of Bridgewater Associates. "Instead of hiding Dalio's shortcomings or attacking the author of the note, Bridgewater's co-CEO copied the email trail to the entire company so that everyone could learn from the exchange."[2] Radical transparency develops trust and commitment from participants. Where have you seen radical transparency in action?

In Matthew 21, Jesus tells a parable of a landowner and the tenants who betray him. This parable is easily misinterpreted by those who assume it is a warning against greed, with the punishment of death for those who withhold money from God. False teachers are happy to

1. J. Clif Christopher, *Not Your Parents' Offering Plate: A New Vision for Financial Stewardship* (Nashville: Abingdon Press, 2008), 12.
2. Adam Grant, *Originals: How Non-conformists Move the World* (New York: Viking, 2016), 189.

allow this misinterpretation to continue, since it deflects away from their own accountability.

However, Matthew 21:45 helps readers see that this is not a warning for church members, but a warning directed at Pharisees and chief priests. Religious leaders (i.e., church pastors and lay leaders) are the tenants charged with caring for the vineyard and the fruit it produces.

Now the question is, will the tenants give to God the produce of the harvest, and will the pastor and lay leaders be responsible with the donations of the church to fulfill God's ministry and mission?

This creates opportunity for the finance committee to demonstrate transparency with its financial operations. It is also effective to state areas where financial procedures, controls, or checks/balances are not yet perfected, and what the church is doing to correct and improve those shortcomings. When church leaders present themselves to the scrutiny of the congregation with honesty, church members develop trust. Church members who trust church leaders and the church's fiscal responsibility will feel more confident that donation dollars are worth giving to the church.

The good news is that Jesus is the vine and we are all the branches, and it is by his love that we can be fruitful and work together so that our fruitfulness and gifts remain dedicated to the household of God. Christ invites us to work together. What a joyful and sweet opportunity it is!

Proper 23: Building Faithfulness on the Way to the Promised Land
Exodus 32: 1–14; Psalm 106:1–6, 19–23

Remember me, O LORD, when you show favor to your people; help me when you deliver them; that I may see the prosperity of your chosen ones, that I may rejoice in the gladness of your nation, that I may glory in your heritage. (Psalm 106:4–5)

The first week of this series focused on staff leadership and fiscal responsibility (two of the three reasons Clif Christopher names for why people give). This sermon addresses "belief in the mission" to focus on the third.

The wide, easy interpretation of the golden calf is to speak against the love of money and how such an idol corrupts individuals. No preacher would be faulted for taking this well-trodden path.

The narrow and difficult path, however, asks how the people came about worshiping the golden calf. Love of money did not *cause* their failure; it resulted from their failure. When Moses delayed too long, fear and anxiety caused panic. Allowing that anxiety to drive them, Aaron asked for gold jewelry to build the false idol they worshiped.

When the people lost sight of Moses (i.e., strong leadership), who stayed focused on the promised land (i.e., a mission of sanctification or the making of disciples to go into the world), they began to fail. Churches that no longer strengthen their members to overcome greater challenges of discipleship will backslide into simply comforting people with self-serving, feel-good activities like entertainment disguised as worship, Bible studies that never grow or change, and charities that foster dependency instead of self-determination. In this anxious state, it is easier to collect rings for golden calves of bigger buildings, frivolous accessories, or nicer comforts that focus on our desires rather than the mission God desires.

Instead of golden calves, the psalm draws focus onto the mighty doings of the Lord who has done great and awesome deeds, as well as God's people who observe justice and do righteousness. The questions for the preacher and church leaders are:

- How has our relationship with Jesus Christ transformed church leaders in the past twelve months?
- What ministries of the church are changing other lives for the better?
- Where can members, constituents, and/or guests give testimonies to how a deepening relationship with Jesus Christ has affected their lives?

Faithful giving is not about just donating, but about supporting missions that bring glory to God and challenge the community to make positive steps toward the promised land.

A wonderful way to start this sermon is with testimonies that speak to these transformations and what the church is doing to facilitate them. What are ways that the church is creating space for new possibilities of transformational ministries? What are the mission and direction of the church for this coming year? How will the church work to lower anxiety and lead into areas that build strength, courage, and confidence?

This sermon creates opportunity to showcase the mission and direction of the congregation and instill trust so that when members give, they know they are not giving to false idols but to missions that bring glory to God. The good news of this sermon is that as God led the Israelites in the desert wilderness, God is continuing to lead with grace and mercy, and as the congregation follows faithfully, the promised land awaits.

Proper 24: God's Imprint on Our Lives
Matthew 22:15–22; Genesis 1:26

Then he said to them, "Give therefore to the emperor the things that are the emperor's, and to God the things that are God's." (Matthew 22:21b)

The last two sermons built a foundation of leadership's responsibility toward God and church members. This sermon explores the spiritual responsibility of every person in the household of God.

To prepare the congregation, begin with examples of the joy, excitement, and thrill one experiences when discovering purpose. Especially consider a college student picking a new career path, a member starting a new career, or a senior discovering a new passion. Intentionally highlight the difficulties faced and how difficulties are balanced by the joy of being who they are called to be. (It may be tempting to use stories of characters who didn't know that they were destined for something great, like Luke Skywalker, Buffy the Vampire Slayer, Hermione Granger, or Harry Potter. However, to do so in this sermon risks disconnecting with the common person.) Exploring these stories prepares listeners to receive the lesson that God has marked every human with a role, an image, an identity that comes with challenge, joy, and fulfillment.

Pharisees and Herodians sought to entrap Jesus by making him choose between respecting the emperor (who thought of himself as a god) and worshiping God. To endorse the paying of taxes would discredit Jesus as honoring a false idol, but to reject taxes would label Jesus as treasonous among Romans.

Jesus, seeing their manipulation, points out that the emperor imprints his face and title on his things. When Jesus says, "Give therefore to the emperor the things that are the emperor's, and to God the things that are God's," the follow-up question is, "Where does one find the image and title of God?" In the first creation story we read, "Then God said, 'Let us make humankind in our image, according to our likeness'" (Gen. 1:26). Jesus avoids their trap, elevating the conversation out of money to a reflection about how we live as participants in the household of God.

As Roman subjects, the people paid taxes to the emperor. As citizens, we pay taxes for roads, education, armed forces, and so forth. As church members, we contribute toward utility bills, staff salaries, classes, and so on. These, however, are nothing compared to what it means to bear God's image and title. We are members of the household of God and called to a holy and sacred duty. Our lives are made to honor God through our prayers, presence, gifts, service, and witness.

This comes with challenge, but like those who have discovered their purpose or calling—no matter what age—difficulties are always accompanied by the joy, excitement, and thrill of doing what we are called to do.

The good news is that God claims us with the imprint of God's image and likeness. Bearing that image is a humbling and sometimes overwhelming responsibility that God entrusts to us, but God believes in us and believes in our ability to live up to that calling in beautiful and amazing ways.

Proper 25: Committed to the Win-Win-Win
Matthew 22:34–46

He said to him, "'You shall love the Lord your God with all your heart, and with all your soul, and with all your mind.' This is the greatest and first commandment. And a second is like it: 'You shall love your neighbor as yourself.'" (Matthew 22:37–39)

The first two sermons focused on church's leadership, fiscal responsibility, and belief in the mission. The third sermon raised expectations of ourselves from being just givers to the church to being members of God's household. This final stewardship sermon explores good stewardship that brings joy and love to God, neighbor, and ourselves.

Last week, Pharisees and Herodians attempted to undermine Jesus with a false dilemma. False dilemmas oversimplify complicated issues by offering only two possibilities, which are never comprehensive and manipulate unsuspecting victims into making bad choices. Tricksters blame the victim for making a bad choice, and victims may even blame themselves. Defending against false dilemmas, wise persons always recognize more than two possibilities.

False dilemmas in economics and game theory are called "zero-sum games," from the idea that if winners earn a plus-one score, and losers get minus-one, the sum of both equals zero. Zero-sum games are competitive, with losers and winners, like checkers or chess. People who live zero-sum lives are driven to eat or be eaten. It is shallow, painful, and lonely to live this way.

Zero-sum games are not life. Real situations include many possibilities, like everyone winning, everyone losing, or everyone gaining different results based on preferences. Two teachers fighting over twelve eggs will discover only through creative conversation that one needs the shells for a craft project, the other needs the yolks for baking, and both teachers can win.

The challenge to stewardship is that money is perceived as a zero-sum game of either (a) generously give to the church and foolishly have no money left, or (b) selfishly keep the money and let the church suffer. This is oversimplified and not creative.

Faithful giving fulfills the greatest commandments of loving God, our neighbor, and ourselves. Faithful giving lets go of fear and competition and considers how courage and joy lead to giving that cares for basic needs while caring for others, the church, and our faith.

Faithful giving does not claim that we deserve all worldly comforts, which do not bring peace. However, if God's care and provision is trusted, it is possible to live peacefully with less, make a greater impact on the world, and grow in joy and happiness. Good stewardship's goal is to grow in love and faithfulness through creativity.

The good news is that God does not want us to suffer, nor does God want our lives selfishly distracted from peace. God desires that life prepare for eternity by helping us be better stewards, that is, creative people who find ways to use money, prayers, presence, service, and witness in ways that love God and others as we love ourselves.

Fall Series 3: Entrusted

Four Parts: Proper 26 through Proper 29

Matthew's Gospel encourages us to accept the mantle of responsibility for the work to which God calls us.

ANTHONY J. TANG

Series Overview Church vitality does not depend on the pastor's charisma, but on how inspired the entire church is to be actively involved, responsible for its own ministries, and caring for each other. When all members see themselves as needed, responsible, and contributing, then amazing transformations can happen. The call to faithful service is not always easy to respond to, but all things are possible when we realize how much God loves us and trusts the church to care for the world.

Tips and Ideas for This Series This series can support a volunteerism campaign. Appeal to natural inclinations toward fairness by emphasizing "We're all in this together" or "Working together to do our part." Groupthink and passing the buck of responsibility can be avoided by having more

	Sermon Title	Focus Scripture	Theme
Proper 26	The Rise of Servant Leaders	Matt. 23:1–12	Helping our congregations move from rights toward responsibility.
Proper 27	Who Is Responsible for My Oil?	Matt. 25:1–13	Jesus will never do for us what he has equipped us to do for ourselves.
Proper 28	Multiplying Our Impact	Matt. 25:14–30	God blesses us with more than can be fathomed, so that we will do good things in the name of Christ.
Proper 29	Entrusted with Each Other	Matt. 25:31–46	Conversation and dignity help us care for the least of these.

volunteer jobs than there are people in the church. Just be sure to have the support of existing volunteers so efforts are not undermined by powerbrokers feeling threatened.

Preachers should beware of implying a theology of works righteousness. Hard work is not for earning salvation or bargaining one's way into heaven. God's love cannot be bought. Rather, because of God's love, we respond faithfully in service to others.

Proper 26: The Rise of Servant Leaders
Matthew 23:1–12

"The greatest among you will be your servant. All who exalt themselves will be humbled, and all who humble themselves will be exalted." (Matthew 23:11–12)

The goal of this sermon is to shift from focusing on rights and entitlements to focusing on responsibilities, from being passive passengers to being active and contributing crew members. The more a church engages servant leaders who take personal responsibility for ministry, the greater its future potential.

Consider beginning with personal stories of difficult and humbling work. Church members could be asked about first jobs or jobs that defined their character or work ethic. Even Pope Francis had early years running tests in a chemical laboratory, sweeping floors as a janitor, and working as a bouncer for clubs.[1]

An opinion piece in a newspaper called on high school graduates to mop their way to success. It said, "A task once considered beneath you could actually be the key to your success. Do the job nobody wants, because, believe it or not, somebody appreciates it. Volunteer to learn and to provide value to others. Find a dream job by first doing the rote tasks in that field, without complaint. Pick up a mop."[2] The author was not simply arguing that hard work leads to success, but that because it benefits other people, we should not forget other internalized benefits.

Unfortunately, many Christians are tempted into thinking that success should result in luxury. Likewise, too many churches believe worship is for entertainment. It does not help that there are televangelists arguing that they need multiple private jets. Granted, the Bible

---

1. Carol Glatz, "In conversations with parishioners, pope reveals he once was a bouncer," *Catholic News Service*, Dec. 2, 2013, http://www.catholicnews.com.
2. T. Bonin, "My Advice to Grads: Start Mopping—Doing Work That Feels Beneath You Always Pays Off in the End," *Wall Street Journal*, May 28, 2018, https://www.wsj.com.

says in Matthew 4:9, "All these I will give you, if you will fall down and worship me," but this invitation is from Satan, not Jesus.

Likewise, it is confusing when Jesus says, "All who exalt themselves will be humbled, and all who humble themselves will be exalted." It sounds like an endless roller coaster, if we do not understand the purpose of God's blessings.

Matthew 23:2–7 helps readers know that God's blessings are not for fame or comfort. The church is not a bank or country club, and membership does not have its privileges. Rather, the greatest among us will be our servant (Matt. 23:11). Jesus teaches that God blesses us so we can use those blessings to be a blessing for others. God made us for faithful service. Christ entrusts us to serve others on his behalf. The Holy Spirit strengthens and equips us to be the hands and feet of God's mercy, kindness, and compassion.

The good news of this sermon is that God believes in us and engages us in holy and spiritual work of humble servanthood. None of our service will ever be forgotten, as Christ exalts those who live humbly.

Proper 27: Who Is Responsible for My Oil?
Matthew 25:1–13

"When the foolish took their lamps, they took no oil with them; but the wise took flasks of oil with their lamps." (Matthew 25:3–4)

This parable's easiest interpretation is that preparation is more valuable than free-spiritedness, and the unprepared will be left behind at Christ's coming. The get-things-done Marthas who feel chastised by Luke 10:38–42 love this interpretation, while the more reflective Marys feel ashamed. But what if this Scripture is not an eschatological warning so much as a reflection about God's interaction with us and natural consequences for failing to take personal responsibility?

God entrusts us all with doing what we can. There is joy and purpose to be found in living to the fullest of our abilities, and something profoundly debilitating about having everything done for us.

Consider beginning this sermon with stories of when someone takes responsibilities away from us, like when a supervisor micromanages by doing what employees were originally assigned to do or when parents call their children's bosses or college professors. This causes others to lose initiative, confidence, and control.

In *Toxic Charity: How Churches and Charities Hurt Those They Help (and How to Reverse It)*, Robert Lupton's first promise in The Oath for Compassionate Service is this: "Never do for the poor what they have (or could have) the capacity to do for themselves."[3] Lupton's research shows that disregarding this promise causes long-term dependency and suffering.

In *Turn the Ship Around: A True Story of Turning Followers into Leaders*, L. David Marquet explains the value of not making decisions for others: "The vast majority of situations do not require immediate decisions. You have time to let the team chew on it. . . . When you follow the leader-leader model, you must take time to let others react to the situation as well. You have to create a space for open decision by the entire team, even if that space is only a few minutes, or a few seconds, long."[4]

By allowing people time to think, teams can rise up and be responsible for their own work and decisions in ways that emancipate and inspire people to do their best.

This parable is not easy, and some may feel the wise bridesmaids were selfish. Perhaps they should have been more understanding, but they also did not treat their peers like helpless dependents or take responsibility away from them. This parable should not be used as justification for not helping people in need, but rather taken to heart as we examine our own actions and motivations. Do we take responsibility where we can, or do we ever want others to step in and do things for us that we could do ourselves?

What about God? Sometimes we may get frustrated and angry with God for not fixing our problems or giving to us what we want. But Jesus Christ believes in us more than we do and the good news is that he equips us to take responsibility for our choices and to find creative solutions for our challenges.

Proper 28: Multiplying Our Impact
Matthew 25:14–30

"For it is as if a man, going on a journey, summoned his slaves and entrusted his property to them; to one he gave five talents, to another two, to another one, to each according to his ability. Then he went away." (Matthew 25:14–15)

> God entrusts us with so many more gifts and talents than we realize, to be used for building up the household of God. What sort of "return on investment" will God receive from us?

3. Robert D. Lupton, *Toxic Charity: How Churches and Charities Hurt Those They Help (and How to Reverse It)* (New York: HarperCollins, 2011), 8.
4. L. David Marquet, *Turn the Ship Around!: A True Story of Turning Followers into Leaders* (New York: Penguin Group, 2012), 91–92.

To connect the congregation with the values and direction of this sermon, consider starting with a reflection about investments. Some investors will entrust their savings to financial advisors. Those financial advisors are paid to review opportunities and work to provide a financial return to the investors. A couple getting married will invest a substantial part of their wedding budget in the photographer in order to get a return in the form of beautiful wedding photographs. Restaurant owners hire chefs and invest in high quality foods, equipment, appliances, and so on, and expect a return on their investment in the form of creative and/or appetizing meals that can be sold to the public.

Whether one has been a business owner or employee, it is likely that one has both invested in others and expected a return, or been the recipient of an investment and expected to produce a creative return on that investment.

This parable is about a wealthy man who trusts his slaves with his property.

When looking at the fact that the servants were given different amounts of talents, we may have feelings of unfairness. However, it is worth asking, "How much was a talent worth?" *The New Interpreter's Dictionary of the Bible* says that a talent is "roughly equal to 6,000 drachmas (greater than sixteen years' wages for a laborer)."[5] So, while there is a difference between having one, two, or five talents, it is also true that each of these servants was entrusted with an extremely large sum of money.

Our neighbors or friends may seem so much more talented or blessed or lucky than we are. It may seem as if life is so much easier for others. But even if others have so much more than us, God has still poured out more blessings into our lives than we know what to do with. How would we live differently if we realized just how abundant God's "investment" in us is?

This challenge can feel intimidating, particularly for those raised with a more "transactional" view of God. It is impossible to "repay" God for all we have been given. That is not the point, nor is it something God demands of us. God's generosity toward us is an invitation to practice generosity in return—with whatever we have received.

The good news is that God believes in us. God has entrusted each and every person with a wide variety and assortment of gifts, skills, talents, opportunities, loved ones, blessings—more than could ever be counted. God entrusted these gifts to us so that we will use them creatively and joyfully to bless others and provide a return to God's glory.

5. Katharine Doob Sakenfeld, ed., "Talents," in *The New Interpreter's Dictionary of the Bible* (Nashville: Abingdon Press, 2009), 5:457.

Proper 29: Entrusted with Each Other
Matthew 25:31–46

"And the king will answer them, 'Truly I tell you, just as you did it to one of the least of these who are members of my family, you did it to me.'" (Matthew 25:40)

This passage is often used as a call to charitable giving. It is that and so much more. Jesus is not generic in describing how people have responded to those in need, but specific about various needs: not "I was poor and you cared for me," but "I was hungry and you gave me food, I was thirsty and you gave me something to drink," and so on. If Jesus was hungry and you gave him clothes, or thirsty and you visited him, would that be counted as righteousness? Your good intentions might count for something, but Jesus praises those who identify and respond to particular needs.

If we met someone on the street in need, how would we know what they needed? In a Las Vegas food pantry that gave food monthly to a good number of families, one volunteer took a day to talk with clients about their specific needs—food and otherwise. At first, clients wondered if they needed to answer questions in a certain way to maintain food privileges with the pantry. Once that doubt was relieved and clients could be honest, they told about their lives and challenges. When asked what would really benefit their lives for self-determination, not one client asked for more food. Many stated that they really wanted help finding jobs. Most striking was that at the end of these conversations, clients repeatedly thanked the volunteer for listening.

Charitable donations are kind and well-intentioned, but too many churches want to solve all problems with food baskets, Thanksgiving turkeys, and Christmas presents. To truly get food to the hungry, water to the thirsty, welcome to the stranger, clothing to the naked, health to the sick, and hope to the prisoner, what is universally called for is listening, respect, and relationship. This Scripture is a call to be in relationship with the least of these.

In *The Anatomy of Peace: Resolving the Heart of Conflict*, one of the characters explains, "When you begin to see others as people, . . . issues related to race, ethnicity, religion, and so on begin to look and feel different. You end up seeing people who have hopes, dreams, fears, and even justifications that resemble your own."[6] Stories of people connecting across differences prepare the church to consider in what ways they too can cross chasms to connect with others who are different.

6. The Arbinger Institute, *The Anatomy of Peace: Resolving the Heart of Conflict* (San Francisco: Berrett-Koehler Publishers, 2008), 185.

God's ultimate desire is that we listen, respect, and grow in relationship and then care for each other's needs. How will our church members listen, respect, and grow in relationship with the least of the community and the world? How will pastors and lay leaders listen, respect, and grow in relationship with the least of the members of the church? How will denominational and regional offices listen, respect, and grow in relationship with the least of its pastors and lay leaders? These are the questions that make a difference to the world.

While everyone has had moments of being goats on the left and also sheep on the right, the good news is that over and over again God places people in our lives to give us new opportunities to learn how to connect across our differences and be in relationship. Our God of second chances creates possibilities for us to be in relationship with the least of these who are members of Christ's family.

Year B

Advent/Christmas Series: Where We Belong

Six Parts: First Sunday of Advent through First Sunday of Christmas, including Christmas Eve

As Christ came to dwell among us, we too seek a place to dwell.

TUHINA VERMA RASCHE

Series Overview Everyone may have a different definition of home and the places where we belong. Some people may find home not in physical spaces, but instead in belonging to a community that accepts us for the entirety of

	Sermon Title	Focus Scripture	Theme
Advent 1	The End of the World as We Know It	Mark 13:24–37	Advent reveals that our endings and beginnings are different from God's beginnings and endings.
Advent 2	Where the Wild Things Are	Isa. 40:1–11	In the midst of wilderness places, God accompanies us home.
Advent 3	Homecoming	Isa. 61:1–4, 8–11	God recognizes our wholeness and brokenness when we cannot remember the places we call home.
Advent 4	Pitching the Tent	2 Sam. 7:1–11, 16	Humanity can try to build a house for God, but God finds creative ways to dwell with humanity.
Christmas Eve	Home in the Word	John 1:1–14	God, as the Word made flesh in Christ, finds a place to dwell with us.
Christmas 1	Reign It In	Isa. 61:10–62:3	God's reign comes about with unexpected people in unexpected places to bring a sense of wholeness in broken places.

who God created us to be. Advent and Christmas are a sort of homecoming. God found a new home among us in the flesh and blood of Jesus Christ. God will find this home again in the second coming of Christ as we await that return. The dwelling places where we find Christ today can be in our mangers, surrounded by parents, shepherds, magi, and a variety of animals—and also through the moves of the Holy Spirit. Sometimes those dwelling places can take us by surprise; sometimes those dwelling places can also be where we experience the most comfort and joy, where we truly belong in creation.

Tips and Ideas for This Series

As the liturgical year begins anew, where do we physically, mentally, and spiritually find ourselves as we make preparations for the coming of Christ? Take paper road maps and printouts from directions on the internet to create a collage of maps evoking different interpretations of home. What are the stops along the way that provide life and sustenance? What are some of the preparations that are needed to seek out those places of belonging? Creating a map of the physical and spiritual places we call home can lead to expressions of how to embody a dwelling place for the Spirit to live and move among us. If people are challenged by talking about home and belonging, what are their yearnings to find those places and spaces? How can we embody those places and spaces for one another in our communities?

Advent 1: The End of the World as We Know It
Mark 13:24–37

"But about that day or hour no one knows, neither the angels in heaven, nor the Son, but only the Father. . . . Therefore, keep awake—for you do not know when the master of the house will come, in the evening, or at midnight, or at cockcrow, or at dawn, or else he may find you asleep when he comes suddenly. And what I say to you I say to all: Keep awake." *(Mark 13:32, 35–37)*

Advent begins by talking about the end of the world as we know it. While it might be nice to think about that sweet baby Jesus lying in the manger when we get to Christmas, we have Mark's Gospel that unsettles us on this First Sunday of Advent. While it would be so much nicer to think of a precious infant, we have to remember that Advent is also about that day and that hour when Christ returns. There is an incredible uncertainty about that day and that hour.

What does that day mean for us? How does that day, when we don't even know the day or the hour, impact us right here and right now?

Think of how we order our days. Some of us may be finishing out part of a school year. There is the end of a fiscal year. Then the calendar year itself is wrapping up in just a few short weeks. It's an end time; it's the end of the world, in a way. This end time is colliding with the start of our church year, a new beginning. During the "end times," when we are finishing up fiscal years, semesters, and the calendar year, we're often tired, burned out, and exhausted. We may be looking forward to some blessed time off. These endings are in contradiction with our faith lives and journeys of newness and being called to be awake.

Think of how we order our time, the chronological passage of seconds, minutes, hours, days, weeks, and such. We see this passage of time on our watches, clocks, cell phones, and whatever other devices we use to keep time, and it feels so nice, so predictable, so measured, and so orderly. But our chronological notions of time can never be compared to or described against God's time. Our way is not God's way. Especially when it comes to the timing of events. God's timing to us may not seem nice, measured, or orderly at all. Sometimes God seems to break into our lives at the most inconvenient times in our everyday lives. But then God's time collides with our time. Today's Gospel is clueing us in to God's time. We have no idea how God's time works or when it works. Jesus tells us that he himself does not know this hour.

How do we know God's time is at work? Because God's timing has been at work throughout the course of history. God has been at work, but on God's time. God works in unexpected and incredible ways. What about that hour, over two thousand years ago, when so many were asleep in Bethlehem? That hour when God unexpectedly broke into our world? That hour when God broke into our world in a manger as a baby, not clothed in majesty and power, but in utter humility and helplessness? As Christians, we cannot write off that unexpected hour.

Advent 2: Where the Wild Things Are
Isaiah 40:1–11

A voice cries out:
"In the wilderness prepare the way of the LORD,
make straight in the desert a highway for our God.
Every valley shall be lifted up,
and every mountain and hill be made low;
the uneven ground shall become level,
and the rough places a plain.

Then the glory of the LORD shall be revealed,
  and all people shall see it together,
  for the mouth of the LORD has spoken." (Isaiah 40:3–5)

There's something scary about being in the wilderness. There's the physical wilderness, the middle of nowhere places that seem empty, desolate, and lacking life. Then there's the theoretical wilderness in our spiritual, emotional, and psychological existence—times when we're alone, destitute, feeling as if nothing will work, that nothing can be done. The internal wilderness of despondency, isolation, doubt, fear, or anger, and wondering, "Where, oh where, is God in the midst of all of this?"

Wandering out in the wilderness leads to fear and the unknown. This passage from Isaiah was written during an intense time in Israel's history. Israel repeatedly turned away from God; the prophets were trying to warn the people to turn from their selfish ways and to turn back to God. The prophets stated that if the Israelites didn't turn back to God, something bad was going to happen. That something bad was the Babylonians. The Babylonians not only conquered Jerusalem; they outright destroyed it. The Babylonians then carted the Israelites away from their home, marching them to Babylon. The Israelites were whisked away from a land that they loved and knew as home. The Israelites were in an awful wilderness in a foreign country, being held against their will in a place they knew nothing about, in a land that wasn't theirs. They turned away from God, and they found themselves out in the wilderness. Yet God was with them in the wilderness of Babylon and in their return home.

In the midst of an unknown, unfamiliar, and scary wilderness, God came to the Israelites with words of comfort. The words from Isaiah aren't the first time God's been in the wilderness with the Israelites. There's the exodus, when the Israelites were fleeing Egypt. God cleared a path for the Israelites out of Egypt in the dramatic parting of the Red Sea. Even in the midst of their complaining, God traveled with the Israelites to their new home.

As time passed, the Israelites turned away from God and did not heed the warnings of the prophets. The Israelites turned away from God and were carted off to Babylonia, leaving Jerusalem in ruins. Yet God cleared a way again and again for the Israelites to return home. Yes, the Israelites may have turned away from their God before the Babylonian exile, but God never abandoned them. God cleared a way out of the wilderness for them.

There's something interesting about Isaiah's words and the words of the Gospel. God is found in the most unexpected of places. God's out in the wilderness. And even if God's people have royally screwed up, God clears a way home for them. God knows our wilderness. God's not just some entity out there, but God, Christ, knows our wilderness experiences—because God's been there too.

Advent 3: Homecoming
Isaiah 61:1–4, 8–11

They shall build up the ancient ruins, they shall raise up the former devastations; they shall repair the ruined cities, the devastations of many generations. (Isaiah 61:4)

When an area that many have called home has suffered severe devastation, can that place truly be called home again? What happens to memory when there has been incredible damage, not just to the land, but also to the emotions of the communities that lived in the area? The sense of recovery becomes not just a single issue, but multifaceted, because of the multitude of factors involved. Considerations such as health and safety and returning home are fairly obvious, but there are new considerations, like caring for the community and land, as well as the need for assistance (whether that be physical, emotional, or spiritual), that begin to emerge.

In the midst of recovering from such devastating events—or even more subtle changes over time—our minds can sometimes play tricks on us. People may be bound to the memories of the past, stating, "Remember then, when life was so good?" There may be a yearning to rely on memories of what a place was like "before." There may be a reliance on memories that can become unreliable. Memories can shift and change, making a place and time further idealized and cherished. The reality of a place and time may omit its fullness of both joys and sorrows. Being bound to the past can keep us from acknowledging the intensity of the present and moving toward the future. Yet God is present in the midst of both joy and sorrow and failed memory. God remembers everything, especially when we are a forgetful people.

In returning to the places we call home, we have to recognize the truths that pulled us away from places of comfort and belonging. If our memory starts to play tricks on us, we will be deceived into thinking about the "good old days," limiting the ability of our imagination to step into an unknown and unexplored future filled with the potential for new growth. We have to be with one another in community to bring our realities together, to reform and reshape places anew, truly exploring what it means to remember and piece together memories of the places that formed us, the places that shaped us, and the places we recognize as home.

Isaiah writes of the reality of mourning, recalling faint spirit, ashes, and former devastations. These were true times of despair, wondering where God was in the midst of turmoil and confusion. The Israelites may have also had their memory play tricks on them, thinking that God caused their despair. Instead of causing their pain, God was with the Israelites in the midst of their suffering, lamenting with them and journeying with them to the land of their exile. God was also present in their celebration and homecoming, restoring their homeland after the disaster of war. This history of God being with God's people is repeated in the most incredible way: God enfleshed in Jesus Christ dwelling with us. Christ lived in the fullness of human existence, embodying joys and sorrows. Jesus also experienced the greatest devastation in the crucifixion.

Advent 4: Pitching the Tent
2 Samuel 7:1–11, 16

And I will appoint a place for my people Israel and will plant them, so that they may live in their own place and be disturbed no more; and evildoers shall afflict them no more, as formerly, from the time that I appointed judges over my people Israel; and I will give you rest from all your enemies. Moreover, the LORD declares to you that the LORD will make you a house. . . . Your house and your kingdom shall be made sure for ever before me; your throne shall be established forever. (2 Samuel 7:10–11, 16)

Home is that place where you feel comfortable, right? Where you can kick off your shoes, maybe (or maybe not, depending on who's in your house) put your feet up on the coffee table, and be your whole and full and entire self. But sometimes the emotional place of home can be elusive. Home can be that mythical land, like in dreams and fairy tales. Thinking about this elusive definition of a full concept of physical, emotional, spiritual, and psychological home makes me think of the people who have formed and shaped us to be who we are today.

When I think of this Fourth Sunday of Advent, I can't help but think of home, and long for that place to fully and wholly and truly be who God created you and me to be. This is the time of year where many of us plan to return to the places and people that formed us, where we can simply be, without having to fully explain ourselves. I think about God's home. Because, really, where does God live? King David, in our Old Testament lesson, is convinced that God needs a better home than a tent. God confronts David and tells him, "Excuse me, all this time you've been carting me around in this tent, have I demanded that you make me a house of cedar? No!" It seems that God's all right with where God is, being among God's people. God delights to be among God's people; God tells David, "I have been with you wherever you went."

Of course, God is the God of reversals and surprises. God tells David, "I will build you a home, for you and your people, and I will establish a dynasty." This home, this dynasty? This is a significant proclamation to come from God. Especially for a people who have lived with displacement, who have a history of wandering, including a good forty years in the desert, having this home is paramount.

Advent reminds us that we're all sojourners. We're all looking for God's kingdom to come, that complete fulfillment of whatever home "is," where we can wholly and fully and entirely be ourselves. Advent reminds of this time of our sojourn, reminds us that we're living in in-between times, reminds us that the fulfillment of the place we can call home is coming not just with the Christ child, but with the second coming of Christ.

Christmas Eve: Home in the Word
John 1:1–14

And the Word became flesh and lived among us, and we have seen his glory, the glory as of a father's only son, full of grace and truth. (John 1:14)

How could God, the Word that was in the beginning, take on our flesh, our bone? Why would God want to do that? The beginning of John's Gospel is beautiful, but sometimes it just doesn't make sense. Why would the Word that was in the beginning, before all creation, want to be in our messy and broken existence? We may never get an answer to why anytime soon. All we know is that it happened. God set aside the distance of the heavens in order to be so close, to be so near, and to make a home with us, whom God created, loves, and saves. God became as human like you and me, as awesome and incredible as that seems.

Jesus, the Son of God being birthed into the world, is depicted on so many Christmas cards. But the pictures on the cards don't tell the fullness of the story. Cards are usually censored and sterile. Not that there's anything wrong with that, but there's something amiss. These cards don't recognize the reality of Christ coming among us by being born into this world. Have you ever seen a Christmas card with Mary and Joseph holding the baby Jesus covered in dirt, grit, and filth? Maybe because the cards have sterile images of glowing halos, well-behaved farm animals, a quiet, sleeping, and peaceful baby, and a couple of calm parents. Think about it: this is about a woman in the throes of labor with her husband finding shelter in a manger filled with animals. What do you think that would really look like? Be honest. If we want to talk about the reality of God taking on human flesh in Jesus and how we're told God entered this world, the censored Christmas card isn't telling the whole story or our story.

The reality of life—well, reality, at least as we know it—is filled with muck. Slop. Highs. Lows. Joys. Sorrows. Messy, and sometimes more uncensored than we can bear. In the midst of an uncensored reality, God took on our nature, took on our form, and came into a very real and broken and beautiful world. The Word made flesh came to truly make our stories and God's story come together, become close and relational and passionate and full of feelings. Because we're still in that season of the illumination, that shine of Christ's birth, with beautiful glowing light that brings warmth and radiance, shining through everything that's messy, dirty, broken, and foul.

Let us remember the Word made flesh that came to live among us, to be with us, and to live out our experiences. This is a gospel of embodiment, not mere words, but the Word.

Christmas 1: Reign It In
Isaiah 61:10–62:3

For as the earth brings forth its shoots,
    and as a garden causes what is sown in it to spring up,
so the Lord God will cause righteousness and praise
    to spring up before all the nations. (Isaiah 61:11)

It all began on an unexpected journey. Wandering around in the wilderness seeking a place of refuge. Wandering to find a new home, a place to lie down, and just to rest awhile. Seeking a place of home and belonging is so vital to being in whole and healthy relationship with one another. This isn't just for Joseph and Mary wandering the outskirts of Bethlehem seeking a place to give birth. This isn't just for the Israelites on their way home after a generation of exile in Babylon. This story is also for us, to find a place where we can wholly and fully be ourselves with one another, where we can rest our heads when we are weary.

In a world where so many are seeking a home and safety, God's message to us this day is to remind us that while nations and kings make attempts to reign in power, God's kingdom is a radically different reign. That reign is shown to us in abundant life and beauty, and God includes us in such a reign. That reign, however, comes to us in a surprising place. We are given the promise to return home. God shows us abundant life and God's own presence in the birth of a first-century Galilean peasant. In this birth God shows us that God's reign not only is radically different, but is bursting with the breath of life, the movement of flesh and bone. God's presence among us, whether that be accompanying us and showing us signs of life along the way or if we're sitting in the shadow of a valley, is a promise to remain constant in the midst of everything. God shows us this promise in full creativity.

We know that God's promise to us will be fulfilled, which then impacts us in the here and now. Knowing where we will end up, knowing God's promise to us will be fulfilled, we can respond to create a different present. A present of hope. A present that is filled with life in unexpected places. A present knowing that fulfillment has come and continues to come and is coming. God's good pleasure gives us the freedom to be engaged in God's created world and in the work of the kingdom that is both here and fully yet to come. God yearns for our response to this free invitation and yearns for a relationship with us.

Epiphany Series: Created Anew

Six Parts: First Sunday after Epiphany through Transfiguration Sunday

Celebrating God's creativity—and our own—in the season of new beginnings.

TUHINA VERMA RASCHE

Series Overview   This series begins at the start of a new year, a time to start over and create the world anew through resolutions, hopes, and dreams. This is an opportunity for a community to explore what it means to be a follower of Jesus in a new calendar year and see Christian identity in a new way. Through Scriptures that span all sections of the Bible, let's discover new and creative ways to explore what it means to be a baptized Christian in the world today.

	Sermon Title	Focus Scripture	Theme
First Sunday after Epiphany	God Created. Now What?	Gen. 1:1–5	God's creativity is made manifest in the continual act of creation that spans space and time.
Second Sunday after Epiphany	Creating Christian Freedom	1 Cor. 6:12–20	Christian freedom is not to do what we please, but in response to God's love for us manifest in Christ, it is to do what pleases God.
Third Sunday after Epiphany	Creativity in Connection	Jonah 3:1–5, 10	God's proclamation is creative, even if we're not ready to hear or speak what God wants to tell us.
Fourth Sunday after Epiphany	Being the Epiphany	1 Cor. 8:1–13	Our bodies and beings matter in Christian community as created in God's image.
Fifth Sunday after Epiphany	Never-Ending Creativity	Isa. 40:21–31	Even in the midst of our own selfishness and destruction, God finds ways to create the world anew.

	Sermon Title	Focus Scripture	Theme
Sixth Sunday after Epiphany	Creating the Extraordinary in the Ordinary	2 Kgs. 5:1–14	Even within the rhythms of an uneventful daily life, God reaches out to us in the most ordinary of places.
Transfiguration	Descending to Share the Story	Mark 9:2–9	In an act of ultimate creativity, Jesus' identity as the Son of God is revealed to us. How do we descend from the mountaintop to share such an experience?

Tips and Ideas for This Series

Epiphany is an opportunity to tap into the creative energy of your community. Decorate parts of your communal space with favorite art pieces from members of the community. Find a way to create a communal art project in this season, such as displaying a blank canvas in a communal area and having people contribute through paint, marker, and/or pasting paper to the canvas. A communal project to unleash creativity can lead to group discussions on the sacredness of creative community and what it means to be made as a maker.

First Sunday after Epiphany: God Created. Now What?
Genesis 1:1–5

In the beginning when God created the heavens and the earth, the earth was a formless void and darkness covered the face of the deep, while a wind from God swept over the face of the waters. (Genesis 1:1–2)

"In the beginning, God created." Those words are amazing. God could have just been sitting around, hanging out, and doing whatever God did before God created. And then God created. Why did God create? Was God bored? Was God lonely? Or was God imagining and wanted to bring that imagination to fruition? Was God ready to build, construct, mold, shape, form, and invent? Did God know what would happen after this creative process took place, where amazing things came out of the chaos, out of the void, out of nothingness?

The creation stories are just amazing, that God creates the heavens and the earth, these amazing creatures, and us. The part that amazes me most is this: "Let us make humankind in our image, according to our likeness." The diversity of everyone on earth, all in God's image, speaks to how God is so creative, so amazing, and so much bigger than what we can ever imagine.

When do you find yourselves at your most creative? Sometimes it is when the mind is at rest, not burdened with the tasks of a day. Sometimes it's ignited by that first sip of morning coffee. Sometimes it's having to think of what life is like and what to do and how to respond to the world around us. We may have to take a risk and wonder "what if?" when we encounter situations that do not have concrete outcomes. In those situations, we might find ourselves in in-between spaces. It's those thin spaces where we see things in a new light and in a new way.

We're currently living in liminality, in an in-between space. We're living in between times of Jesus who walked among us around two thousand years ago, and we're waiting for Jesus to return to us, to fully reconcile the world and God's creation to our creator and creative God. Liminal spaces are weird. Sometimes they're awkward. They can also be uncomfortable. They can also be outright beautiful. There are opportunities to do things we haven't done before. There are opportunities to be so very creative.

As we experience the start of a new year, picture the time like a blank canvas stretched out before you. What will you create in this void? Remember that it was out of the void, out of chaos, that God created the earth and the seas and the birds and the snakes and us. God was so creative in wanting to know our experiences, how we live, what we feel, and what we do, that God came to us in the person of Christ. When I think of what Christ did for you and for me and for creation, reconciling us to God, forgiving us our sins, dying and rising, that amazement and wonder is amplified. Not only did God create; God wanted and continues to want to be a part of creation, beside and in and through you and me.

Second Sunday after Epiphany: Creating Christian Freedom
1 Corinthians 6:12–20

"All things are lawful for me," but not all things are beneficial. "All things are lawful for me," but I will not be dominated by anything. (1 Corinthians 6:12)

Few preachers get excited at the prospect of a lectionary passage that uses the words "fornication" and "prostitute" repeatedly. Why did Paul write a letter that could be interpreted to be emanating fire and brimstone? Paul couldn't sugarcoat his words, because he wrote this letter to a church in trouble. Either the early church in Corinth didn't understand the early Christian teachings, or the Corinthians were misinterpreting messages to suit their needs, because a fixation on food wasn't the only issue in the church of Corinth. There's a list of issues, such as lawsuits, marriage, how to prepare and distribute the Lord's Supper, and liturgy. Such fixations were preventing the people of Corinth from knowing the freedom of being in community with one another. Paul was trying to guide the church, much like a shepherd guiding sheep when the sheep are lost and going astray.

Where were the Corinthians going astray? They were misinterpreting freedom, taking advantage of the idea that "all things are lawful" for those with freedom in Christ. When children are trying to be independent of their parents, they try to self-identify by moving away from control. Part of self-identification is finding ways creatively to bend the rules, seeing how far regulations can be tested. Hearing they were free, many of the Corinthians thought that this gave them license to do whatever they wanted; but as Paul reminds them, "not all things are beneficial," lawful though they may be.

The Corinthians acted on the indulgence to consume whatever they wanted, believing that this could happen without consequence. (This sort of indulgence may be what prompted some of us to make New Year's resolutions a few weeks ago!) In all this consumption, the Corinthians turned inward on themselves to focus on their own needs. In turning inward and acting upon their own indulgences, they were not able to live fully and creatively in a community that God desires. Their supposed "freedom" was misused, leading the Corinthians to indulge their desires, mislead others, and be in bondage to a new master. The Corinthians misinterpreted Christian freedom. But then, what exactly is Christian freedom?

Christian freedom is rooted in self-giving agape love, love without limits, without boundaries, and without restrictions. We are so radically loved by our Creator that we are compelled to create a world of radical love toward our neighbors. Loving limitlessly and creatively is not easy when people have their hearts turned inward on themselves and their own needs. Consider whether your efforts at self-improvement this year are turning your heart outward toward others or further inward, agonizing over diets or exercise regimens. Let your freedom from overindulgence free your heart to love others more abundantly, creating a community that expresses the love that God intended and created for us.

As Paul writes to another church community, the Galatians, "For freedom Christ has set us free. . . . For you were called to freedom, brothers and sisters; only do not use your freedom as an opportunity for self-indulgence, but through love become slaves to one another" (Gal. 5:1a, 13).

Third Sunday after Epiphany: Creativity in Connection
Jonah 3:1–5, 10

When God saw what they did, how they turned from their evil ways, God changed his mind about the calamity that he had said he would bring upon them; and he did not do it. (Jonah 3:10)

Can you remember the Ten Commandments in order? Many can name the first two commandments, which are God naming God's self to us and God defining a desired relationship with us. These two commandments set the foundation for the other eight commandments, which determine our relationship with one another. The commandments connect us to God and to one another. But there are times when Israelites neglected or broke those connections.

There was a need for prophets with challenging words that would arise from within a community to remind people about their need for connection, in relationship with God and one another. As time stretched on from the first disconnect from God in the garden of Eden, human history has been filled with more and more disconnects from God, both great and small. There's historical evidence of institutions believing one thing, yet God's call for the world being radically different in that belief. There are also personal disconnects; we may be struggling with our own relationship with God, or not wanting to listen to God if we are being called to a vocation or ministry. If we don't want to listen to God, we may think there is an opportunity to run far away. But in running away, who are the people we encounter along the way? What can they show us about being in community with one another?

Jonah, an unwilling messenger, spends much of his time running away from being in relationship with God. Jonah attempts to disconnect himself from God, but through some creative means, God is able to reconnect with Jonah. Jonah encounters people who reveal their relationship with God, but instead of Jonah seeing these people as a model, he is tossed to and fro until he begrudgingly accepts God's call to travel to Nineveh to deliver a message of repentance.

Attempting to flee Israel altogether, Jonah encounters foreign fishermen who respect God more than he does. After God uses a fish to rescue him, Jonah begrudgingly travels to Nineveh, shouting that God will destroy the city for its evil ways, but like the fishermen who toss Jonah from the boat, the people of Nineveh are also an example of what it means to connect again with God. The people of the city are so grieved by God's proclamation through Jonah that they mourn deeply. God sees how the people of Nineveh turn from themselves and back to God, and God does not bring disaster upon the city.

In this time of Epiphany we need to have continual reminders of who we are to God and to one another. As God sent Jonah to Nineveh, God sent us a proclamation. God sent us a proclamation of not just word, but of Word made flesh. God sent this embodied proclamation to remind us of who we are to God and to one another. Even when we're disconnected and distracted, God uses creative ways to connect us to God and to one another.

Fourth Sunday after Epiphany: Being the Epiphany
1 Corinthians 8:1–13

Knowledge puffs up, but love builds up. Anyone who claims to know something does not yet have the necessary knowledge; but anyone who loves God is known by him. (1 Corinthians 8:1b–3)

Some days I am consumed by what weighs me down in daily life. I cannot see the forest for the trees, because I am so consumed with myself, really to the point where I'm self-absorbed and I forget the physical and spiritual presence of my neighbor beside me. I then remember the fullness of the body of Christ, who have let their prayers rise up like incense, holding me in a sacred space in the midst of being consumed. Because of those prayers and the community that raises them up, the Epiphany continues to be revealed. Every person here is created in the image of God and is a creative and unique epiphany of how God works in the world. Through God's creativity working through us and through our intercessions, the Holy Spirit says, "I've got you. You are a part of the body of Christ, and there are members of the body who are supporting you."

What I love about the Epiphany of our lives of following Christ is the opportunity to see God in our neighbor. That's just how creative God can be: that in wonder and amazement, we can turn to our neighbor and see the image of God in one another. This is God revealing to us that God is relational. God loves us and cares for us and wants to be with us.

Paul, in his letter to the church of Corinth, was talking to the church about what it means to be the body of Christ, and how distractions can pull us away from that body—namely, for the Corinthians, the controversy over eating food sacrificed to idols. What we do to one another, how we treat ourselves, and how we treat one another matter. Paul reminds the people of Corinth not to let their knowledge about the meaninglessness of idols create a "stumbling block" for those newer to the faith. While knowledge "puffs" us up with arrogance, love "builds" others up in their faith, and in turn the whole body of Christ. Paul reminds the Corinthians they were not their own person as a member of the church.

Paul is also speaking to us today. Not only do we exist for Christ; we are also created to exist for one another, to accompany one another, and to be accountable to one another. We gather in community so that if a sibling in the faith struggles, the community can accompany them. It's both daunting and terrifying, because being in community comes with incredible responsibility for one another. Sometimes it takes a member of the community to be an epiphany for us, to show us where we are headed. God sent us a reminder of God's creativity in the flesh of Jesus, but even when people encountered God's creative work in flesh and bone, there were still struggles and doubts. Our world is undeniably broken, and such brokenness affects us all.

Sometimes we cannot see the forest for the trees. How wonderful that God created each of us in God's image to reveal God's presence in the world in a new, different, and creative way. How has God revealed God's self to you in this Epiphany?

Fifth Sunday after Epiphany: Never-Ending Creativity
Isaiah 40:21–31

Have you not known? Have you not heard?
The LORD is the everlasting God,
    The Creator of the ends of the earth.
He does not grow faint or grow weary;
    his understanding is unsearchable.
He gives power to the faint,
    and strengthens the powerless. (Isaiah 40:28–29)

Isaiah hearkens back to the beginning of time when God created the earth from the void. God named this creation as a series of good days. As time created distance between God's creation and the people of Isaiah's time, people forgot the goodness in many ways, and yet God envelops us in the creativity of life, death, and resurrection.

Isaiah speaks to a weary people, downtrodden by circumstance. Isaiah reminds them that they are under the wing of the One who created the entire universe, who knows and understands all things. Can we too be deemed "good" creators, even in the midst of a broken world? As we live out our own creative callings, all the while wrestling with our own struggles and catastrophes, do we stop to ponder where our creativity is rooted? Does a creative act serve one's self, or the greater good? Is the creative act to hoard what doesn't belong to you, or is it based in a community?

In the midst of power struggles between nations and the struggles we may find closer to home, many individuals and institutions can take credit for creating, whether that be a political system, a set of values, or influences on how people can live their lives. Yes, this can be viewed as a form of creation, but not as how God intended for us. Creative endeavors are meant to be life giving and life sustaining, much like those first days of existence in Genesis. Some of the "creative" endeavors we see in the world claim such titles, but when the veil is lifted, the life-giving and life-sustaining characteristics are questionable at best.

While we are created as creators, Isaiah continues to remind us of our origin story, that while we are created in God's image, we are not God's equals in a broken humanity. Even if our attempts to imitate creation are not perfect, it doesn't mean that we grow tired and weary and give up. When we create for and with one another, something amazing can happen. Wherever two or three are gathered, ideas can bounce around, excitement and tension can fill the space, and a new creation can be birthed into the world through the power of the Holy Spirit.

Today's passage reminds us of the identity of the ultimate Creator, and that the creative process in God's created world and within us is never ending. If we were to turn to our communities and turn toward God, where could our creativity take us? What could it embody? What could it represent?

Sixth Sunday after Epiphany: Creating the Extraordinary in the Ordinary
2 Kings 5:1–14

But his servants approached and said to him, "Father, if the prophet had commanded you to do something difficult, would you not have done it? How much more, when all he said to you was, 'Wash, and be clean'?" So he went down and immersed himself seven times in the Jordan, according to the word of the man of God; his flesh was restored like the flesh of a young boy, and he was clean. (2 Kings 5:13–14)

It's easy to pass over the daily, ordinary practices and people in our everyday lives. Part of it is our regular routines; if we perform an action or see a person time and time again, we may not truly notice what is happening and who is around us. There are also invisible people all around us, individuals and communities whom society views as unworthy and unacceptable.

If someone told us that our lives would radically change by brushing our teeth one particular morning or listening to a word of prophecy from a barista as he handed us our coffee, what would our natural reaction be? I know my immediate reaction would be of disbelief. I'd probably laugh, thinking about how my life could change while scrubbing my teeth clean. I'd probably scoff at the barista, internally thinking something was wrong with him.

What if we could remember that there are extraordinary events in ordinary places? What if we could hold a space for a message of faith from a person we would least expect? What if Naaman disregarded the words of a foreign girl who was deemed a mere servant? What if Naaman paid attention to the "shoulds" of the world, taking in messages only from people in power in extraordinary places? Naaman had every opportunity to laugh at his wife's servant, a young foreign girl who had no standing in the land of Aram. We could surmise that Naaman's body would have still been plagued by leprosy.

And what of ordinary elements? Water is a very ordinary element. When Naaman hears that he needs to wash seven times in the Jordan River, he outright scoffs at Elisha. Naaman pretty much asks Elisha, "Do you know who I am?" Why would a powerful general have to perform such a simple task in order to receive healing? We are reminded of this when Naaman goes to wash seven times in the Jordan River, and the extraordinary happens in the most ordinary of elements. Naaman is healed through his encounters with the ordinary.

God is immense and expansive and cannot be defined and contained in mere words. Yet God knows us enough and so yearns to be in a relationship with us that God finds ways in daily and ordinary life to be present with us. I wonder how often we've passed over where God has been, just waiting for us to take notice? Think about the ordinariness of water. Think of baptism. How often is baptism simply "getting the baby done"? That's just something the church does, gathering around a font, using water, and then having smiling friends and family take pictures.

How often, in the washing of our hands, bathing, or taking a sip from a glass, do we remember the extraordinary event that has taken place? God comes to meet us in the most common and ordinary of elements to redefine and recreate our relationship with God and one another. We were created anew when the extraordinary came to meet us in the most ordinary of elements and experiences.

Transfiguration: Descending to Share the Story
Mark 9:2–9

Six days later, Jesus took with him Peter and James and John, and led them up a high mountain apart, by themselves. And he was transfigured before them. (Mark 9:2)

Mountaintop experiences are layered experiences. If it's a clear day, there is the ability to take in views for miles on end. Depending on where this mountaintop is located, the peak may be calm and quiet, away from the bustle of daily life taking place at the mountain's base. Depending on the experience, mountaintop sensations don't last forever. Who would tell the story of the sights, smells, and sounds if no one ever returned from the pinnacle? If this is in the context of a journey, there is the ability to see where to go next, what dangers may be in a path, what resources are available to sustain life, and to notice if there has been a path already trodden by those who have journeyed before.

Mountaintop experiences are also places of creation and relationship. It is the place for mere humans to experience just a part of God's fullness of presence. It was at the top of Mount Sinai that God came to Moses with the guidance of right relationship with God and with one another. It was at the top of a mount where Elijah went to mourn and lament, but heard the still, small voice of God in the whirlwind to keep on with where God's call would take him. It is the place that brings clarity in the midst of chaos. It is the place where we can see fully what lies before us. It is also a place we cannot seem to stay forever; there is only so much space at the top of a mountain. Also, how would we know of such wondrous experiences if people did not make the descent to report on what happened to them?

On this final Sunday of Epiphany, Transfiguration Sunday, we are witness to a wondrous mountaintop experience with Jesus and his disciples. We are witness to God's creativity in revealing Jesus' identity not just to the disciples but also to us. God reminds us of previous mountaintops, previous relationships from those pinnacles, and previous voices "crying in the wilderness." What a creative story God tells us through this mountaintop scene, showing us who God is throughout the course of history, and also today.

This creativity of God in the person of Jesus doesn't end. God continues God's creative nature to reach out to us today through the moves of the Holy Spirit. Over the waters of baptism. In the profound nature of the Eucharist. We are also made to be creative beings on a journey. How do we come down from the mountaintop? What do we do with this holy creativity that has been gifted to us?

Lenten Series: The Power of Sacrifice

Six Parts: First Sunday in Lent through Palm Sunday

Jesus shows us how subversive radical self-sacrifice can be.

BRANDAN J. ROBERTSON

Series Overview   Lent has become a vain ritual where Christians give up small, often insignificant vices as they prepare themselves to contemplate the passion and resurrection of Christ. But what if Lent was meant to be much more radical and transformative than that? The fundamental

	Sermon Title	Focus Scripture	Theme
Lent 1	Expand Your Mind	Mark 1:9–15	The heart of Jesus' gospel is to continue expanding our perspective and changing our direction.
Lent 2	What Matters Most	Mark 8:31–38	Jesus calls us to focus on giving up our lives in order to gain a more abundant life.
Lent 3	The Destruction That Brings Life	John 2:13–22	Jesus assaults the systems of privilege and power that perpetuate marginalization and oppression.
Lent 4	The Spotlight of Grace	John 3:14–21	We explore the call to own our participation in injustice and to shine a light on the powers that perpetuate it.
Lent 5	Sacrificial Bravery	John 12:20–33	Jesus' bravery in the face of impending death should inspire and challenge us.
Lent 6 (Palm Sunday)	Joy before Sorrow	Mark 11:1–11	We explore our addiction to power instead of sacrificial service.

call of Jesus to all who follow him is to sacrifice themselves and their lives for the good of their friends, neighbors, and even enemies. However, this call is far more easily preached than practiced. In this Lenten series, we will examine the tangible ways that Jesus demonstrated sacrificial living in his day and age, and the powerful, world-shaking ramifications that his sacrificial life had on his society in his day, while posturing ourselves to imitate Jesus in our day.

Tips and Ideas for This Series

This series takes a nonconventional approach to Lent, playing on the ideas of power, privilege, and oppressive systems and contrasting them with Jesus' assault on the power structures of his day through a simple but difficult path of sacrificial service. One suggestion would be to feature a different marginalized group in your community every week to speak about the ways that they have faced injustice and ways that your community of faith can be engaged in working for their liberation and equality. This practical application of the theological exposition you will be engaging with every week—even, or especially, if it makes people uncomfortable—will certainly bring home the point of this series and of the Lenten season.

Lent 1: Expand Your Mind
Mark 1:9–15

Jesus came to Galilee, proclaiming the good news of God and saying, "The time is fulfilled, and the kingdom of God has come near; repent, and believe in the good news." (Mark 1:14b–15)

At the start of Lent, a season that calls us to the very heart of the Christian story, it makes sense that we begin with the cornerstone of what it means to be a disciple of Christ: the gospel. While many have articulated versions of the gospel that include ideas about substitutionary atonement and the depravity of humanity, in this week's reading we are given the opportunity to hear the gospel as Jesus preached it, and it's much simpler than most of us have ever learned. The gospel that Jesus actually preached is the proclamation that the kingdom of God is being manifest in the world and to participate in it, we must "repent" and "believe" in *that* good news.

Biblical scholar John Dominic Crossan suggests that when Jesus speaks of the kingdom of God, he's not actually talking about some divine reality that he expects to emerge from the heavens at some point in the future but, rather, is asking his disciples to imagine what the world might look like if God were on the throne instead of Caesar. The invitation was to begin working to make that vision a manifest reality in the world, and the way that this was accomplished was through "repenting" and "believing."

What I find stunning is that, like so many ideas in Christianity, the word *repent* doesn't actually mean what we've been taught it does. In almost any Christian context, the idea of repentance, especially tied to the proclamation of the gospel, has to do with asking God to forgive us for our moral failings. In a more progressive environment, repentance may be defined as turning from a damaging action or belief and choosing a better way. But the word translated "repent" here is the Greek word *metanoia*, which literally means "expanding your mind"—to work to move from our finite human perspective and expand to a broader, wider, divine perspective. At the heart of the gospel is the call to change the way that we see the world, to expand beyond our rigid boundaries and beliefs and begin to see things in a new way. Oh, that Christians would have embraced *this* kind of repentance throughout our history!

The way that Jesus invites us to respond to the news that there is a better, more righteous way to live and be in the world is to expand our thinking and to believe in the possibility of the more just and generous world that he demonstrates in his life and ministry. It all begins with a willingness to change our perspective, to see things differently, which is a sacrifice that requires great humility. True repentance means humbling ourselves to embrace a posture of empathy, a posture of listening, a posture of exploration, and a willingness to change the way we think, act, and live based on what we learn.

As we begin Lent, it is essential that all of us begin with a posture of repentance—the sacrificial posture of understanding that our perspective is finite and that God is so much bigger than our singular worldview or beliefs.

Lent 2: What Matters Most
Mark 8:31–38

"For those who want to save their life will lose it, and for those who lose their life for my sake, and for the sake of the gospel, will save it. For what will it profit them to gain the whole world and forfeit their life?" (Mark 8:35–36)

The words that Jesus proclaims in this week's Gospel reading are perhaps some of the most difficult words that he will preach over the course of his ministry. They are difficult because he reiterates, multiple times, his call to "come and die" for the sake of the kingdom. One interpretation of this call is to understand that Jesus was calling his early disciples to literal martyrdom, something that many of them would ultimately experience.

But the Christian tradition has always understood an even more difficult meaning beneath the surface of these words. Jesus' call is to "lose their lives for the sake of the gospel," which means lose their self-centeredness for the sake of manifesting the more beautiful world that God desires. This call is, in many ways, more difficult than the call to martyrdom. It's one thing to physically die; it's another to live a life in which one continually dies to one's own self-interest for the good of one's friends, neighbors, and even enemies.

We can be sure that this latter interpretation is what Jesus is getting at, based on his famous proclamation in this passage: "*For what will it profit them to gain the whole world and forfeit their life?*" Jesus says that there are those who gain "the whole world"—meaning wealth, notoriety, success, relationships, and so on—but in so doing "forfeit their life." All of us, at the core of our being, know that the pursuit of earthly gain is ultimately unfulfilling and will leave us longing for more. We see stories of celebrities and billionaires who have everything that all of us have been conditioned to desire, but end up spinning out of control because they have discovered the lie that is at the heart of the modern American dream. Wealth, fame, sex, and success do *not* lead to true and lasting joy. In fact, they leave a gaping hole that no *thing* can fill.

Jesus is teaching us that by giving up our attachments to material gain and turning from selfishness to selflessness, we actually can find the peace and meaning that all of us are looking for. All of us know that this is true, but few of us have the faith actually to give up our selfish pursuits of whatever we think will bring us joy and begin sacrificially serving others. Perhaps this is the more challenging and more transformative posture for us to take in this Lenten season. Let's make Lent not about giving up certain foods or habits but, rather, about daily turning our attention off of ourselves and joyfully, sacrificially serving others. As difficult as this practice will most certainly be, we have the promise of Jesus that we will "save our lives" and experience "abundant life" if we make this pursuit of dying to ourselves through sacrificial service our regular practice.

Lent 3: The Destruction That Brings Life
John 2:13–22

"Destroy this temple, and in three days I will raise it up." The Jews then said, "This temple has been under construction for forty-six years, and will you raise it up in three days?" But he was speaking of the temple of his body. (John 2:19–21)

In this famous passage of Scripture, we see Rabbi Jesus engaging in a number of symbolic, activist efforts. Entering the temple courts and overturning tables, Jesus was showing at once a profound lack of respect for the powers that controlled the operations of the temple, both political and religious, as well as a profound *respect* for the "true religion" that Jesus' brother James will later say is "to care for orphans and widows in their distress, and to keep oneself unstained by the world" (Jas. 1:27).

One of the core themes in the life and teachings of Jesus was highlighting the ways in which the Jewish religious system in Jerusalem had become a force of oppression and wickedness instead of liberation and love. He was quick to expose the unjust ways of the religious authorities and call them to a posture of sacrifice, something Jesus was quite aware very few of them would accept. By carrying out this dramatic demonstration in the temple courts, Jesus had surely caught the attention of not only the patrons, but the religious leaders and government officials who would have immediately tried to put an end to Jesus' demonstration, lest he cause a riot. With their gaze fixed on him, he declared, "Destroy this temple, and I will rebuild it in three days."

The author of the Gospel tells us that Jesus was cryptically prophesying about what would be done to his body in his inevitable crucifixion and subsequent resurrection. This may be true, but there is an even deeper meaning contained in this passage. Jesus is making a statement that is reiterated time and time again throughout the New Testament: that the Spirit of God doesn't dwell in temples or systems or organizations, but rather in flesh-and-blood human beings. Jesus' double meaning in this passage is that this temple isn't important after all. It could be destroyed and it would be rebuilt in his very body, the vessel through which the Spirit of God actually dwells.

Jesus also prophecies many times about the physical destruction that would one day come to the physical temple. He was aware that this sacred place would be around for only a short period of time, and tried to help people realize that they didn't need the temple and its trappings to be connected to God. In fact, the temple and everything that it represented had become a hindrance to people connecting with the Divine, and in fact became a force of oppression and injustice.

So, when Jesus speaks of destroying the temple, as radical as it would have sounded to his listeners, he's also hinting at a deeper reality: that institutions, religion, and hierarchies were not necessary at all, that God was available to all and through all, if we would only open our eyes and behold.

Lent 4: The Spotlight of Grace
John 3:14–21

"For all who do evil hate the light and do not come to the light, so that their deeds may not be exposed. But those who do what is true come to the light, so that it may be clearly seen that their deeds have been done in God." (John 3:20–21)

Today's passage is perhaps the most famous portion of Scripture in the world, containing Jesus' declaration of God's unconditional love for the world manifest through Jesus. But following Jesus' famous declaration, the author of the Gospel adds some penetrating commentary about human nature and the power of the light of God. Grace is God's unconditional acceptance, regardless of our behavior or disposition toward God. The writer of John says that the light (which he earlier describes as "God" in chapter 1) reveals the motives of everyone's heart. He says that those who desire to do evil, to perpetuate systems of injustice, are opposed to the light and even *hate* the light, because it reveals to themselves and to everyone else their true nature. He continues by saying that those who are committed to living in truth are drawn to the light, because it reveals their pure heart and true desire for justice and peace.

This is the profound paradox of grace: in order to receive it, one must go through the painful process of exposing one's inner brokenness and sinfulness. Until one's sins are exposed, there is no reason to seek out grace. But stepping into the light, even with the promise of grace and forgiveness, is hard to do. It may very well change the way others think about you; there may be temporal consequences; at the very least, it will require us to make changes and live differently. We may sacrifice part of our reputation, or at least our self-image. The process is uncomfortable, but unless we are willing to step toward God and light, we will allow our inner brokenness to fester, which will only chip away at our humanity and perpetuate wickedness in the world around us.

Lent is a season of owning our brokenness, taking an account of the impact our wrongdoing has on our lives, on our world, and on those around us. It's a season when we set aside time to go through the painful process of bringing our dark and ugly parts into the light of God's truth, allowing ourselves and others to see all the ways that we are in need of healing and grace. It's a terribly difficult process, but it is also liberating. Once we step into the light of God with every part of ourselves exposed, we have the profound gift of hearing Jesus proclaim the words that he says early on in our Gospel reading: "*I have not come to condemn the world, but to heal it!*"

Healing, salvation, and liberation are ours. But the first step is owning our flaws and failures, and being willing to bring them into the light. Then, and only then, can we bask in God's glorious gift of grace.

Lent 5: Sacrificial Bravery
John 12:20–33

"Now my soul is troubled. And what should I say—'Father, save me from this hour'? No, it is for this reason that I have come to this hour. Father, glorify your name." (John 12:27–28)

In our reading this week, we get a glimpse into the humanity of Jesus. As he lies prostrate in the Garden of Gethsemane, just outside of the city of Jerusalem, considering the pending consequences of the subversive movement he has led, he faces an incredibly difficult choice: he can turn away from the city, the epicenter of political and religious power, where his message is needed most and the consequences of preaching an anti-imperial message are nothing short of execution. Or he can walk forward into what will be certain death, and become a powerful witness against the oppressive violence of humanity. His whole life has led him in this direction, but as he faces the moment of sacrifice, he begins to second-guess his choices.

In this brief passage, you can almost imagine Jesus' inner dialogue: "Is this really worth it? Couldn't I make more of an impact among the small fishing villages? Why do I need to stare power in its face? Am I really ready to give my life for this cause?" Who among us wouldn't ask the same questions? And who among us wouldn't turn back when faced with the death penalty? Yet, in this fragile moment where Jesus' human nature is on full display, we see the profound divine strength and resolve that marked his life and ministry. "I am deeply anxious, but should I seek to be delivered from these consequences? No! This is the very reason I have come into the world. God, glorify yourself through me."

These are the words of a martyr, of someone willing to stand with extraordinary bravery in the face of stark consequences, so that his message will be heard. In this moment, we see the frail humanity of Jesus intermingled with the divine strength of the Christ. In this moment, he chooses not to take the easy road, the path of least resistance, but to do the only thing that will truly transform the world, even at the high cost of his own life. In this moment, Jesus breathes deeply and resolves to make his way into the city to stare the oppressors in the eye and shine a spotlight on the corrupt ways of the empire. In this moment, Jesus makes the choice to be brave and thus to transform human history forever.

As we walk this Lenten journey toward the cross, may we take time to reflect on the sacrificial bravery of Christ. May we remember that he is like us, often distressed and perplexed by the choices that lie in front of us, the choice to stand up and speak out or to remain complacent and comfortable. But in his moment of deepest distress, leaning on the strength of his Creator, he resolves to take the hard path. And in so doing, he transforms the world for good. May his bravery become our bravery, and may we heed his oft-spoken words to his disciples to "Go and do likewise."

Lent 6 (Palm Sunday): Joy before Sorrow
Mark 11:1–11

Then they brought the colt to Jesus and threw their cloaks on it; and he sat on it. Many people spread their cloaks on the road, and others spread leafy branches that they had cut in the fields. Then those who went ahead and those who followed were shouting,
   "Hosanna!
     Blessed is the one who comes in the name of the Lord!
     Blessed is the coming kingdom of our ancestor David!
   Hosanna in the highest heaven!" (Mark 11:7–10)

Our Gospel reading this week places us in the middle of a really odd scene. Jesus, who has throughout his entire ministry rejected even the appearance of being a person of power and honor (he tells his disciples not even to call him Rabbi!) willingly rides into Jerusalem on the back of a donkey, while his disciples wave branches and shout "Hosanna," a welcome typically reserved for kings and prophets. We have no indication that Jesus resists this display of praise and triumph; in fact, he seems to go along with it happily. What exactly is going on here?

As we've already explored in previous weeks, Jesus' gospel is a call to people everywhere to stop finding their hope in systems and institutions of power and, instead, to find liberation and salvation in the Spirit's dwelling in the ordinary and the unremarkable. Jesus is well aware that his disciples likely believe he is going to be the messianic figure that Israel is hoping for—a ruling king, who commands an army and destroys the forces of Rome that have been oppressing the people of Israel for generations. And constantly, Jesus subverts this expectation, declaring peace instead of war, self-sacrifice instead of violence, service instead of seeking to rule.

In this instance, Jesus is allowing his disciples to see him as a messianic ruler, knowing full well that in just a few days, he will be arrested, tried, and likely crucified, without resistance or calling for a revolt. The contrast Jesus is preparing to display with his life is stunning. Indeed, he is the Messiah, but one who will lay down his own life to reveal the evil of the empire and the religious establishment. He has spent his entire ministry trying to communicate this to his disciples, with no real evidence that they have understood. Now he is going to demonstrate the power of the way of the kingdom by paying the highest price.

On this day, the disciples are rejoicing. They believe that at last, Jesus has stepped up into the role of being a messianic liberator. Indeed, he has. But in a way that will in just a few days leave them stunned. The kingdom that Jesus leads is not one where a monarch will sit on a throne and rule over the people, but one where the leader kneels at the feet of the poorest, sickest, and most broken within the kingdom and declares, "You are loved and liberated to be who God has created you to be." This is the subversive, upside-down kingdom that we are called to meditate on in this season of Lent.

As we enter Holy Week, may we reflect on the ways we believe and participate in false gospels rooted in power and privilege instead of sacrifice and service. If we do not repent and turn from these ways, we too will experience the painful sorrow that the disciples are about to experience—for the systems of privilege and power cost nothing less than our lives.

Easter Series: Living in a Postresurrection World

Eight Parts: Easter Sunday through Pentecost Sunday

What it means to have faith in the resurrected Christ.

BRANDAN J. ROBERTSON

Series Overview
One of the central messages of the Christian faith that is most often overlooked is that Christ is present in and through all things, which means that everything is sacred and every moment is holy. From Easter to Pentecost, we will explore the good news that Christ is risen—not just physically from the grave some two thousand years ago but in every aspect of our lives and world—and how to live in awe of the mundane moments of our ordinary lives. This series begins with focusing on the resurrection of Jesus, a single person, and leads us to Pentecost, where we understand the way in which the entire faith community and indeed the world is resurrected in the Spirit of Christ.

	Sermon Title	Focus Scripture	Theme
Easter Sunday	He's Not Here	Mark 16:1–8	Christ does not always appear in the ways that we think he should, but he is always present and always giving new life.
Easter 2	Seeing Is Not Believing	John 20:19–31	Faith is stronger than what we can see with our eyes.
Easter 3	Got Fish?	Luke 24:36b–48	Sharing a meal with a stranger is more important than understanding or having the right answer.
Easter 4	Truth and Action	1 John 3:16–24	Faith is lived in the doing, not just the believing and declaring.
Easter 5	Abide in Me	John 15:1–8	We abide in Christ in order to bear good fruit in the world.

	Sermon Title	Focus Scripture	Theme
Easter 6	True Friendship	John 15:9–17	The call to sacrificial love is the key to experiencing God.
Easter 7	The Ways of the World	John 17:6–19	We don't belong to the world, but we are in the world to be the incarnations of Christ for all.
Pentecost Sunday	A New Temple	Acts 2:1–21	We explore what it looks like to live in Spirit-saturated Christian community.

Tips and Ideas for This Series

This series seeks to draw on the theme of living in the presence of the risen Christ in our day-to-day lives—a practical draw for Easter visitors who may seek a primer to the faith. In that regard, it may be beneficial to invite members of your faith community to share ways that they have seen and/or experienced the risen Christ in their own lives and world. By sharing a testimony each week (like the initial "witnesses" to the resurrection of Jesus), you are building a case for the final appeal of the series on Pentecost, where, in the words of St. Theresa, we declare, "Christ has no body on earth but ours!"

Easter Sunday: He's Not Here
Mark 16:1–8

As they entered the tomb, they saw a young man, dressed in a white robe, sitting on the right side; and they were alarmed. But he said to them, "Do not be alarmed; you are looking for Jesus of Nazareth, who was crucified. He has been raised; he is not here. Look, there is the place they laid him. But go, tell his disciples and Peter that he is going ahead of you to Galilee; there you will see him, just as he told you." (Mark 16:5–7)

Jesus is always subverting our expectations of him. Easter is perhaps the greatest subversion of all. At the beginning of last week, the disciples think Jesus is their long-awaited political Messiah, riding into Jerusalem on a donkey. On Friday, they watch as their hopes and dreams are crucified high above the city, as Jesus demonstrates that he is not willing to fight, but to forgive his enemies. And on Sunday, as the disciples sit in a state of utter hopelessness and shock, the greatest miracle in history occurs. Christ rises from the grave, subverting death and all the systems that came against him, desiring to put an end to his gospel through a show of brute force.

Mark's account here is arguably the least dramatic of the Gospels' resurrection stories. Some women arrive at the tomb on Sunday morning, and are simply greeted by a calm young man who tells them: "*Jesus isn't here. He's risen from the dead. Go and tell the others.*" And that's that. It's a mystifying experience, and they struggle to believe it's true. After all, if Jesus is alive, then where is he? He doesn't immediately appear to them in any recognizable manner.

So many of the accounts of his appearances after the resurrection have Christ showing up to people who don't immediately recognize him. In Luke 24, he appears as a traveler who becomes recognizable only "in the breaking of bread." In John, he's a gardener who becomes recognizable when he calls Mary by name. And even when he stands in the midst of his disciples, they seem to doubt that it's really Jesus, prompting Thomas to demand to see his wounds. Why do the writers of the Gospel accounts go to such great lengths to let us know that the resurrected Christ is so *unrecognizable*?

I want to suggest that Easter's message is much more expansive than the proclamation that Jesus rose from a literal grave two thousand years ago. What if Easter's message is that the Christ is risen, not just in one single body, but in every person and throughout all creation? What if Easter is the realization that Christ is present and at work in the world *through* us—through a gardener, a traveler, and even in simple rituals like the Eucharist. The risen Christ can be encountered every day through the mundane and ordinary moments, if we only have the eyes to see.

Christ is risen indeed, through you and me. May we take time this Easter to gaze at the beauty of the light and life of the Divine that surrounds us at every moment of every day.

Easter 2: Seeing Is Not Believing
John 20:19–31

Jesus replied, "Have you believed because you have seen me? Blessed are those who have not seen and yet have come to believe." (John 20:29)

As we contemplate the Christian mystery of the resurrection of the Christ, it's easy for us to get caught up in the questions that stem from our modern minds: Did Jesus really rise from the dead? Was it physical? Was it spiritual? Does it really matter at all? Even for the earliest

Christians, believing that Christ rose from the grave required a great deal of faith. In today's reading, we enter into a famous postresurrection scene where the disciple of Jesus named Thomas doubts the other disciples' declaration that Jesus has risen from the grave.

We, as modern Christians, are often tempted to give Thomas a bad rap, labeling him "doubting Thomas." But if we put ourselves in that situation two thousand years ago, I believe most of us would find ourselves in the very place that Thomas finds himself. He has devoted likely three years of his life to following this renegade rabbi, and he watches as all his hopes are destroyed, when the empire hangs Jesus high upon a cross to die. The sorrow and dread he must feel is unimaginable. Jesus isn't just a religious figure for Thomas, but a physical embodiment of hope for liberation from the oppressive hand of Rome. Many leaders rose up in this period of history claiming to be "the one" who would liberate the Jewish people, and all of them ultimately failed.

Thomas believes Jesus is different, and yet, after the events of Friday, it seems that Jesus is just the same as every other would-be Messiah. So, when the disciples rush into the room where Thomas is and declare that Jesus is alive, his skepticism is merited. He is cautious about getting his hopes up, especially for a claim as outlandish as this one. He says, "Unless I physically see Jesus, with his wounds and all, I will not believe these reports."

This is a very reasonable desire indeed. It's at this moment that we are told that Jesus "appears" in the room, and Thomas is astounded as Jesus invites Thomas to feel the wounds in his hands and side. Upon this display of proof, Thomas declares, "My Lord and my God!" and believes in the resurrection. Then Jesus declares these perplexing words: *"Do you believe because you have seen? Blessed are those who have not seen and yet believe."*

Scholars generally agree that these words were likely not spoken by Jesus but were added by the author of the Gospel of John to communicate a message to Christians throughout the ages: Thomas is given the chance physically to encounter Jesus after he has died, but those who believe in the resurrected Christ but never see his physical body, they are truly blessed. Think about it. If you saw Jesus physically, would your faith be changed in any significant way? Sure, Thomas gets the rational proof he desires, but the real question is, once he sees this proof, does it transform his commitment to follow in the way of Jesus?

In this way, faith is perhaps more profound and powerful than sight. Whether or not we believe in a physical or literal resurrection ultimately seems quite trivial when we reflect on the true call of the gospel to live a life modeling Jesus' posture in the world. Our faith is not about a singular event in history—whether or not Jesus rose physically—but, rather, about whether we will allow Christ to rise within our hearts and lives as we seek to embody his path of self-sacrificial love in the world.

When we think about our faith this way, demanding evidence for the stories of Scripture seems really trivial. Thomas's request falls short of the real evidence that is necessary to legitimize the Christian faith: a life that lives the way of Jesus on earth as it is in heaven.

Easter 3: Got Fish?
Luke 24:36b–48

While in their joy they were disbelieving and still wondering, he said to them, "Have you anything here to eat?" They gave him a piece of broiled fish, and he took it and ate in their presence. (Luke 24:41–42)

In last week's reading, we reflected on how seeing and confirming the resurrection of Jesus actually had very little to do with *following* Jesus. In this week's reading, we build on that concept. Here we have some unnamed disciples among whom Jesus appears. After they hear Jesus' testimony about what has happened to him and see his wounded hands and feet, just like Thomas, Jesus asks them to share some of their food with him.

What I love about this passage is that in verse 41 we were told that "in their joy they were disbelieving and still wondering." These men were given the gift of "sight"—Jesus showed them evidence of his death and resurrection—and even as they were filled with joy at the thought of this story being true, they were still *disbelieving and wondering.* They had what so many millions of Christians have longed for since—physical proof of Jesus' resurrection—yet that didn't convince them to follow Jesus.

One might expect Jesus to get frustrated with these disciples. How could they not believe? How could their hearts be so hardened? But he doesn't do that. No, instead of seeking to prove to them who he is or what has happened, he instead asks to eat with them, to share a simple meal around a table with them. The prerequisite of Jesus' fellowship wasn't belief, wasn't agreement, and wasn't devotion. Jesus sat with them at the table and ate, a symbolic gesture in the first-century Jewish culture of acceptance and union.

Some may read this account as Jesus further trying to prove that he was physically raised from the dead (eating a physical fish could help add proof to this claim). That may be the case, but I think that what we see here is probably more likely Jesus demonstrating yet again what matters most in the postresurrection world: All transformation begins, not with evidence or reasoning, but with simple fellowship around a table.

Around a table, we see each other not as ideologies or enemies, but as humans. Around the table, we share radical hospitality and grace. Around a table, we are equals, partaking of the same food and the same drink. And after rising from the table, we are more likely to be open and inclusive of those whom we might not have been so willing to accept before we sat down and supped together.

Our faith was birthed around a table and is symbolized by a table. It is meant to be a faith that feeds us all, regardless of what we believe, how we identify, or how we live. It is a faith that is demonstrated most profoundly through radical hospitality and inclusion, not through rational arguments and proof. When we invite our friends, our neighbors, and our enemies to join us at the table, perhaps we are giving the most powerful witness to the resurrected Christ that is possible—one that will certainly transform hearts and lives for the better.

Easter 4: Truth and Action
1 John 3:16–24

How does God's love abide in anyone who has the world's goods and sees a brother or sister in need and yet refuses help? Little children, let us love, not in word or speech, but in truth and action. (1 John 3:17–18)

What is the heart of the Christian faith? Many in the modern church would answer that question by naming a list of doctrinal beliefs that in theory would transform the way one sees the world. But when one examines the teachings of Jesus and the early teachings of the apostles, another message emerges: Christianity is about *doing* far more than *believing*.

Action and belief are not opposed to each other, but in our epistle reading today, we are told that there is to be an emphasis on our *actions* and our *truth telling*, rather than on believing or declaring our faith in God. The writer of the epistle goes so far as to suggest that the love of God isn't in someone's heart if they see someone in need but choose not to act. This echoes the teaching of James, the brother of Jesus, who condemns those who would say, "Be blessed," to someone in need instead of offering a tangible hand of healing.

In the postresurrection world, we are called to be the incarnations and channels through which Christ is manifest in the world. Theresa of Avila famously declared, "*Christ has no body on earth but ours.*" And it seems that this is the sentiment that the earliest followers of Jesus understood. Unless we are willing to make our faith in the way of Jesus real through living the sacrificial life that Jesus taught, then how can we say we have been transformed by the gospel of Jesus? If we aren't willing to speak the truth about our addictions to wealth and power, then how can we say that our lives are centered on the *agapē*—unconditional and equalizing love—of God?

It's far easier simply to *believe* in Jesus and to *pray* for God to meet people's needs. This sort of religion falls dramatically short of what Jesus himself embodied and taught his disciples. Unless we are willing to follow the example of Jesus, sacrificing ourselves, our comfort, and our privilege for the good of our "other," then we truly haven't understood Jesus. And if we aren't *compelled* to follow in this path because of the overwhelming grace and love of God that we've experienced, then it is likely that we haven't truly encountered the world-shattering love of God.

The writer of the epistle says that our faith will be legitimized by how willing we are to actually embody it and to tell the truth, even when it costs us. This is the challenge that all of us are called to rise to in this postresurrection world.

Easter 5: Abide in Me
John 15: 1–8

"Abide in me as I abide in you. Just as the branch cannot bear fruit by itself unless it abides in the vine, neither can you unless you abide in me. I am the vine, you are the branches. Those who abide in me and I in them bear much fruit, because apart from me you can do nothing." (John 15:4–5)

What does it mean to *abide in Christ*? One of the central claims of the Christian faith is that, in some form, Christ is risen and active in the world. He is not simply a spiritual teacher who lived and died two thousand years ago, but the Spirit of light that pulsated within him is at work in the world today. For those of us who would identify as more "progressive," talking this way can feel rather uncomfortable. We would rather rationalize and demythologize our faith, making it strictly about morals and ethics, rather than about some sort of spiritual relationship to Christ.

But another undeniable aspect of what it means to live in a postresurrection world is that we are invited to an intimate spiritual relationship with Christ. Through prayer, meditation, contemplation, and service, we are invited to open the eyes and ears of our souls to perceive the living and active Christ at work in and around us at every moment of every day. Jesus himself knew this. Not only did he center his life on outward service to the poor and the oppressed, but he also serviced his own soul regularly through prayer, fasting, retreat, and contemplation. Through this process, Jesus cultivated an intimate and personal relationship with the creator and sustainer of life, even calling God "Abba," a term of endearment literally translated as "Daddy."

If our commitment to the way of Christ is going to have an enduring impact on our lives and the life of the world, it must be rooted in regular encounters with the Divine. We must know God, not as an abstract reality, but the very ground of being and source of our lives, the source from which the unconditional love we hope to manifest in the world originates. Jesus promises that those who root themselves deeply in "the vine" of the Spirit will "bear much fruit," meaning that they will be personally nourished and able to be effective incarnations of Christ in the world.

This week, we are being called to turn inward, to establish our own personal connection to God as the prerequisite to being channels of renewal and healing in the world. We need to discern what it looks like for us to experience the resurrection in our own souls, and determine which practices and postures help us to feel most connected to God and to our true inner selves. Unless we begin our work as followers of Christ here, it is unlikely that our faith will remain vibrant and active; we will be unable to bear good fruit in the world.

Inner peace begets outer peace, inner wholeness begets outer wholeness. This is the rhythm of authentic discipleship.

Easter 6: True Friendship
John 15:9–17

"This is my commandment, that you love one another as I have loved you. No one has greater love than this, to lay down one's life for one's friends. You are my friends if you do what I command you." (John 15:12–14)

Think about your best friend. What was an attribute that they displayed that earned them your relational commitment and trust? If we think about this question, one of the most common answers is that said best friend "would do anything for me," which is a way of saying that this friend is loyal, selfless, and sacrificial on your behalf. Someone who puts your needs above their own and overflows with affection for you—that's a signature sign of a great friend.

As those who are living in the light of the resurrection of Jesus, we are called to reflect on what following Christ in the realm of relationship looks like. In today's famous passage from the Gospel of John, Jesus is speaking to his disciples, to whom he relates more as friends than as "students" (which would be the common expectation in a discipleship relationship). In the friendship Jesus shares with his disciples, he embodies sacrificial selflessness for these individuals whose own faithfulness to him constantly wavers. In other words, Jesus is the example of a *true* friend . . . the disciples, not so much.

Jesus sums up all the commands in the Hebrew Bible in the singular phrase, "Love one another." This is the theme of his ministry, the heart of his teaching. And in relation to friends, this is the same command Jesus comes back to: sacrificial love for each other. Jesus says that true friendship is a willingness to serve and sacrifice—even one's own self-interest and life—for the good of another. In this way, Jesus raises the standard of friendship from a simple version of *philia* love, the Greek word for "brotherly love," and presents a relationship based on *agapē* love, meaning unconditional love.

To live as incarnations of the resurrected Christ in our relationships is to be willing to see *all* interactions with *all* humans through the lens of *agapē*, sacrificial love. Jesus ends his teaching saying, "You are my friends if you do what I command." What he's *not* saying is, "In general, do whatever I say, otherwise I won't consider you my friends." No, he is saying that when his disciples finally obey his command to *love each other as one's self,* then they will finally cross the line into authentic friendship. This week, let's reflect on what it looks like to be sacrificial friends for the relationships in our lives. How can we better embody Christ's love and grace to those in our relational spheres?

Easter 7: The Ways of the World
John 17:6–19

"They do not belong to the world, just as I do not belong to the world. Sanctify them in the truth; your word is truth. As you have sent me into the world, so I have sent them into the world." (John 17:16–17)

This week's Gospel reading comes from what has become known as the "high-priestly prayer," a prayer that Jesus offers at the end of his life, as he sees his crucifixion looming and is wrestling with the deep affection he has for his disciples. One of the most famous lines in this prayer comes from verse 16, "[My disciples] do not belong to the world, just as I do not belong to the world." But what exactly does this mean?

The Gospel of Jesus is always one of tension. It calls us to embrace our present moment and reality, while also straining toward a more just and generous reality. Jesus isn't teaching us that we are to separate from the world with all its diverse peoples. Rather, he calls us to live by a different set of standards, a different rhythm of living, a different reality. The kingdom of God, as Jesus calls it, isn't a singular city that exists somewhere in the universe, but the gradual transformation of *this world* into the more beautiful world that God desires.

Manifesting the kingdom of God on earth as in heaven requires that we reject "this world"—the engrained ways of thinking, seeing, and being that humanity has bought into. This means thought patterns like "the American dream," which promises that everyone can and *should* seek wealth, status, and fame as a means of finding fulfillment in life, or patterns that tell us that we are just cogs in a much bigger social and political wheel who can't actually make a difference in the long run.

Both of these thoughts represent the consciousness of the "world," and millions of people buy into them. If we settle for them as "true," then we cannot be effective followers of the way of Jesus, whose core teachings directly contradict these ways of living. While Jesus calls us to reject the thinking and ways of "belonging to the world," he at the same time prays that we would be sent "into the world," clearly an indication that, in general, we're not meant to separate ourselves and form alternative societies and subcultures but, rather, to live according to the rhythm of the kingdom *in the midst* of "the world" and, in so doing, to entice others to live according to this new way of seeing and being in the world.

This week, may we take time to reflect on the ways that we have bought into and live in sync with the systems and thought patterns of "the world" that directly contradict the path that Jesus embodies. Once we identify the myths that we live into, may we intentionally seek to dismantle them in our own lives, in favor of gradually adapting and adopting the way of Jesus to fit our own culture and context. When we do this, we not only become channels through which the light of Christ is manifest, but we will also be compelling witnesses who draw others toward the way of Jesus, thus fulfilling his high-priestly prayer.

Pentecost: A New Temple
Acts 2:1–21

When the day of Pentecost had come, they were all together in one place. And suddenly from heaven there came a sound like the rush of a violent wind, and it filled the entire house where they were sitting. Divided tongues, as of fire, appeared among them, and a tongue rested on each of them. All of them were filled with the Holy Spirit and began to speak in other languages, as the Spirit gave them ability. (Acts 2:1–4)

The Pentecost story is one of the most dramatic and perplexing events in the history of early Christianity. What exactly is happening and why? And is it relevant to the life of Christians in the twenty-first century?

The Pentecost story is the fulfillment of a prophecy from the book of Joel in which it is declared that in "the last days," the Spirit would be poured out from heaven on all people equally, and the systems and structures that had divided humans for so long would be dissolved. God would be in all, through all, and for all. God would be revealed not to reside in temples made by humans, but rather in the true temples of the Spirit, human beings themselves.

Using this imagery of the temple of God moving from a physical location in Jerusalem to within the hearts of every human, we see in Acts 2 a powerful metaphor for the new thing that God desired to do in the world. In the Hebrew Bible, when the tabernacle and temple were first established, the people knew God was present within the Holy of Holies, because God appeared as a wild flame of fire above the temple; this was called the *shekinah* of God. From the very earliest days of the temple, the prophets continued to say that the rituals of the temple were nothing more than *shadows* of a coming reality that all people would experience. This is ultimately what Joel is prophesying.

God's love is not limited to the people of Israel. God's presence is not limited to the temple. The prophecies of Pentecost were prophecies of a day when the temple, with all its exclusive rights and potentially burdensome religious laws, would be done away with, and the revelation of God's presence in all and through all would be experienced. In Acts 2, the *shekinah* of God appeared above the heads of people from every nation, tribe, and tongue. A new community was birthed, one not bound by law but liberated by grace. A new day had begun, a new revelation that God's dwelling place was within all people, and absolutely no one was excluded. Together, united in the midst of all our diversity, we become the new temple through which the glory of God is made manifest on earth as in heaven. All are welcome to be a part of this new reality, and in fact, all already are a part of it. The question is whether or not our eyes and ears are open to see and perceive this new reality.

After all, Jesus said we must be spiritually reborn in order to *see* the kingdom of God pulsating around us.

Summer Series 1: More Than Meets the Eye

Four Parts: Proper 4 through Proper 7

Discovering God's surprises through Paul's Second Letter to the Corinthians.

KYLE E. BROOKS

Series Overview   In nature, things are not always what they appear to be. The mineral pyrite (also called fool's gold) has a pale yellow color and shine that give it the *appearance* of real gold. The graphite in a pencil is hardly as valuable as a diamond, but graphite and diamonds are just different forms of the same element: carbon. Appearances can be deceiving, and it can be difficult to see the deeper substance without closer examination. For Christian believers, it is necessary to examine our surroundings carefully in order to perceive how God might be showing up in them. Power, faith, transformation, and salvation often appear in ways we do not expect. God's work is radical, unusual, and often surprising, working behind the scenes and beneath the surface. This series, drawn from Paul's second letter to the church in Corinth, focuses on the various ways that members of the Christian community are called to look closely and deeply at where, when, and how God works beyond our expectations.

	Sermon Title	Focus Scripture	Theme
Proper 4	Something within Me	2 Cor. 4:5–12	God's power works through modest means.
Proper 5	Seeing beyond Suffering	2 Cor. 4:13–5:1	We put our suffering in perspective.
Proper 6	Changing Seasons	2 Cor. 5:6–10 (11–13), 14–17	Life in Christ brings thorough transformation.
Proper 7	No Time Like the Present	2 Cor. 6:1–13	Don't delay embracing God's grace.

Tips and Ideas for This Series

Since this series is all about close examination and seeing beyond the obvious, consider using imagery in worship that could be viewed or interpreted in multiple ways. You might use extreme close-ups of ordinary objects, or images of optical illusions. For instance, there is the classic picture that looks like an elderly woman in one view, and then a young woman in another view. Another way to play with this theme is imagery showing the commonalities between seemingly different things. The example in the series overview about graphite and diamonds could be an object lesson. Beyond visual aids, it could be useful to ask congregants to take time in the week between worship gatherings to observe and reflect on ways that God unexpectedly shows up in daily life, as a way of preparing for and engaging the teachings in the series.

Proper 4: Something within Me
2 Corinthians 4:5–12

But we have this treasure in clay jars, so that it may be made clear that this extraordinary power belongs to God and does not come from us. (2 Corinthians 4:7)

What do we know about Corinth, the place where Paul founded one of the early church communities? Well, it was a cosmopolitan place, composed of people from various ethnic backgrounds, lifestyles, and religious beliefs. It was also a seaport, making it a valuable site for trade and commerce. Corinth was, in many ways, a model city in the Roman Empire. It was also known for its significant slave trade, sexual perversion, and general moral corruption. At first glance, it hardly seems like the ideal setting for a new church. But what does Paul do? Plant a church in Corinth.

You can imagine that Paul is thoroughly aware of the various cultural influences that might impact this fledgling community. The members of the Corinthian church would have come from varied backgrounds and experiences, different social norms and values. Such differences can be a challenge for a new community trying to agree on common practices and commitments. In this passage from his Second Letter to the Corinthians, Paul uses language and images that reflect tensions of difference and paradox: light in the midst of darkness, treasure in clay jars, perseverance despite persecution, life that surpasses the work of death. He highlights an important reality: we do not preach *ourselves*: we preach Jesus Christ as Lord. That knowledge enables us to deal with the tensions of difference and paradox that arise in our lives.

The image of clay jars is significant. They would be the equivalent of plastic storage containers today: cheap, easily replaced, perfect for leftovers. The idea of putting treasure in them is utterly ridiculous. You would think a treasure would be stored in a secure space, tucked away and protected.

Yet the passage directs our attention to the fact that the treasure *is* in clay jars, and it is in no way diminished by its container. On the contrary, it stands out even more because the container is unassuming and unexpected. Corinth would have been a surprising place for a church. But truthfully, it is even more surprising that human beings are carriers of the treasure of the gospel at all. Paul makes it clear that we carry the death of Jesus with us, and through our own mortal lives, the life of Jesus is enfleshed and expressed daily to the world.

There is a saying attributed to Henry Stanley Haskins: "What lies behind us and what lies ahead of us are tiny matters compared to what lies within us." This is an important point. Paul would have been writing to people who came from different, perhaps checkered, pasts. They would have faced challenges trying to build and sustain a Christian community within a tumultuous Corinthian culture.

Paul does not deny these realities. Rather, he points to the reality that pushes against and overcomes them: the power of God is in us, and God is glorified through this. It can be easy to fixate on our imperfections, our struggles, and our surroundings. As Christian believers, we are not promised lives of ease and comfort. However, God's presence in the midst of our journey enables us to maintain hope in knowing that something powerful lies within us, strengthening us for whatever lies ahead.

Proper 5: Seeing beyond Suffering
2 Corinthians 4:13–5:1

So we do not lose heart. Even though our outer nature is wasting away, our inner nature is being renewed day by day. (2 Corinthians 4:16)

Paul's encouragement to the Corinthians is couched in a sober reality: life is hard, and sometimes it will break us down. From illness, injury, and the wearing down with age, the ailments of our physical bodies are a reminder that our lives in them won't last forever. Despite these facts, Paul's attention is on the inner life that is renewed daily. Within the context of day-to-day challenges, he reminds his audience that suffering is not *all* there is. There is life and possibility to be seen and embraced.

This perspective starts with a spirit of faith. Verse 13 emphasizes that such a spirit prompts us to believe and to speak. There is an internal conviction that prompts an external statement. Paul grounds this belief in the knowledge that the power that raised Jesus is the very same power that will raise us. This is intriguing, because you can't have a resurrection without first having a death. It seems, then, that Paul is not offering some pie-in-the-sky motivational speech. He's not trying to reduce real struggles to a case of mind over matter. He's saying that a perspective of faith is the key to *enduring* the struggle. Yes, it'll be tough. But we can make it.

Theodicy is the attempt to make sense of divine goodness and providence in light of the existence of evil and suffering. It is always tricky to talk about the meaning of suffering or the ways to handle it. Many times, the explanations I've heard have been absolutely terrible. People will say, "God never gives us more than we can bear" or "Suffering builds character." Those are hard words to swallow when you've seen people collapse under the weight of tragedy or you've watched bad things happen to good people. It can be downright infuriating to listen to people trying to tell you how you should think about your own suffering.

The problem of theodicy is nothing new, and it certainly hasn't disappeared. As human beings, but particularly as Christian believers, we have to reckon with our relationship to real suffering. Being faithful doesn't mean we escape hardship or hurt. In fact, there may be times when attempting to be faithful places us in situations of suffering. But Paul's words are not aimed at making suffering disappear. Instead, he is focused on the internal spirit and mind-set that enable people to face their suffering with renewed strength and courage.

The presence of God and the renewing of our spirits don't necessarily end the difficulty. Affliction and divine consolation are two major themes throughout Second Corinthians. Divine power doesn't necessarily end the affliction, but it guides our spiritual understanding of it. From an outsider perspective, it may seem as if nothing has really changed. But for Paul, the attention of the believer is not dominated by temporary circumstances. Instead, it is focused on the eternal glory of God, on a reality beyond what we can naturally perceive.

Seeing *beyond* suffering doesn't mean we don't see the suffering. It means believing that our suffering is not the last word. It means trusting that the God who has resurrection power can indeed renew our spirits each and every day.

Proper 6: Changing Seasons
2 Corinthians 5:6–10 (11–13), 14–17

So if anyone is in Christ, there is a new creation: everything old has passed away; see, everything has become new! (2 Corinthians 5:17)

Growing up in the Midwest, I was accustomed to having discernible seasons. We had sweltering, humid summers, followed by crisp, colorful autumns and blankets of ice and snow in the winter. Springtime was always a respite after long, dark days and cold temperatures. By the time the spring flowers were in full bloom, it seemed as though winter had never happened.

Of course, winter *had* happened. And in its deepest throes, I would anticipate the days when I could walk around in shorts and T-shirts again. I envisioned those moments when all would become new again. The possibility of re-creation is at the heart of Paul's declaration in verse 17. The entire passage builds up to this moment, in which everything becomes new.

It takes confidence and faith to walk the path toward new creation. Verse 7 is familiar enough: "for we walk by faith, not by sight." More easily said than done, especially when the environment around me belies the season. Sometimes you get chilly days in the spring or unseasonably warm days in December. We often see and feel things that don't align with our present understanding of the seasons of our lives.

Why does Paul emphasize faith over sight? Perhaps he knew that the circumstances of the Corinthians might be discouraging to them. Their life as a church community certainly had its peaks and valleys. What we experience may not look or feel like what we expect from life as the church. We are reminded that the church is made up of people who are all too human and imperfect. We don't always resemble what we are becoming. Paul makes the point that God is at work in our hearts and consciences in ways that may belie what we and others observe with the naked eye. We are prepared inwardly to face our outer world with new faith and courage.

We can draw important lessons from a most difficult season in Jesus' human journey: his path toward crucifixion. The death, burial, and resurrection of Jesus underscore the cycle of death and life that is also embedded in the life of the church. Paul is adamant about how his audience should identify with the life of Jesus, and that identification pushes them (and us) to take on a changed perspective. While death might normally prompt feelings of despair, the giving of one's life in love affords another way of thinking about our response to it.

The power of Christ's resurrection brought about a new season in the life of the church, even when things appeared bleak.

There is no avoiding death and suffering in human life. They come and go, much like the seasons, though with far less rhythm or predictability. Even so, to share in the death, burial, and resurrection of Jesus the Christ is to participate in the changing of seasons, to enter into new creation. It is not a denial that the old seasons of our life ever existed. It is a confident affirmation that new seasons are on the way. We have a reason to live, because we know the renewal and transformation of life are at work even when we can't see them.

Proper 7: No Time Like the Present
2 Corinthians 6:1–13

As we work together with him, we urge you also not to accept the grace of God in vain. For he says, "At an acceptable time I have listened to you, and on a day of salvation I have helped you." See, now is the acceptable time; see, now is the day of salvation! (2 Corinthians 6:1–3)

There is a saying that procrastination is the thief of time. All of us have some experience with putting things off. We do it for different reasons: anxiety about failure, lack of structure, the unpleasantness of what needs to be done. But there are times when the urgency of the moment requires us to overcome our hesitancy and seize the opportunities in front of us.

This passage of Paul's letter carries that sense of urgency, as Paul implores the Corinthians to accept the gift of God's grace. Grace is a central concept to Christian theology. It speaks to the free, unearned act through which creation is restored to God. We need not *work* for it, but it must be *accepted*. Paul urges his audience to do so without delay, to accept restoration in God.

In verse 2, Paul quotes from Isaiah 49:8 when he writes about the "day of salvation." This quote comes from Second Isaiah, which is focused on the theme of consolation for God's people at the tail end of Babylonian exile. It calls to mind the fact that situations of exile and struggle are not new. The Israelites knew something about the struggle to wait on God—hoping and expecting what, at the time, remained unseen—and centuries later the words of Isaiah were fitting for the Corinthians.

Why is it so difficult, then, to embrace the grace of God? What stands in the way of that possibility? Well, I imagine it has to do with the same reasons people procrastinate. Paul describes at great length the challenges and difficulties that he and others faced in trying to communicate the gospel to others. The life of a person who embraced God's grace still involved enduring hardships and dreadful circumstances. But Paul's pursuit also led to the practice of greater patience, love, and truth.

Making progress, whether naturally or spiritually, often means embracing the full spectrum of possibilities that accompany it. Throughout the fourth, fifth, and sixth chapters of Second Corinthians, Paul seems to be making the point that we can't measure the meaning or value of our pursuits by the way things appear. The goodness in God's grace is truly valuable, but it does not erase the real challenges of everyday life. Cycles of life will find us wrestling with life and death, joy and sorrow, hope and despair. Even with the best of intentions, our aims and means could be misunderstood.

So why the urgency? Who would be in a rush to experience this kind of life? I try to imagine what it meant for the Corinthians to try and build a church community in a setting that seemed antagonistic to their goals. In a context with very different social, political, and spiritual norms, it seems there would always be conflicts. There would never be a perfect moment to go all-in on following the way of Jesus.

Procrastination often pushes us to wait for ideal conditions that may never exist. The fear of potential struggles and failures can cause us to come to a standstill. The gift of God's grace is not a simple solution to all of life's ills. It is a transformative perspective and way of life that enables us to recognize God's presence and power even in the direst situations. Grace transforms our view of ourselves and of others. We take the good with the bad, in ourselves and in the world, and recognize that neither of those defines us. Rather, through God, we are empowered to define *our* response to life. That is a possibility worth accepting without delay.

Summer Series 2: Everyday Prophecy

Four Parts: Proper 9 through Proper 12

Examining four prophets, we see how we too can respond to God's call.

KYLE E. BROOKS

Series Overview

It is easy to the view the prophets of the Hebrew Bible as marginal characters in strange circumstances distant from our contemporary times. But there are tremendous lessons to be garnered from watching the way prophets responded to their everyday situations. The prophets were known for the ways they critiqued the systems and figures of power and privilege in their time and space. The ongoing life of the church demands prophetic address that both attends to personal need and empowers communal action in the service of justice and righteousness in the world. The work of the prophet is not based on status or talent, but on presence and availability to the call of God. This four-week series will investigate how that call is carried out in everyday ways that make a profound difference.

Tips and Ideas for This Series

One intriguing idea could be displaying "profiles" of the prophets in the common areas of the church, highlighting interesting back-

	Sermon Title	Focus Scripture	Theme
Proper 9	Ezekiel: React or Respond	Ezek. 2:1–5; Ps. 123	How do we respond to God's call?
Proper 10	Amos: On-the-Job Training	Amos 7:7–15; Ps. 85:8–13	Our habits are more important than our titles.
Proper 11	Jeremiah: Looking for Good Shepherds	Jer. 23:1–6; Ps. 23	God models caring for God's people.
Proper 12	Elisha: More Than Enough	2 Kgs. 4:42–44; Ps. 145:10–18	God's provision is abundant.

ground info about the prophets in the series. The idea is to make them more familiar to congregants and to demystify some of the aura around these figures. You could also offer space for congregants to reflect on their own sense of call, asking how our own everyday work might be like or very different from the biblical prophets.

Proper 9: Ezekiel: React or Respond
Ezekiel 2:1–5; Psalm 123

The descendants are impudent and stubborn. I am sending you to them, and you shall say to them, "Thus says the Lord GOD." Whether they hear or refuse to hear (for they are a rebellious house), they shall know that there has been a prophet among them. (Ezekiel 2:4–5)

If you've read the books of the prophets in the Hebrew Bible, you know well enough that the prophets were often charged to deliver difficult messages. For most people, delivering difficult news is not an easy task. People don't respond just to the message; they respond to the *messenger* too. In this passage, Ezekiel is made to stand and given a charge to deliver a message to a difficult audience.

The people of Israel have been in rebellion, and this is the latest round in the ongoing saga between God and God's people. Interestingly, we get a clear description of how the ancestors and their descendants have been stubborn and resistant to God. But we *don't* get an explanation of exactly what Ezekiel is supposed to say to them. What seems clear is that, regardless of how the people respond, God wants them to know that a prophet is among them.

Ezekiel was part of a priestly family, and so he had been trained in the rites and rituals of the priesthood. He was equipped and prepared to be a spiritual leader for the people of Israel. This position would have commanded some respect and status. But if the people had been rebellious for generations, they weren't exactly keen on whatever the spiritual leaders were saying or doing. I imagine that rebellion had a lot to do with frustration at their situation of exile. It can be difficult to talk to God when your circumstances cause you to wonder if God is even listening.

A significant sermonic lesson is to be found in the question of how we respond to the voice of God. Ezekiel is in a position to speak to the people of Israel because he responds affirmatively. God invites him into conversation. Any conversation involves some measure of responsive communication, a back-and-forth dialogue, an exchange of information and ideas. To be truly prophetic might mean to facilitate the necessary communication between God and God's people.

How people respond to that communication makes all the difference. In Psalm 123, we have a model for response. The psalmist offers a message of contrition and a desire for mercy. The psalm is an acknowledgment of the place God holds in the life of the people. It communicates the relationship between those who serve and the one who is worthy to be served. It expresses a desire for a response from God. It is a call for divine dialogue.

What has God called us to, corporately and personally? This will vary depending on our individual lives or our particular congregational communities. I believe we are called to be present in our world and to facilitate the engagement of people with the glory of God. Both in Ezekiel's response and the psalmist's words, we see the necessity of putting aside rebellious ways and opening our ears and hearts to God's voice, God's grace, and God's mercy.

Rebellion is a natural *reaction* to difficult messages. I think of the growing pains we go through as we transition through adolescence, moving from childhood into adulthood. Sometimes that transition involves rebellion, as we resist the things we have been told and try to find our own way. Sometimes we walk away from dialogue and cut off communication. But at some point we hopefully recognize the value of conversation, of coming together and reasoning, even when we disagree. I believe we are called to divine dialogue with God, to wrestle with difficult moments in our lives and to find ways to live faithfully in the midst of them. Rebellion is an easy reaction, but the prophet and the psalmist show us what it means to respond conscientiously to God.

Proper 10: Amos: On-the-Job Training
Amos 7:7–15; Psalm 85:8–13

Then Amos answered Amaziah, "I am no prophet, nor a prophet's son; but I am a herdsman, and a dresser of sycamore trees, and the LORD took me from following the flock, and the LORD said to me, 'Go, prophesy to my people Israel.'" (Amos 7:14–15)

When people ask you about yourself, do you tend to tell them who you are or what you did/do? Do our roles make us, or do we simply inhabit those roles? Maybe both of these ideas are true to some extent. I believe that we are not *what* we do, but we are shaped by *how* we do it. Still, at times, there may be a risk in losing ourselves in a role, of negating who we are in order to fit into an ideal.

Amos doesn't seem to have that problem. In fact, he is quite an ironic figure: a prophet who denies being one. In fact, he makes it clear that he's a shepherd and a gardener. He is neither a prophet nor a prophet's son. He is making a claim that he is not a part of a particular lineage or that he has inherited status. Amos is rejecting a title. He is also rejecting an ideology, an identity that is not his own. In his day there were temple prophets who were essentially on the royal payroll, but Amos is distinguishing himself from that group. He is not a prophet for hire. He is defined not by his affiliation but by his response to God's call. He was already busy with his own work when God called him to prophesy.

Amos's prophesies are not exactly sunshine and roses. In fact, his message is pretty direct and severe: the people of Israel are going to be militarily defeated, and the house of King Jeroboam is going to fall. This is not good news to the religious leader in Bethel, Amaziah the priest. He believes Amos's words are treasonous and tells Amos to go away and ply his prophetic wares somewhere else.

Amos's response to Amaziah is critical. It tells us something about Amos's everyday life, which prepares him to be a prophet, regardless of his title. Nothing suggests Amos became a different person because of his assignment. Rather, he brought *himself* to the work. It's worth asking, what kind of person does Amos become in the midst of his daily work . . . before he is called to his prophetic work? He is a herdsman (shepherd) and a dresser of sycamore trees (gardener). He is acquainted with dirty work that produces the conditions for things to flourish and live. Shepherds make sure a flock is well nourished, while gardeners manage the growth of plants. Amos is a cultivator of living things. We might think of Israel as a living organism, whose nourishment and growth are dependent on shepherding and gardening. Amos has developed life-giving habits, the practices of herding and pruning. Amos is proof that our habits outweigh our titles. What we do, day in and day out, reflects our character and identity.

The selection from Psalm 85 gives us a picture of a God who cultivates God's people with salvation and peace. The imagery is telling: glory that dwells in the land, faithfulness that springs up from the ground, righteousness that looks down from the sky. The land, the ground, and the sky are all intertwined in the life of the shepherd and the gardener, who recognize their participation in the beautiful dance of the natural world. God's engagement with the people mirrors Amos's engagement with creation. That is a model to follow and embrace. True prophets reflect a close following of God's ways in the world.

Prophetic life, it seems, is not about grand gestures, sweeping proclamations, or public titles. It may be about the daily habits of cultivation and maintenance that enable life to flourish. It may be found in the herding and pruning that help life to grow in the healthiest and most meaningful directions. Through Amos and the psalmist, we receive a lovely reminder that "prophet" is less a title and more a disposition. To be faithful to our daily labor and calling is truly prophetic.

Proper 11: Jeremiah: Looking for Good Shepherds
Jeremiah 23:1–6; Psalm 23

Therefore thus says the LORD, the God of Israel, concerning the shepherds who shepherd my people: It is you who have scattered my flock, and have driven them away, and you have not attended to them. So I will attend to you for your evil doings, says the LORD. (Jeremiah 23:2)

Psalm 23 may have been the first psalm I ever memorized as a child. Even now, it flows smoothly off my tongue with little effort. But what strikes me now is how differently this passage reads when held up against the narrative of shepherds in Jeremiah 23. Psalm 23 is a beautiful picture of the psalmist's recognition that the Lord offers care and provision in a way that mirrors a shepherd's gentle yet firm guidance of sheep. It reflects the holistic care for tangible, emotional, and spiritual needs. These are the marks of good shepherds.

Jeremiah 23 paints a different picture, one that condemns the leaders who have been anything but good shepherds. The passage speaks to a time of restoration after exile. We know that times of exile were a recurring theme in the history of the people of Israel. It seems that this scattering of the people is tied to the malpractice of their leaders, whose actions and attitudes led them astray.

Jeremiah was a strong critic of the royal and religious authorities. His prophetic declaration is an indictment of Israel's leadership at the highest levels. What we find here in chapter 23 is a brief sort of sermon that not only decries poor leadership but also promises reformation. The language of shepherding is meaningful because it suggests a kind of intimacy and closeness; it is hard to be a shepherd and not smell like the sheep. In order to truly shepherd people, you have to meet them where they are and be attentive to their needs. Jeremiah had a front-row seat to the desolation and despair of the people of Israel. He would have known just how much they needed restoration.

In verse 3 Jeremiah expresses God's message of gathering the very people whom God drove away. It is an image of a God who both punishes and restores, who disciplines and delivers. It is worth asking how this squares with our impression of the shepherd in Psalm 23. To know God as a shepherd is to know a complex relationship. The sheep and shepherd enjoy closeness, but that relationship is not always easy. Sheep have minds and wills of their own. Perhaps the love and care of a shepherd doesn't always appear that way to the sheep. At times, it may feel like restriction or constraint.

To be saved by the shepherd may not mean a life of total comfort or ease. But if the end of the Jeremiah passage is any indication, it should ultimately look like a restoration of justice, righteousness, and safety. The long-term well-being of the people seems to be at the heart of God's message through Jeremiah.

The passages for this week remind me that the relationship between God and God's people is dynamic, not static. It is always evolving, as we come to understand more about God's will for us and the world. Think of the various ways we are called to examine this shepherd-sheep dynamic in our own lives. Who are the people who are entrusted to our care? Under whose care have we had to live? In a world often characterized by abuses of power and authority, the prophetic challenges of the Scriptures here call us to resist business as usual and pursue the way of the good shepherd in our everyday relationships.

When we are entrusted with a measure of power and authority—as pastors, employers, guardians, coaches, and the like—it is our responsibility to operate in ways that model justice, righteousness, and safety. We are called to shepherd people, not turn them into prey. To love and care for those in our lives, particularly the most vulnerable, is to live in a way that tends to their deepest needs.

Proper 12: Elisha: More Than Enough
2 Kings 4:42–44; Psalm 145:10–18

A man came from Baal-shalishah, bringing food from the first fruits to the man of God: twenty loaves of barley and fresh ears of grain in his sack. Elisha said, "Give it to the people and let them eat." But his servant said, "How can I set this before a hundred people?" So he repeated, "Give it to the people and let them eat, for thus says the LORD, 'They shall eat and have some left.'" (2 Kings 4:42–43)

One of the most meaningful and gracious acts of care we can perform is providing a meal for someone. It is a way of meeting a tangible need while also offering personal connection. Food is a necessity, but preparing and serving it with kindness and intention can elevate food to be part of an act of love. To recognize another's hunger and seek to meet it is to demonstrate compassion and concern that attends to the heart and soul as well as the body and nourishes the whole person.

This is the situation in which we find the prophet Elisha, who has been busy in the work of tending to God's people. In 2 Kings 2, we find him succeeding his mentor, Elijah, whose own life and work nourished Elisha's prophetic growth. In their final moments together, when Elijah asks Elisha what he can do for him before he departs, Elisha asks for a double portion of Elijah's anointing—an inheritance that will feed his own spiritual life.

The generosity of Elijah becomes clear in Elisha's own actions in 2 Kings 4. Here he is with the prophetic guild, who are now learning from his wisdom. Chapter 4 highlights Elisha's movements through different towns and the encounters he has with various people: a widow with two children, a wealthy Shunammite woman, and the company of prophets. In every instance, there are acute needs related to debt, health, and sustenance. There are conditions of crisis that require some immediate response.

Elisha does not have the *material* resources on hand for meeting the needs of these people. What he *does* have is a powerful faith and witness that compel people to seek his counsel in times of need. Elisha demonstrates a consistent and confident response to the situations of the people he encounters. What is also significant is that he has meaningful relationships with the people he helps. He is acquainted with the widow's late husband, who was a prophet. He has a long-standing relationship with the wealthy Shunammite woman and her family. He is a mentor and guide to the guild of prophets. This suggests that God's provision is not merely material but relational; it is concerned about the whole person.

Psalm 145 brings this idea home for us. It offers praise to the God who lifts up the falling and the bowed down, who is a source of provision and encouragement. It is not the kind of praise that simply offers thanks for fulfilling an immediate need. Rather, it is the praise that speaks to an encompassing spirit of generosity and care. The open hand speaks to the relationship God shares with God's people, as a continual support.

The miraculous provision in 2 Kings 4:42–44 is an intersection of modest means and confident faith. The man from Baal-shalishah comes with an offering for Elisha, and Elisha directs it to the people. He speaks confidently, asserting that God has promised not only provision, but abundance beyond their needs. The miracle unfolds at the extremity of human ability. There isn't enough food. There is, however, faith that God can work with people willing to give what they can. And sure enough, everyone is fed, with food to spare.

I am reminded of a saying I once heard from a pastor: "When God wants to bless you, it isn't with things, but with people." Elisha is a model of God's provision and blessing in the form of faithful people who will lead the way with confidence and boldness. His relationship with God makes him a conduit for God's desire to bless and sustain people. To participate in God's abundant generosity is to become people who facilitate that giving through our very lives and being. Yes, we need the basics of life: food, shelter, health, freedom from debt. We also require the relationships that create community and ensure that we are nourished as whole people. Elisha offers a prophetic witness that models adapting to immediate human needs and caring for the human through relationship.

Summer Series 3: Soul Food

Four Parts: Proper 14 through Proper 17

Biblical food and table metaphors invite us to a feast of discipleship.

KYLE E. BROOKS

Series Overview   The metaphor of the bread of life is a popular image. Bread is a basic staple food, filling and made of simple ingredients. It is plentiful and readily available. In calling himself the bread of life, Jesus speaks to his identification with the needs and interests of the everyday person. It is also a profoundly sacrificial theme; Jesus invites us to *consume* him, to eat and drink of his life. But Jesus does not originate this imagery. In the writings of Proverbs, we find an invitation to eat and drink from the table of holy wisdom. This consumption is more than metaphorical. It means internalizing the ways, the thoughts, the imagination, the disciplines of righteous life. This series explores the idea of how our own lives are transformed from the invitation to partake of life-giving realities. The four passages lift up important teachings that can deepen our understanding of how life in God feeds our souls.

	Sermon Title	Focus Scripture	Theme
Proper 14	Eat to Live	John 6:35, 41–51	Jesus offers sustenance for the soul.
Proper 15	An Appetite for Instruction	Prov. 9:1–6; Ps. 34:9–14	Wisdom leads us to fulfilling life.
Proper 16	Hard to Swallow	John 6:56–69	The way of Jesus is not an easy path.
Proper 17	Dirty Hands and Clean Hearts	Mark 7:1–8,14–15, 21–23	Our hearts reveal our true devotions.

Imagery in worship and bulletins could reflect the different kinds of cuisine that make up a traditional meal for people in the congregation. Soul food is but one form of cultural "comfort food," so it could be meaningful to actually invite congregants to share in a communal meal, bringing their own family or household favorites to share. It could be useful to highlight explicitly ways the congregation can engage in practices of sharing and soul nourishment, not just at meals but in everyday interactions, both inside and outside of the congregational space.

Proper 14: Eat to Live
John 6:35, 41–51

Jesus said to them, "I am the bread of life. Whoever comes to me will never be hungry, and whoever believes in me will never be thirsty." (John 6:35)

As a child, I always anticipated holidays, largely because they meant my grandmother would be baking her homemade yeast rolls for dinner. They were special because they took hours of preparation: mixing and kneading the dough, waiting for it to rise twice, forming it into small rolls. After a while, the aroma of baking bread would fill the entire house, and I would anxiously await the chance to eat a roll fresh out of the oven.

The Jews in Jesus' company, however, were *not* so excited about his proclamation that bread had arrived. The audacity of his statement seemed unbearable to them. Who has the nerve to call *themselves* bread from heaven? Much less a homegrown guy like Jesus? I mean, they knew him from the neighborhood. Surely he couldn't be serious.

But he certainly was. And Jesus' concern was not the believability of his claim, but the power in its fulfillment. This makes sense in light of the overall tenor of the book of John. The book of John differs from the Synoptic Gospels in that it focuses on different events of Jesus' life and thematically underscores Jesus' divinity. From the first chapter of the book, we get an emphasis on "the Word made flesh" that dwells among us, the Son of God. Jesus' claim is an extension of the author's own testimony about who Jesus is.

Jesus' declaration that he is the bread of life suggests a few things to me. Jesus is concerned with feeding the spiritual lives of the people of God. His statement is an invitation to a spiritual meal, to an ongoing communion. It is an invitation to intimate engagement with his own life and example. To be living bread is to be an everyday staple, not an occasional treat. Jesus is pointing toward his daily, consistent presence as a source of grace and truth.

What's more, the bread imagery connects to the history and future of the children of Israel. Jesus notes that their ancestors ate manna in the wilderness. We recall that manna was a means of sustenance given to them by God's hand. It was intended as only a temporary measure to help them endure the desolation of the wilderness. It was for survival, and it got them through their journey. Jesus does not discount this; he does, however, differentiate his purpose. The bread of life is not for wilderness survival, but for ultimate thriving. It is a call to eternal life that transcends mortal limitations.

Jesus is inviting people not just to stay alive, but truly to *live*. He is calling us back to the first chapter of John, where we read that all who receive the Word made flesh obtain the right to become children of God. We are invited to be a part of the family of God, to inherit a new vitality and energy.

Jesus' offering has important implications for our present lives. Jesus is both bread of life and daily bread. Through him, we have the opportunity to slow down and appreciate the goodness of grace and mercy in our everyday lives. To partake of the bread of life is to sit, to sup, to savor. Each day, we can anticipate the goodness of God's grace and mercy manifested in the bread of life. This is the food our souls need.

Proper 15: An Appetite for Instruction
Proverbs 9:1–6; Psalm 34:9–14

Wisdom has built her house. . . . She calls from the highest places in the town, "You that are simple, turn in here!" To those without sense she says, "Come, eat of my bread and drink of the wine I have mixed. Lay aside immaturity, and live, and walk in the way of insight." (Proverbs 9:1a, 3b–6)

As I have grown and matured, my tastes and appetites have changed. Foods that I used to loathe—Brussels sprouts, asparagus, broccoli— have become some of my favorites. I still crave the occasional sugary treat, but I have learned to enjoy my green vegetables. It is beneficial to have an appetite for things that are actually really good for my well-being.

This week's passages from Proverbs and the Psalms speak to the cultivation of healthy appetites for ways of life that will bring us to flourishing ends. The book of Proverbs gives us a wide-ranging collection of wise sayings and instructions for practical living. In particular, Proverbs 9 directs our attention to divine wisdom and her ways.

Wisdom is personified as a woman who manages and cultivates her household. This image of wisdom as a woman is notable and varied throughout Proverbs, as well as in the book of Job. In the preceding chapter, Proverbs 8, we find an extended treatment and exaltation of wisdom. She is of great value and highly sought after. She is positioned as a teacher and instructor whose lessons will lead her students to joy and life.

The role of keeping a household is no small task. It requires a multitude of skills and the wise execution thereof. Wisdom comes to teach and lead by example. In Proverbs 9, she is a model of preparation: she has built a home, and she has prepared a feast. What's more, she has invited the simple, the ignorant, those in need of a seat at her table. She is willing to share her abundance with those in great need.

It is important that Wisdom *invites* people to her table. Her guests don't necessarily seek her out, but they absolutely *need* to be eating from her table. The feast of Wisdom invites us to a process of transformation: abandon immaturity, live, and walk with insight. Wisdom is cultivating an appetite for instruction and spiritual growth, a desire for deeper and more fulfilling life.

The psalm dovetails beautifully with this appetite, asking directly, who desires life? Life is found in the fear of the Lord. It is sharpened and developed by being wise with our words, abandoning evil, and seeking after goodness and peace. Verse 10 is pivotal; it speaks of the young lions who go hungry, while those who seek the Lord lack nothing. Lions are predatory animals who chase after their prey for their daily meals. This requires tremendous effort. The implication is that the young lions expend their energy but come up empty. The psalmist declares that the pursuit of righteous life will not leave us hungering for something else.

If everyone had an appetite for Wisdom's offerings, she probably wouldn't have to call out from the highest places in town. Quite often, what we want and what we need are at odds with each other. But sometimes the only way to shift our tastes is actually to try something new. Wisdom is an acquired taste. It demands something more from us than just blissful comfort and uncaring activity. If we would be wise, we must adopt the spiritual diet that matures our minds, our mouths, and our motives. Soon enough, Wisdom won't have to call us; we'll come running to her, hungry for more.

Proper 16: Hard to Swallow
John 6:56–69

But Jesus, being aware that his disciples were complaining about it, said to them, "Does this offend you? Then what if you were to see the Son of Man ascending to where he was before? It is the spirit that gives life; the flesh is useless. The words that I have spoken to you are spirit and life." (John 6:61–63)

Jesus had a penchant for saying hard things. I don't mean that his statements were necessarily difficult to understand (though folks do interpret his words in a variety of ways). I mean that his words were often difficult to accept. He did not shy away from bold statements about his life, his purpose, or the work required to live with godly power and purpose.

It is no wonder then that even his first disciples had trouble accepting his teaching. Eating flesh and drinking blood sounds gruesome. But Jesus doubles down and says that *this* is the way to life. The disciples are resistant to this teaching, and Jesus calls them on it.

What makes this teaching difficult? At the very least, it just seems difficult to grasp. Is Jesus speaking metaphorically, or does he expect us to take it literally? We could take his words as an allusion to his eventual last supper with his disciples. The preceding chapters of the book of John give the impression that Jesus is up to something with his references to food and eating.

Jesus, as usual, is seemingly not concerned with what's plausible. The things he suggests seem strange at first blush. Consider chapter 4, in which Jesus meets the Samaritan woman and tells her about living water that will satisfy every thirst, or subsequently when he tells his disciples that he has food to eat that they don't know about. Here again his references to food and drink are confusing for the people who hear them. But Jesus gives us clues to his meaning. Living water is the source of continual spiritual renewal. Jesus' food is the work and will he was sent to fulfill on earth.

Perhaps this reframes how we think of eating his flesh and drinking his blood. It is common to refer to those related to us as our "flesh and blood." This means we share a bond and a lineage, a common ancestry. What if eating the flesh and drinking the blood of Jesus meant taking on a whole new level of identification with the deep substance of his life? This is a powerful notion. It might mean taking on both the spiritual empowerment of living water *and* the weighty responsibility of the work and will of God.

The difficulty of Jesus' teaching may be less about the idea of consuming flesh and blood and more about just how much this requires of his hearers. He is not advocating mere religiosity or ritual practice.

He is calling for life-changing spiritual commitment. The text records Jesus telling the disciples that the spirit gives life, and the flesh is useless. In other words, it's not enough to *perform* commitment; we have to *live* it and *embody* it.

No wonder so many of the disciples left Jesus that day. So many of them who literally followed Jesus could not follow his words to their spiritual conclusion. Jesus knew that the path ahead of him was not for the faint of heart. His words pushed his followers to ask if that path was really for them. Jesus invited all who would hear to join him in this journey, to eat and drink of his life. We are given the same opportunity. Chances are, it's hard for *us* to swallow too. Still, this is the choice that is before us. There are no shortcuts or easy ways to the spiritual growth Jesus offers us. It is only through faith that we are able to accept it in spirit and in truth.

Proper 17: Dirty Hands and Clean Hearts
Mark 7:1–8, 14–15, 21–23

Then he called the crowd again and said to them, "Listen to me, all of you, and understand: there is nothing outside a person that by going in can defile, but the things that come out are what defile." (Mark 7:14–15)

To be quite honest, I think the Pharisees get a very bad rap as people who are judgmental, critical, and overly concerned with minor details. But in their own context, the Pharisees were among those charged to maintain religious traditions and practices of the Jewish people. Their roles were important for the reinforcement of sacred communal identity. Here in the seventh chapter of Mark, Jesus' encounter with the Pharisees and scribes strikes me as a conflict of priorities.

Verses 1–5 describe how the Pharisees gathered around Jesus and observed him and his disciples eating "with defiled hands." The author even writes two verses just to explain their ritual practices for washing and the reasons for them. Their attention to cleanliness wasn't just a random concern. It was a way of honoring the traditions of their elders.

Traditions can be a wonderful way of keeping us connected to our histories, reminding us of who we are and where we come from. But without meaning or relevance, traditions can become just rote practices, things we repeat simply because we're used to doing them. They can bring us comfort and familiarity, but sometimes they can limit our understanding of the moment we're in.

There is practice and there is purpose; Jesus clarifies that there is a difference. He responds to the question of ritual tradition with scriptural tradition, recalling the message from Isaiah 29:13: people's words are better than their hearts. Traditions, doctrines, and human-made customs *look* good, but often they don't reflect the habits of the heart. If Jesus is quoting from Isaiah, he's speaking to a long-standing problem of religious performance overshadowing spiritual commitment.

This is an important distinction. It recalls 1 Samuel 16, where the prophet Samuel is reminded by God to look not at the outer appearance but at the heart of Jesse's sons. Samuel passes over the older, more robust brothers in favor of the young boy, David, who tends the sheep. Literally, he has a dirty job, but his devotion to his work and to God ultimately shows his character.

Traditions can be picked up and put down. Our hearts, however, stay with us, and what they produce will ultimately reflect the content of our lives and intentions. We may differ in the body of Christ around particular customs or practices of religious devotion. But the products of our hearts tell the story of our deepest commitments. Jesus runs down the list of defiling things that the human heart generates: deadly acts, despicable attitudes, devious ways. Paying lip service to God does nothing to disrupt that flow. Jesus knew this, and he did not mince his words in spelling out just how much our hearts can hurt our witness.

Our prayer ought to be that of Psalm 51:10: "Create in me a clean heart, O God, and put a new and right spirit within me." The transformation of the heart results in new habits that will impact our outward presence. Something on the inside begins working on the outside, and it leads to true change in our lives. The pursuit of a clean heart is a private matter that becomes public only over time. No wonder Jesus is critical of those who try to use public displays to cover up private intentions. Eating with dirty hands might offend some sensibilities, but living with dirty hearts is the truest offense in the sight of God.

Fall Series 1: A Good Life

Five Parts: Proper 18 through Proper 22

Wisdom for living well, from Proverbs, Job, and Esther.

AMY K. BUTLER

Series Overview | Our lives don't just happen to us—we build them through our decisions and our actions. How can we live in a way that will allow us to look back on the lives we've lived and pronounce them good? The lectionary's Old Testament readings during this stretch of Ordinary Time give us a taste of the Bible's Wisdom literature as well as stories like Esther's, showing us through pithy poems and extraordinary circumstances how we can build for ourselves "a good life."

	Sermon Title	Focus Scripture	Theme
Proper 18	A Good Name	Prov. 22:1–2, 8–9, 22–23	Have you made a name for yourself? What do people think when they hear your name?
Proper 19	A Good Mind	Prov. 1:20–33	Living a good life means training your mind, filling it with what you want your life to reflect to the world.
Proper 20	A Good Community	Prov. 31:10–31	Who are the people you keep around you? The people in your community either build your character or chip away at who you are trying to become. Choose carefully.
Proper 21	A Good Cause	Esth. 7:1–6, 9–10; 9:20–22	What are you living for? Living a good life means being on this earth for a reason.
Proper 22	A Good Practice	Job 1:1; 2:1–10	With all the swirling demands of life, what practices keep you grounded? Choose good ones.

This series will begin when folks are returning from summer travel and starting fall programming—coming back to "real life." Complement this series with some practical educational opportunities like parenting or money management. This would be an especially good time to offer a class on end-of-life issues (legal, medical, spiritual); small groups could read books like *When Breath Becomes Air* by Paul Kalanithi, *Everything Happens for a Reason and Other Lies I've Loved* by Kate Bowler, or *The Bright Hour* by Nina Riggs.

Proper 18: A Good Name
Proverbs 22:1–2, 8–9, 22–23

A good name is to be chosen rather than great riches, and favor is better than silver or gold.
(Proverbs 22:1)

I got married back in the days when the question of hyphenating your last name was quite the subject of heated conversation. I ran with a group of students in the religion department at my university who were dedicated feminists; it would seem in my group of friends that taking your husband's name when you married was a sure sign of giving in to the patriarchy. I surely didn't want to do that, but I was conflicted. My name and my future husband's name didn't really sound that great when hyphenated. Further, my maiden name had been a lifelong source of teasing, and I'd always longed for the day when I could be called something else. I was describing my dilemma to one of my women's studies professors one day: should I hyphenate my name just to avoid the appearance of surrendering to an oppressive and unjust system? My professor looked at me for a moment and then said, "Your maiden name and your married name hyphenated sound stupid. Why would you want a name that sounds stupid?"

She had a good point. In the end I chose to take my husband's last name . . . but I did *not* give in to the patriarchy!

The book of Proverbs is part of the biblical collection of Wisdom literature. Some of the Wisdom literature in the Bible is presented in the form of poetry, song, or story, but the book of Proverbs is a collection of little pearls of wisdom, short words of advice for living a good life. In this chapter of Proverbs the writer insists that having a good name is worth more than almost anything else in life.

The writer of Proverbs, of course, was not talking about whether you have a last name that sounds sophisticated. No, this advice is about making a good name for yourself, building a solid reputation, so that when someone hears your name, the person who comes to mind will be someone of excellent character. Be thoughtful and kind; make wise decisions about how you spend your time and resources; be humble; choose for yourself a good community; make generosity your hallmark; fill everything you do with justice. Living life this way, making a good name for yourself, will surely pay off in the end. The sage writes: "One who loves a pure heart and who speaks with grace will have the king for a friend."

You know how the saying goes: "You never get a second chance to make a first impression." An article in *Business Insider* takes this on with some suggestions for how one might make a great first impression. Among them? "Listen 10x more than you talk." "Shift the spotlight to others." "Choose your words carefully."[1] Good advice; I'm sure the author of Proverbs would agree. Here in chapter 22 the writer is asking us to consider: How do you want to be seen in the world? What mark will your life leave on the lives around you?

Proper 19: A Good Mind
Proverbs 1:20–33

How long, O simple ones, will you love being simple? How long will scoffers delight in their scoffing and fools hate knowledge? (Proverbs 1:22)

I have a friend who tells the story of his large southern church where more than five hundred people would come to the church gym for Wednesday night supper every week. Staff would cover the floor of the gym with blue plastic tarps in order to protect the gym floor. The staff lived in fear, my friend told me, of someone tripping on the edge of a tarp, falling, and being injured.

One night, sure enough, it happened. An elderly member was walking from the buffet line to her seat at the table and her toe caught on the edge of one of the blue tarps. Down she went, sprawling, her food flying everywhere. Of course many people in the gym that night ran over to help, including five doctors who were members of the congregation.

As they leaned over the woman trying to help her, they looked around at each other and realized that every single one of them was . . . an ophthalmologist. Five eye doctors who were extremely well educated and knew quite a lot about the health of the eyes, but weren't quite sure how to help the woman on the floor. Eventually another

1. Jeff Haden, "9 Powerful Ways to Make a Great First Impression," *Business Insider, December* 12, 2017, https://www.businessinsider.com/9-powerful-ways-to-make-a-great-first-impression -2017-12#9-and-readily-admit-your-own-failings-9.

member of the church, a young man who had graduated from high school just a few years before and decided to skip college to become an emergency medical technician, ran over and made sure the woman had not been injured in her fall. Later, one of the five doctors laughed about the experience, "I wasn't sure if she was injured at all, but her eyes looked pretty good!"

We find ourselves again this week in the book of Proverbs, a collection of short wisdom sayings that adds up to some good advice for how one might live a good life. Today the writer of Proverbs lauds the benefits of a good mind—of seeking knowledge as a way of life so that we might show up in the world with a curiosity that opens our lives and connects them to others and to the larger story of human life together.

As evidenced by the story above, this kind of knowledge does not always correlate to our levels of education. Gaining wisdom means sustaining an openness to growth and change, to widening the boundaries of our worlds so that God's Spirit may continue to mold us and shape us into the persons God created us to be. This is less about acquiring a body of knowledge and more about a posture of possibility, of seeing the world and our lives with a sense of hopeful anticipation.

The speaker, personified Wisdom, laments those who think they have nothing more to learn, who seem to plug their ears and close their eyes to all life is trying to teach them. Living a good life means being open to change and growth, to cultivating a good mind that connects us more deeply to God and to the world around us.

Proper 20: A Good Community
Proverbs 31:10–31

A capable wife who can find? She is far more precious than jewels. The heart of her husband trusts in her, and he will have no lack of gain. (Proverbs 31:10–11)

When my daughter Hannah was in third grade, she performed in the school talent show. I showed up to cheer her on in what she'd told me was a dance routine her friend Robin had organized. Imagine my shock and chagrin when a small group of girls, including my daughter Hannah, got up on stage and commenced a dance routine to Justin Timberlake's song "SexyBack." Imagine, if you will, an eight–year-old version of a striptease performed for a large group of parents. I was mortified. After the performance I rushed up to Hannah to express my strong disapproval. Her little face was crestfallen at my response and a little baffled. "How did you come to be involved in something like this?" I asked Hannah. She explained that Robin had chosen the song for the group, and they all thought it was a great idea. After we got home, Hannah and I had a long talk about choosing friends, because the community you choose to surround yourself with will certainly determine your ability to "live a good life."

Our passage today comes from the final chapter of Proverbs, and it's one of those you either love or hate—nothing in between. The shelves of Christian bookstores are filled with books describing how one might be a good wife, based on the direction in this passage, and our Bibles give this passage headings like "The Wife of Noble Character." And boy, is this woman amazing. Not only is she "lacking nothing of value"; she cooks dinner every night, runs a thriving business, takes care of the poor, dresses beautifully, and doesn't worry about the future. In short, she's someone who is easy to hate. She sets a standard that is flatly impossible to meet, and her example is readily invoked to encourage or, alternately, shame anyone who reaches for one of those books in the Christian bookstore.

I got to thinking, however, that there might be another way to look at this "Wife of Noble Character" passage. What if this advice from our Wisdom literature is not really a guilt-inducing list of to-dos for all of us women out there, but more the description of the kind of person we should be choosing to fill our lives? This instruction, after all, isn't directed at the woman herself, but at the person who is seeking a worthy partner.

Many of the characteristics of the woman described in Proverbs 31 are not just characteristics a good Christian woman should strive for; they're actually great qualities to find in any partner or friend. Think of how your life is impacted for the good when the people closest to you actively care about your well-being; exercise responsibility and care for the things they own; show empathy and kindness to those less fortunate. Keeping such company will encourage you to be generous and trustworthy too. When you think about what it takes to live a good life, the community you choose to surround yourself with can determine whether that happens.

Proper 21: A Good Cause
Esther 7:1–6, 9–10; 9:20–22

On the second day, as they were drinking wine, the king again said to Esther, "What is your petition, Queen Esther? It shall be granted you. And what is your request? Even to the half of my kingdom, it shall be fulfilled." Then Queen Esther answered, "If I have won your favor,

O king, and if it pleases the king, let my life be given me—that is my petition—and the lives of my people—that is my request." (Esther 7:2–3)

The Google offices in downtown Manhattan are like an adult version of Disney World. Around every corner there's a "nourishment station"—a snack bar or coffee shop or entire restaurant featuring celebrity chefs in rotation. Everything is free, of course. There are Ping-Pong tables all over the place, scooters to ride up and down the long, carpeted hallways, and little rooms with glass walls and comfortable chairs and lots of whiteboards to foster creativity. The idea, our tour guide told me, was to make work a place where employees wanted to be, a place they'd love to spend time. Google's approach seems to be working: Google's employees work longer days than most, and many of them eat all their meals at work, creating more opportunities for collaboration and creativity to flourish.

This may be good for Google. I'm not sure what it does for a society of professionals who already tend to spend too much of their energy and lives working—to the detriment of other parts of life. Still, Google has hit on something that many of us long for: a need to have something in our lives—whether it's our professional work or not—that *means* something. As one employee said, "Our managers don't want us to wake up in the morning to come to a *job*. We want to wake up and come to our *life*—to be spending our time doing something that really matters."

Our assigned Hebrew Scripture reading today comes from the little book of Esther. Readings from Esther don't appear often in our lectionary, and that's too bad, because this is a great story. Esther was a young Hebrew woman whose parents or grandparents had been carried away to exile in Persia. After her parents died, Esther came to live with an uncle, Mordecai, who was a palace official and aide to the most powerful leader in that part of the world at the time, King Ahasuerus. Esther is selected by Ahasuerus as his queen and ascends to one of the highest positions in the land. This was a miraculous turn of events, as there was a man in the king's team of advisors, Haman, who hated the Jews and who cooked up a plan to get rid of them once and for all. Esther took the brave step of revealing her nationality to the king and begging for the life of her people. In the end, it was Haman who was executed, and the Jewish people were saved by the brave action of Queen Esther.

You may have heard a verse commonly quoted from the book of Esther, when her uncle Mordecai tells her she has come into this position "for such a time as this." She knew for sure that her life meant something, that she had a cause to live for, that when she was gone, people would know what she cared about. How many of us long for our lives to mean something, for us to have a good cause to stand for? A good cause is a critical essential if we want to live a good life.

Proper 22: A Good Practice
Job 1:1; 2:1–10

There was once a man in the land of Uz whose name was Job. That man was blameless and upright, one who feared God and turned away from evil. (Job 1:1)

I recently visited my parents in their home in Hawaii. In their kitchen on the side of the refrigerator is a calendar—old school, with squares for each day and landscape pictures at the top. On almost every week-day of the month, there was a big red X, made with a permanent marker obviously applied with relish. When I asked my mother the meaning of the Xs, she proudly told me that she gets to mark an X on her calendar for every day that she attends water-exercise class at the YMCA.

I must have looked a little confused, so she went on to explain: if she was able to document attendance at water exercise class for forty-five times over the course of the year, her health insurance company would send her a check for $200.00. "It's only July and I've already made it to 45!" she told me proudly.

It's a good practice, one the likes of which I often begin soon after January 1 but rarely continue all the way into July. My mother is wise to undertake a practice like this; it will pay off in increased mobility and good health as she approaches her eighth decade. And there are other practices we can undertake that, put all together, will help us to live a good life—little things that build upon each other and result in long-term payoffs.

Our Hebrew text today is a quick summary of the story of Job, to whom we're introduced with quite a description. Job was "blame-less and upright," someone who "feared God and turned away from evil." We know that he lived a disciplined life that included running a successful business, leading a large family, and faithfully following God. Despite living an exemplary life, he is hit with blow after blow of major life tragedies. He loses his family, his farm, even his health, in an attempt by Satan to try to get him to curse God and die. But while he mourns deeply and indulges in some self-pity, the text says that "in all this Job did not sin."

The book of Job is not a historical account of the life of one man who faces total destruction but keeps his faith anyway, and then his life is restored to him. The book of Job is a mythical story, meant to teach a lesson. But what lesson can we learn from Job?

Well, there are many, of course. An important one may be that cultivating good practice, good habits, in our lives helps us to live good lives—even in the face of difficulty. What do I mean by good practice? The daily routines that keep us close to God and close to each other, that help us do our part in healing the world, and that make our lives impactful. These will be different for each of us, of course, and we learn from the book of Job that good practice does not ensure an easy life. Though we long for a formulaic approach to living a good life, in hopes that all will go well for us as a result, nothing in our lives is guaranteed. What we do learn from Job's story is perhaps the lesson that these pillars of good practice can be the touchpoints that offer stability—something to hang on to when the waves of life threaten to roll over us.

Fall Series 2:
Take Up Your Cross

Three Parts: Proper 23 through Proper 25

A study in discipleship from Jesus' encounters in Mark 10.

AMY K. BUTLER

Series Overview Earlier in Mark's Gospel, Jesus told a crowd that if any would follow him, they should "take up their cross." These three consecutive passages in Mark 10 give us a little more insight into what Jesus was talking about. Interactions with a rich man, disciples James and John, and a blind beggar each reveal part of the challenge of taking up our cross. This series looks closely at the different parts of this act of discipleship and what it means for our day-to-day lives.

Tips and Ideas for This Series This series will focus on some critical teachings of Jesus that make up the core of discipleship. It may be appropriate to pair a preaching of this series with a study of Dietrich Bonhoeffer's *The Cost of*

	Sermon Title	Focus Scripture	Theme
Proper 23	Pick It Up	Mark 10:17–31	Following Jesus' command to take up your cross begins with a conscious decision to pick it up.
Proper 24	Refocus	Mark 10:35–45	What does it mean to actually carry your cross? Sometimes, like James and John, we have the wrong idea of what it means to follow Jesus.
Proper 25	Ask for Help	Mark 10:46–52	Following Jesus' command to take up our cross cannot be done individually; we need help, and that help comes from our community and from God.

Discipleship. Reading groups for the book could carry on in the form of discipleship groups to encourage one another in carrying our crosses.

Proper 23: Pick It Up
Mark 10:17–31

Jesus, looking at him, loved him and said, "You lack one thing; go, sell what you own, and give the money to the poor, and you will have treasure in heaven; then come, follow me." When he heard this, he was shocked and went away grieving, for he had many possessions. (Mark 10:21–22)

There are many occasions in the New Testament story of Jesus in which he just says the most offensive things. Most of these things have to do with the heart of the gospel message, what I like to call the worst marketing slogan ever: "Take up your cross and follow me." Today's passage from Mark's Gospel is, in my opinion, one of the saddest stories in Jesus' interactions with the people he is trying to give his gospel message.

There is a wealthy young man who really wants to be a follower of Jesus. He runs up to him one day and falls to his knees, begging Jesus to tell him what he needs to do to inherit eternal life. "Follow the commandments," Jesus tells him, and the young man is sure relieved to hear that. "I've been doing that my whole life long!" he tells Jesus. But then Jesus adds a little caveat: "Go, sell everything you have and give the proceeds to the poor." The blood must have drained from the man's face when he heard that, because the text tells us he is a very wealthy man. Give everything up? Can't I just ease my way in, a little at a time? You mean I have to be all the way in?

There Jesus goes again, shooting himself in the foot. I bet that young man would be a great addition to Jesus' group of followers, but then Jesus has to start up with that terrible marketing again: Take up your cross, sell what you have, give up your life. These are just not the most compelling messages, and they certainly will not grow your fan base.

But here it is: the very beginning point of being a disciple. You can't move past the initial informational session unless you're willing to go all-in—right from the beginning—to lean over and put your hands on the splintered beams of that cross, to struggle with all your might to lift it up off the ground, to hoist it onto your shoulder until your shoulder fits right in the corner where the beams cross, and to get walking—sometimes lifting the cross off the ground a few inches, sometimes dragging it because it's so heavy and you're so tired.

That's the starting point of discipleship, an expression that we're really all-in and willing to bear the cost and the fatigue and the pain of living the gospel message. Why? Because Jesus has so taken us with his message of God's radical love for the world that we're with him: we think it might be worth even our whole lives to live the gospel.

That's not often how faith is depicted, is it? If it was, my guess is churches would be even smaller than they are now, and being a Christian in America might not be so socially acceptable or politically malleable. Radical sacrifice isn't a very popular message. Jesus says it starts here: going all-in—not turning away in disappointment as the rich young man does, but by picking up your cross and following him.

Proper 24: Refocus
Mark 10:35–45

James and John, the sons of Zebedee, came forward to him and said to him, "Teacher, we want you to do for us whatever we ask of you." And he said to them, "What is it you want me to do for you?" And they said to him, "Grant us to sit, one at your right hand and one at your left, in your glory." But Jesus said to them, "You do not know what you are asking. Are you able to drink the cup that I drink, or be baptized with the baptism that I am baptized with?" (Mark 10:35–38)

Sometimes we get lost along the way. Even if we are brave enough to pick up our cross or sell what we have or set out with enthusiasm after Jesus, we then get a little confused, we lose our way and wander off in the wrong direction, and before we know it, we've totally lost our focus. This seems to be what happened to James and John, the sons of Zebedee, who had gladly set down their fishing nets, given up everything, and followed Jesus. But just a few chapters later, they have completely lost their focus, convinced somehow that following Jesus included ascending to positions of influence and power. They had picked up their crosses, but then they got a little lost.

My sister lived for several years in Rapid City, South Dakota. One summer, when all our siblings came together to visit, we decided to take the kids to see Mount Rushmore. There were nine children then in the assembled group of all my siblings' children. Nine children under the age of seven.

We piled them all into various car seats in several vehicles and set off, then unloaded them and herded them up toward the Rushmore visitors' center. On the way up the paved path to the visitors' center, however, there were a couple of ice cream vendors, and someone in my family decided we'd create a special memory by getting all nine of the cousins ice cream and watching them eat their ice cream in the hot afternoon sun. Well, you can imagine what that scene was like. Ice cream scoops toppling off cones onto the sidewalk, dripping ice cream, and not nearly enough napkins, ardent protestations that it wasn't fair: "His ice cream cone is bigger than mine!" What a nightmare.

Finally, we got all the kids somewhat cleaned up and herded them into the visitors' center overlooking Mount Rushmore. The visitors' center is a modern, serene reception area with one whole wall of floor-to-ceiling windows. These huge windows give the best view you could possibly have of the Mount Rushmore monument, and there were tourists calmly gazing over the scene as we all came in together. As we herded our little group of kids in to see the monument, I started feeling rather alarmed. They had, as you can imagine, hands covered with ice cream, sticky fingers ready to smear all over those pristine windows. As others peered into the view of the monument, I ran around trying to keep those kids in line. "Keep your hands off the windows! People can't see the monument if your fingerprints mess up the windows!" All the adults were running around, looking over our shoulders for lurking park rangers ready to reprimand us as our children pointed and smeared their hands all over the view of Mount Rushmore.

At long last, my sister decided it was time to go. And on the way down the mountain, with all the kids buckled into their various child safety seats, I suddenly realized: I didn't see the monument. I couldn't tell you whose face was carved into the rock at Mount Rushmore, or why anybody would want to go see the monument at all. All I could think about was sticky fingers making a mess all over the glass looking out over the monument.

Sometimes it's easy for us, followers of Jesus, to wander off the path even while carrying our crosses. We get distracted by other concerns. We lose focus on the path of discipleship, and we need to step back and refocus.

Proper 25: Ask for Help
Mark 10:46–52

They came to Jericho. As [Jesus] and his disciples and a large crowd were leaving Jericho, Bartimaeus son of Timaeus, a blind beggar, was sitting by the roadside. When he heard that it was Jesus of Nazareth, he began to shout out and say, "Jesus, Son of David, have mercy on me!" (Mark 10:46–47)

Jesus encounters a blind beggar named Bartimaeus in today's Gospel lesson. In Jesus' day, folks with physical conditions that prevented engagement in typical societal roles often had to support themselves by asking for the help and compassion of others. Perhaps Bartimaeus had become accustomed to asking for help after years of begging for enough resources to survive. Whatever the case, the people around him were uncomfortable with the way Bartimaeus persistently called out to Jesus, begging Jesus to notice him, come alongside him, and give him the help he so desperately needed. But Bartimaeus persisted, and Jesus heard him and healed him. I wonder if the people around him learned the lesson Bartimaeus had to teach them that day: an important part of being human in the world, an important part of being a disciple of Jesus Christ, is asking for help.

Cultural Christianity, often underpinned by a theology of individual salvation, has damaged a biblical understanding of corporate salvation—the fundamental truth that we need each other to be God's people in the world. In the challenging task of following Jesus in this world, of carrying our cross, we must learn to ask for help.

Every time our world holds an Olympic Games, some story of human triumph inevitably emerges. In 1992, at the summer Olympics in Barcelona, Spain, that story was the story of Derek Redmond, a British track-and-field athlete who had trained for years to run the 400-meter relay. He had about one lap around the track left to go when he felt a snap and fell to the ground in pain: his hamstring had torn. As medics rushed to the track to help him, Derek struggled to get up and keep going—he was determined to finish the race. In excruciating pain, however, he couldn't keep going without help. It was then that his father, running in from the stands, jumping over barriers and pushing away security, ran to his side, put an arm around his son, and helped him limp the rest of the way until he crossed the finish line to the roars of the crowd.

The crowd went wild when they saw Derek Redmond limp across the finish line with the help of his father, perhaps because they knew a fundamental truth of human life and of the life of faith: we cannot walk this path alone. What's more: we don't have to. Carrying our cross as we follow Jesus in the way of discipleship is not a solitary mission. We need the help of each other, and we need the help of God. Let us not be afraid to ask!

Fall Series 3: More Than Enough

Four Parts: Proper 26 through Proper 29 (Reign of Christ)

A stewardship series about living with a sense of abundance, not scarcity.

AMY K. BUTLER

Series Overview

This series is about living with a sense of abundance, not scarcity. We're taught to hoard what we have, that more is better, and that we'll never have enough. But that sense of scarcity does not compute in God's economy, where there is more than enough for everyone and where our lives are enriched by living generously and assured of God's abundance. This could be used as a stewardship preaching series, emphasizing generosity and giving as spiritual practice.

Tips and Ideas for This Series

Taking place in November, the topic complements our cultural focus on appreciating all we have. In contrast to an overflowing cornucopia, however, consider imagery that evokes simplicity and contentment—a

	Sermon Title	Focus Scripture	Theme
Proper 26	Enough to Love	Mark 12:28–34	God's abundant love flows through us and out to the whole world.
Proper 27	Enough to Give	Mark 12:38–44	Without the discipline of tithing, a fear of scarcity takes over.
Proper 28	Enough to Know	Mark 13:1–8	It doesn't take a genius to see trouble in the world—but it takes faith to see good.
Proper 29 (Reign of Christ)	Enough to Live	John 18:33–37	Recognizing God's reality changes everything.

message that we don't have to have a lot for it to be *enough*. Collateral supporting the series (bulletin covers, a logo, special offering envelopes, a special online giving opportunity) should use this imagery and will generate congregational enthusiasm for this emphasis. On Reign of Christ Sunday, the final Sunday of the series—and of the church year—it might be helpful to create a special worship ritual that symbolizes our willingness to live into God's abundance.

Proper 26: Enough to Love
Mark 12:28–34

One of the scribes came near and heard them disputing with one another, and seeing that [Jesus] answered them well, he asked him, "Which commandment is the first of all?" Jesus answered, "The first is, 'Hear, O Israel: the Lord our God, the Lord is one; you shall love the Lord your God with all your heart, and with all your soul, and with all your mind, and with all your strength.' The second is this, 'You shall love your neighbor as yourself.' There is no other commandment greater than these." (Mark 12:28–31)

If there ever was a word that these days was used to excess (and in mostly frivolous ways), it would be "love." So, what a gift it is to have this text, which asks us to spend time imagining and wondering about what this means for us to love God with our whole heart and soul and mind and strength, and our neighbors as ourselves.

Advertisements would have us believe that love is a feeling, that love equals happiness, that love with a partner is what completes you. Yet loving with your strength, mind, and soul surely widens the scope far beyond the realm of feeling, to commitment, to making a choice about how we treat someone. Love of God means the love of what God loves, which means loving all people. It means living out what it would look like if we as the church and society actually loved whom God loves, with the extensive and unrestricted love of God. This is not a love limited in space to a romantic relationship or a nuclear family or limited in depth to times it is convenient. This is abundant love. Love enough for the whole world.

If you've done even a few weddings, it's likely that the couple has asked that some portion of 1 Corinthians 13 be included. I used to roll my eyes inwardly just a little when that Scripture was chosen, but not anymore. I relish the idea of using a wedding as a reminder that though the day often seems to say the opposite, love is not about things being beautiful and having no doubts about how you'll make a life with another person. Love is not about being happy or having your needs met just as you want them. Love is about choosing to live in faithfulness even when you don't want to. Love is about a high calling to move beyond the common narrative to deep and abiding commitment to living life the way God calls you, as a couple perhaps, but as individuals together, whether you're in a marriage or a faith community or both.

At a wedding a few years ago, the couple came from a Quaker background, so the small, intimate affair included all of us sitting in a circle entering silence for ten minutes (!) while those who wanted to speak could. As it turned out, the silence was what we all needed. We were on a porch at the beach and could hear the wind and the water and nature all around. It was holy time. Coming out of the silence, the brother of the groom read part of 1 Corinthians: "Love is patient. Love is kind. Love is not envious or arrogant or boastful or rude . . ." The more he read, the more emotional he got. It was as though all of us were really hearing these words as what God models and hopes for us. It wasn't a sentimental moment about the couple whose vows we were there to witness, but hope for all of us to trust in God's love and what the world might look like if we could choose this kind of love in all our living: "It bears all things, believes all things, hopes all things, endures all things. Love never ends."

This is the kind of love God has for us and the kind we are called to embody for the whole world—a love that fills our own hearts to the point we have more than enough to give.

Proper 27: Enough to Give
Mark 12:38–44

A poor widow came and put in two small copper coins, which are worth a penny. Then he called his disciples and said to them, "Truly I tell you, this poor widow has put in more than all those who are contributing to the treasury." (Mark 12:42–43)

"Show Me the Money" was the tag line in a popular movie a while back, *Jerry Maguire*. The character saying that line was looking for the biggest paycheck he could get, but it's a telling statement. Show me the money—show me where it is, show me where it's going—and I'll be able to tell a whole lot more about you than you might want me to!

Our checkbooks and our budgets—personal and institutional, local and national—are moral documents, indicative of our priorities, indicating not just what we say we care about, but what we really do value.

But when it comes to giving, we tend to give in to our society's insistence on scarcity. Giving is good and important, of course, but not at the expense of my personal security! When it comes to thinking about how much we give, we begin to ask questions based in scarcity, questions like these: How much is everyone else giving? What is my fair share? What am I getting in return? Fair's fair, after all.

Questions like these reflect limitations in our understanding of resources, of God's generosity creating enough space for all of us. The biblical model for giving, by contrast, is 10 percent of our income—10 percent off the top, regularly—a spiritual practice that reflects a stubborn dependence on God's faithful provision. It requires faith that you have enough to give!

Speaking of tithing, it's important to remember that if God's given you 100 percent of what you have, then honoring God by returning just 10 percent of that goodness to support financially God's work in the world is not too much to ask. Of course, how much you give depends on your individual circumstances, but even if it's just a few dollars a week, for the time being, for those with such limited, restricted discretionary funds, you need that habit. You need that discipline. You need that exercise. You need that commitment. You need that expression of your priorities.

Our idea of what's "enough" to live on will always keep ballooning, if we let it. The current of our culture will sweep you away. It will take you where it wants to go—unless you fight it, unless you intentionally, mindfully resist it. That's where a tithing priority, or some sense of a regular generosity, comes in: to give us a tool in our resistance to the scarcity of the world around us. When we manage to give like the widow, not the scribes, we will soon realize that we have more than enough to give.

Proper 28: Enough to Know
Mark 13:1–8

"When you hear of wars and rumors of wars, do not be alarmed; this must take place, but the end is still to come. For nation will rise against nation, and kingdom against kingdom; there will be earthquakes in various places; there will be famines. This is but the beginning of the birth pangs." (Mark 13:7–8)

Life as a woman in the world is filled with wonderful things, and some challenging. In my experience, there is one trend that's on the rise, something about which I am deeply concerned. Webster's defines it officially:

man•splain

man' splān/

verb

(of a man) explaining (something) to someone, typically a woman, in a manner regarded as condescending or patronizing.

Along with almost every woman I have ever met, I can tell some stories about mansplaining, but I had an experience recently that might win a prize. I had been asked to end a meeting with a short devotional thought, so I read Wendell Berry's beautiful poem "Manifesto: The Mad Farmer Liberation Front." The poem talks of the world we hope for, and contains this phrase:

Ask yourself: Will this satisfy
a woman satisfied to bear a child?
Will this disturb the sleep
of a woman near to giving birth?[1]

After the meeting, a gentleman came up to me to express his disapproval of the poem. "The poem you read is inaccurate," he said. "What do you mean, 'inaccurate'?" I asked him. "I'm a doctor," he told me. "You might not understand this, but women don't sleep while they're giving birth." I looked at him, but I couldn't think what to say. "Giving birth is very painful," he continued. I still couldn't think of anything to say. "Women often scream because the pain is so intense—believe me, I've seen it!" After a few more silent beats, I turned to the woman next to me and said, "He just explained to me what it feels like to give birth!"

True confession: I sometimes feel how I felt in that moment when I read this passage in Mark's Gospel with its reference to birth pangs. I always wonder whether Jesus—Son of God though he was—had any business at all talking about how it feels to give birth. But I'm going to give Jesus' mansplaining a pass here, because I understand what he's trying to say. The world around us is in bondage and decay; it's groaning with the deep pain of broken bonds and pain-filled separation. We are torn, frayed, and broken, and it doesn't take a genius to see that all around us there is suffering.

When reading this passage, it's easy to get caught up in the details of this apocalyptic event Jesus and the disciples seem to be discussing, but it's plain to see that the world is already (and, dare we say, has always been) full of wars and rumors of wars, natural disasters

---

1. Wendell Berry, "Manifesto: The Mad Farmer Liberation Front," from *The Country of Marriage* (New York: Harcourt Brace Jovanovich, 1973).

and famines. But as followers of Jesus, people of God in the world, we have seen enough to know that another reality defines our lives and can define our world. We have enough evidence of the goodness of God all around us to insist that the brokenness we see is not the final story.

Proper 29: Enough to Live
John 18:33–37

Then Pilate entered the headquarters again, summoned Jesus, and asked him, "Are you the King of the Jews?" . . . Jesus answered, "My kingdom is not from this world. If my kingdom were from this world, my followers would be fighting to keep me from being handed over to the Jews. But as it is, my kingdom is not from here." (John 18:33, 36)

How would our lives change if we lived with the idea that we already have enough: enough to love, enough to give, enough to know, enough to live? I suspect the change would be staggering, because living with a sense of abundance is literally divine—God's way of looking at the world. Our human way, by contrast, is so mean, so limited, so scarce. We constantly are hemmed in by what we can't do, have, know, love, give, hope, try. We end up actually limiting the work of God in our lives and in the world. By contrast, God is full of endless possibilities and unlimited resources. All we have to do is shift the way we see our lives and the world to reflect the abundance God wants for us all.

Our lectionary presents us today with a small part of Jesus' passion narrative, as told in the Gospel of John. Jesus has just lived through one of the hardest nights of his life: a last supper with his disciples, hours of tearful prayer in the Garden of Gethsemane, and the brutal betrayal of a friend—of several friends—that has found him in the headquarters of Pontius Pilate, the Roman governor who is trying as hard as he can to defuse a civil crisis. Pilate doesn't really care about Jesus or his message. What he does care about is the possibility of civil unrest, the disruption of his easy life, and possibly the disapproval of his superiors. It's almost with a sense of exasperation that Pilate asks Jesus a simple question: "Are you the King of the Jews?"

Pilate doesn't get a straight answer from Jesus, because Jesus doesn't seem to be sharing his perspective. If he saw the situation as Pilate sees it, he would be overcome with fear of the sure disaster that lies ahead. But instead, as Jesus tries to explain to Pilate, "My kingdom is not from this world." In other words, Jesus is saying that the reality from which he sees the world is not limited to the power and politics of the Roman regent in Galilee, or even the rulers of the temple in Jerusalem. God's reality, the power of God in the world, is so much bigger than the immediate disaster. Perhaps that larger perspective gives Jesus the courage to live into the larger reality instead of being dismayed by the bleak reality of the immediate situation.

This can be a critically important lesson for us as we think about how to live into God's expectation of abundance and generosity. The immediate reality we face is not the whole story; God is always doing something bigger, something that leads us toward wholeness and hope. And embracing that reality—God's reality—can give us enough courage and strength to live and to create a world where others can too.

Year C

Advent Series: Boundless

Six Parts: First Sunday of Advent through First
Sunday of Christmas, including Christmas Eve

God offers us so much more than we could ever want or need.

MIHEE KIM-KORT

Series Overview This Advent series focuses on the second readings of each lectionary week as framed by the traditional New Testament readings found in the Gospel of Luke. The thread throughout the epistle passages offer us a fresh encounter with the familiar themes of joy and anticipation. In a culture saturated with the pursuit of material abundance, especially during this season, this series offers space to consider how we

	Sermon Title	Focus Scripture	Theme
Advent 1	Boundless Love	1 Thess. 3:9–13; Luke 21:25–36	We practice looking to what seems small, because these are expressions of the boundlessness of God's love.
Advent 2	Boundless Joy	Phil. 1:1–11; Luke 3:1–6	We practice joy by expectantly making space for the way it can surprise us.
Advent 3	Boundless Peace	Phil. 4:4–7; Luke 3:7–18	We become peacemakers by orienting ourselves toward others.
Advent 4	Boundless Hope	Heb. 10:5–10; Luke 1:39–45 (46–55)	We practice hope by seeing the world upside down.
Christmas Eve	Boundless Spirit	Titus 3:4–7; Luke 2:1–14 (15–20)	We practice openness to God's spirit whenever we confront the darkness.
Christmas 1	Boundless Life	Col. 3:12–17; Luke 2:41–52	The boundlessness of God's life poured out for us in the incarnation continues beyond Christmas.

might recover the sense of wonder of God's boundless presence as love, joy, peace, hope, spirit, and life, even as we rehearse once more the anticipation and longing for God's entrance into the world.

Tips and Ideas for This Series

Imagery for this series should evoke wide-open possibilities, abundance not of the material sort but of the spiritual. An open gift box with an untied ribbon might make a good visual, making an intangible message a little more tangible as people imagine what the uncontainable gift might be.

Advent 1: Boundless Love
1 Thessalonians 3:9–13; Luke 21:25–36

And may the Lord make you increase and abound in love for one another and for all, just as we abound in love for you. (1 Thessalonians 3:12)

We're in the stage of life with our children when every year Advent is filled with anticipation—the children ask us daily, how many more weeks, how many more days, how many hours until it's Christmas? They seek out all manner of signs, like when certain decorations go up—those familiar garlands and lights on the railing of the stairs and on the mantle over the fireplace. We don't put everything up at once, but a few things here and there each day or weekend, and watch their delight with every new piece they encounter throughout the weeks.

In our imperfect attempts we try to make space by attending to the source of what makes the season meaningful to us, by going back to the basics, that is, simply God's love. Although it is mostly exhausting, their impatience, their frantic and frenetic counting of the minutes and hours, and their state of near-desperation instruct us as the parents and grown-ups. I revel in their unhindered longing for fulfillment of the promise of Christmas, a story about God's presence in the world that suddenly becomes so much more real during this month.

Of course, the children are likely longing for that moment they tear into the small pile of mismatched wrapped boxes and shapes under the tree. So it makes for numerous opportunities to talk about what we're doing and why we're doing it, without diminishing their perspective or their experience. But we try to savor the story of God's love realized in the birth of Jesus the Christ by paying attention to what is ordinary, even mundane, in the everyday.

I love what Kathleen Stewart writes in *Ordinary Affects*: "The ordinary is a thing that has to be imagined and inhabited. . . . This is no utopia. Not a challenge to be achieved or an ideal to be realized, but a mode of attunement, a continuous responding to something not quite already given and yet somehow happening."[1]

God's love is in these ordinary things. So we practice looking to what seems small and insignificant because these are expressions of the boundlessness of God's love too, which compel us and draw us to God's self.

Gazing at what is normally around us, instead of passing it by and seeing it as a sign of the season. Being present in the mud and muck, the water, the laughter, the skies, the bite of a cold wind, the pink of a child's nose and cheeks, the fleeting thoughts and difficult-to-describe emotions. Embracing the ordinary. Leaning into the ordinary. Growing in the ordinary. Looking out for the ordinary and how it might lead us to kneel at God's feet, kicking softly in that bed of hay, covered in dirt and cow hairs, his blankets and swaddling loose, and the sound of gurgles and slow blinking . . . to kneel before God incarnate over and over again. It makes sense . . . to approach God's very first human throne, we would be led there not by a burning bush or even a choir of angels but by something as ordinary as a star and a road.

Advent 2: Boundless Joy
Philippians 1:1–11; Luke 3:1–6

I thank my God every time I remember you, constantly praying with joy in every one of my prayers for all of you, because of your sharing in the gospel from the first day until now. (Philippians 1:3–5)

One Sunday morning I went to the 9 a.m. service, and after dropping the kids off at Sunday school I left to brunch with a group of moms. We observed together that there is something about this season with all the twinkling lights, trees, and dreamy music that weighs heavy on us. Perhaps it is the superficial, gooey feeling that comes from too much hot chocolate and cookies, presents with fancy bows, and big toothy smiles that feel like an affront to harsher realities—the constant turmoil of war, violence, and poverty happening all around the world. Maybe instead of more glitz and shine, what we need is more darkness.

1. Kathleen Stewart, *Ordinary Affects* (Durham, NC: Duke University Press, 2007), 127.

But it's a season of joy so exuberant that it bursts through the cracks of our world's darkness. With each candle that is lit for Advent, more light shimmers in that darkness.

That Sunday morning I left to have brunch was actually the Sunday of the children's pageant, which we did not have the kids participate in that season. But apparently Desmond and Anna nonetheless put on quite the show. Instead of staying in the child-care room, they let themselves be whisked away to sit with their church grandparents somewhere else. Their daddy, who happens to be the pastor, got up to do the welcome and opening prayer when Desmond decided to army crawl up the center aisle to practice his somersaults. He continued to roll forward toward the chancel with the associate pastor, Rachel, trying discreetly to coax him back. As Andy got to the middle of the prayer, Desmond needed more than a gentle nudge; so Andy walked over to pick him up and finish the prayer with him. He asked Desmond if he wanted to sit with Pastor Rachel, to which Desmond responded with a loud, resounding "No." Andy left to take him down to the nursery. Of course, during this whole time, Anna was sitting perfectly peachy.

Needless to say, there was a lot of laughter. But why would a story like this provide any more light into the darkness for me? Because there are days when I feel ready to pick up and leave it all behind. I want to drop the kids off at one of the grandparents' houses and drive west until I hit the Pacific. I want to cover my head with my blankets, lock the door, and never leave my bed. Meanwhile, Desmond is doing somersaults down the center aisle, having completely forgotten that I'm a terrible mother, and that I yelled at him that morning, and maybe gave him only Goldfish crackers for breakfast. I can't help but marvel at them, because it feels like no matter what I'm doing or not doing right, they seem to be undeterred by it.

No matter the circumstances, joy seems always to be on the periphery of their vision. They are ready to laugh and ready to make us laugh too. And maybe the joy is the *surprise*: when it bursts, when it catches us off guard, and when we're looking for something else in that parched land, when we're thinking we need water, but it's the crocus, bright and yellow, persevering in that cracked earth that is the real oasis.

We practice joy by expectantly making space for the way it can surprise us. It's these stories and pictures of boundless, unfettered joy, a joy that persists, a joy that defies convention and category or what makes sense, where valleys are filled and mountains are laid low, crooked paths straightened and rough paths are easy on our feet— that's the stuff and surprise of joy.

Advent 3: Boundless Peace
Philippians 4:4–7; Luke 3:7–18

Do not worry about anything, but in everything by prayer and supplication with thanksgiving let your requests be made known to God. And the peace of God, which surpasses all understanding, will guard your hearts and minds in Christ Jesus. (Philippians 4:6–7)

I can pick my mother's voice out in a crowd of a thousand people. She has a distinct way of saying my name. And I can always tell what kind of mood she's in, based on how she's saying it in the moment. When I was younger, she would call my name and my little brother's name when it was time for dinner. If it was high pitched and shrill, I would run the other direction, because that meant she had found something I had broken or a maybe a chore I had neglected or had not finished, and that meant she was not thrilled with me. Sometimes it would be playful, sometimes sarcastic. She mastered snark long before it became a thing, sometimes biting and cutting, sometimes gentle and soothing.

I imagine many of us, even with eyes closed, could pick out our parents' voices. Or teacher's voices. Or grandparents' voices. Or the voice of some other loved one or friend. Because when you love and care for someone, they become a part of you—there are echoes of who they are within you—and something about them resonates in you. That person and that voice anchor us, comfort us, and give us peace. They steady us.

We are hungry and thirsty for good news and that inexplicable peace that comes with knowing the promise of God's faithfulness and love. But the peace isn't given just for us alone. I think about the Beatitudes, and the bit about peacemakers being children of God. We are all children of God, and we are all called to be peacemakers.

I have longed for a particular kind of peace for a while now—the sleeping kind, the quiet kind, the one that I breathe in as I look in my rearview mirror at the children asleep clutching books and stuffed animals. Maybe the peace that we make isn't always between humans who are fighting and arguing or going at it over some stupid toy. Maybe the peace that we make isn't necessarily treaties or compromises or resolutions. Maybe the peace is simpler than that. Maybe we make peace within ourselves when we see that we are children of God, and remind others of that truth as well. Conflict and struggle are inevitable, but so is God's steadfast love. We are all children of God, endeavoring and flailing as we try to make sense of life and family and work. Maybe that peace is something to be practiced in our families first, with our children and spouses. Maybe that peace is tenuous and fragile, like human life; but it is still real, it is still promised, because it is God-breathed into our bones and marrow.

This peace is not always calm and quiet. Look at John the Baptist in today's Gospel text. We have modern models of it in Martin Luther King Jr., Gandhi, Mother Teresa, and even in the unexpected and unlikely, in Ferguson protestors, and in poetry readings, slut walks, vigils, and marches, and when we gather together on Sunday mornings. It's when flesh and blood cry out together for peace, call out the absence or lack of it, and seek to coax it out of the cloaked darkness that tries to hide inequalities, disparities, and discrepancies, and the truth that every human being was created for full and abundant life.

Advent 4: Boundless Hope
Hebrews 10:5–10; Luke 1:39–45 (46–55)

Consequently, when Christ came into the world, he said,
  "Sacrifices and offerings you have not desired,
but a body you have prepared for me;
  in burnt offerings and sin-offerings
you have taken no pleasure.
  Then I said, 'See God, I have come to do your will.'" (Hebrews 10:5–7a)

We arrived at the Freedom School, housed by a church in a large inner-city neighborhood. The students greeted us by running at us clapping and shout-singing like my own children, but enunciating a lot more clearly:

G-O-O-D M-O-R-N-I-N-G
GOOD MORNING (WOOT WOOT)
GOOD MORNING (WOOT WOOT)

The children led us into a bright space with flying leaps and cartwheels. We watched sixty children stomp the floor not only with their feet but their bodies and voices, and we could feel it in our bones too. This was hope unbound, in the flesh and blood, an image of the body of Christ, dancing, singing, whooping. And it was contagious. They sang a song about "being strong and finding that what's inside helps them to resist the wrong." I found myself weeping quietly. Because I cry any time kids are playing and singing hard—sometimes out of weariness and sometimes from being filled up by the sight.

Sometimes hope results in laughter, like Abraham and Sarah when they were gifted with Isaac, and sometimes hope falls from our faces in tears, sweat, and blood.

During a visit to another church that embodies hope, I met Savannah, who is a rail in pink T-shirt and shorts decked out in bright kicks. Hair falling just to her shoulders made her look a little older than her nine years. She was quiet and shy but with smiles so huge as she explained the art on the wall that was hers. I wondered if she was someone who normally needed to be coaxed to talk aloud. I could almost see her buzzing with pride and excitement. I looked behind her to see the influence of Matisse and Monet in these tissue-paper and crayon pieces. Above us there were light bulbs hanging down from the ceiling like huge raindrops suspended in time. It was a lovely effect—these tiny angels that stayed a little above our heads and reminded me that even when the sun is streaming into the room, the light inside is just as necessary.

What does it mean to perform hope? We sing, we create, we lift up. We embody it as we chant and step across the room. We express it in our art as we play with colors and mediums. We share stories; we explore with our songs—ones that we know and ones that we make up; we trample the darkness beneath our feet, clutching each other's hands with shouts of WOOTWOOT. Watching and listening, I felt as though I'd entered their dreams a little, but they were dreams that felt so real and true, as if the songs of declaration in today's texts had come alive with bodies, voices, skin, and cells. And this is church: walking, stomping, shout-singing these dreams.

Mary's Magnificat—"magnificat" meaning song of praise, literally magnifying and lifting up God, the God of the margins—is a powerful and poetic expression not only beautiful and good because it's true. It is about watching and waiting on God's faithfulness, God's liberation, and the hope of wholeness and healing, of redemption and liberation, present in her very body, in the growing baby within her body. Likewise, Christ's song expressed in Hebrews is a manifestation of newness and dedication to God's will for the world. We practice hope by seeing the world upside down, believing that God will turn things that are upside down, right side up, when God's kingdom breaks through to our hurting world.

Christmas Eve: Boundless Spirit
Titus 3:4–7; Luke 2:1–14 (15–20)

But when the goodness and loving kindness of God our Savior appeared, he saved us, not because of any works of righteousness that we had done, but according to his mercy, through the water of rebirth and renewal by the Holy Spirit. (Titus 3:4–5)

I can't remember if I was afraid of the dark when I was a child. I do remember that my younger brother was always a little uncertain at night. It probably didn't help that he had an awful older sister that loved to hide in his room and jump out to scare him at every possible chance. When it was time to sleep, he had a little Snoopy nightlight. Somehow it comforted him—that small, tiny light. It was just as much the goofy cartoon character as the warm glow that allowed him to see a little and slumber in peace at night.

When the twins were babies, we got asked one question often: How are they sleeping through the night? We usually laughed in response. Sleeping peacefully at night seemed like an urban legend. In fact, "sleeping like a baby" had a whole new meaning for us, and those who used the phrase to mean sleeping deeply and soundly clearly did not have babies. It was quite the obsession for us, almost the center of our lives—trying to understand sleep, sleep issues, sleep patterns, sleep routines, sleep associations.

We had good months, hard months, easy weeks, and weeks that seemed as if they would never end because no one was getting any sleep; even Ellis, our boxer dog, would look sluggish some days. Then, when Desmond figured out how to stand on his own, he took to pulling himself up by clutching the rail and rattling his "cage," bellowing to be let out. This was happening for every nap and when we put him down to sleep at night. At night his shouting turned into screeching and eventually all-out crying, and when I went to check on him, he always had big tears in his eyes. I knew there was something about separation anxiety at this stage, but I was beginning to wonder if he also felt anxious in the dark too. Whether it was I or his daddy, it was remarkable that as soon as we picked him up, he stopped immediately. One thing comforted him in those moments: being in our arms.

With a tender tone, like the whispers of a parent speaking into the ears of a wailing baby, God gathers Israel in her arms and says, "Here I am." God's spirit is poured out, a reminder that we do not sit in darkness alone. In Christ, God's boundless spirit is illuminated like a lamp for us all to see.

We experience the light of Christ in numerous ways—like through an encouraging word or the sharing of a meal. Even as we table together, as we break bread and share God's cup of reconciliation, in this simple feast we experience the "goodness and loving kindness of God our Savior" (Titus 3:4), the promise of world-changing salvation.

We practice openness to God's spirit whenever we confront the darkness. If there's anything I believe about following the Christ, the Christ of the triune God, it means that we keep showing up where there's hurt and darkness. It's where God needs us, because someone has to do the diligent work of speaking up, reaching out, and telling God's saving story. Even when we don't understand, even when we are guilty or complicit or fragile or confused, even when it doesn't make sense, even when we are despairing, we go out, we show up to be with people and be Christ's light in the world. We pray. We light candles. We hold hands. We chant. We prophesy. We speak beauty and goodness. We share God's grace. We shout, "Yes, Lord, here I am." We whisper, "God, pour out your Spirit upon us."

Christmas 1: Boundless Life
Colossians 3:12–17; Luke 2:41–52

Let the word of Christ dwell in you richly; teach and admonish one another in all wisdom; and with gratitude in your hearts sing psalms, hymns, and spiritual songs to God. And whatever you do, in word or deed, do everything in the name of the Lord Jesus, giving thanks to God the Father through him. (Colossians 3:16–17)

One year, I missed Christmas Eve. The youngest, Ozzie, brought in the scourge that had three out of five of us (mommy and twins) devastated for the week. Laid out on the couches. Covered in all manner of bodily liquids and smells. Christmas Eve came quickly, and we were scrambling to find clean pants for Desmond that he hadn't thrown up on in the last few minutes. He ended up wearing very comfy dark blue sweats with his tie and sweater. Anna was lovely but listless in her green dress with her hair matted from lying down all day. But Ozzie was fine. Fine, with a vengeance. As if he was making up for lost time, he was almost indignant at our lack of energy.

We lasted about fifteen minutes. I sang a duet with the music director—an old carol to a French melody. When we finished I felt as if I needed to collapse and lie down immediately. The kids looked so pathetic too. Looking at Ozzie made me feel even more exhausted. I made an executive decision and we went home, which was not much of a relief, even though everyone went to bed fairly willingly after only a few reminders that Santa would come if they went to sleep *now*. I looked at the pile of presents that needed wrapping and the kitchen overrun with half-full sippy cups and clothes piled up on every flat surface. I wanted to wither away. I cleaned the kitchen, wrapped a few presents, threw clothes into the baskets, and left a note to Pastor Daddy to finish the rest—which he did, saint that he is, thankfully.

I missed Christmas Eve. The hymns. The candles. The children. The sermon. The laughter and hugs, handshakes, and greetings. The moment when it feels as if the earth shifts slightly, as if she's remembering the weight of the angels' presence or the despair of humanity lightened by the newborn cry of a baby. The breath of hope collectively exhaled into the air that seems to crystalize for a moment as on a cold morning.

But not that time. Not for me. Time and exhaustion and stress and my own children's cries swallowed up any possibility of it. Now the Christmas season is here, but the main "event" is over, and all I can really think about is *we are still a week away from the end of this holiday break.*

Mary missed Christmas Eve too. She was having a baby, after all. But Christmas, all the waiting, hoping, watching—it presses on. It keeps on. It keeps on. It keeps on. I can't help but think of Mary and the words of the hymn "Mary, did you know?" Not, did you know that your baby would be a miracle-worker, teacher, activist, prophet, and savior of the world? Rather, *did you know you would be consumed by the breath and heartbeat of your child?* Did you know that your life would no longer be yours? Saying yes not only to being *theotokos*— the bearer of God—but simply the bearer of a child? The bearer of a little universe with his own galaxies, sun and asteroids and falling stars, where you would continuously feel the ebb and waves of his gravity?

I feel Jesus' presence more thinking about mothers these days. I think about Trayvon's, Antonio's, Tamir's, Renisha's, Michael's, Aiyana's, Nizah's, Kayla's, Rekia's, Eric's, John's mothers. How life presses on boundless and undeterred in their flesh and blood, though that blood is spilled daily, and though for centuries black bodies have borne and continue to bear this violence and death. Because I don't know what I would do if my life and love, my whole world was stripped away from me. Mary knows about this horrible loss too. She anticipated it. How she lived with that knowledge from day one without complete collapse is beyond me.

The boundlessness of God's life poured out for us in the incarnation continues beyond Christmas. The waiting continues beyond Christmas, as we both live and look forward to the kingdom. Even as illness and pain and loss make their mark, we participate in the boundless life of Christ.

Epiphany Series 1: Living with Joy

Four Parts: Epiphany to Third Sunday after Epiphany

Living with purpose and joy in our everyday lives.

MIHEE KIM-KORT

Series Overview

This series, based on stories from early in Jesus' life and ministry, explores what it means to live a meaningful, joyful life. Themes of identity and vocation offer an alternative to the "fresh start" or "clean slate" mentality common in the beginning of a new year with its emphasis on resolutions and plans. By contrast, this series helps us find the joy already present in our lives and reflect on God's continuous presence and inspiration for our daily living.

Tips and Ideas in This Series

Invite congregants to reflect on the things that bring them real joy in life, potentially writing them on mural paper displayed for that purpose. Include a testimony each week from someone in the congregation who experiences great joy in ways pertinent to each week's

	Sermon Title	Focus Scripture	Theme
Epiphany[1]	Led by Joy	Matt. 2:1–12	Vocation: God leads us by attending to our deepest joy.
First Sunday after Epiphany	Baptized in Love	Luke 3:15–17, 21–22	Identity: God knows and names us in love, and shapes us in that love.
Second Sunday after Epiphany	Called to Delight	John 2:1–11	Celebration: God persistently calls us to feast and delight in God's presence.
Third Sunday after Epiphany	Blessed for Good	Neh. 8:1–3, 5–6, 8–10; Luke 4:14–21	Selflessness: God invites us to share goodness with all.

1. The congregation can observe Epiphany on the Second Sunday of Christmas if January 6 does not fall on a Sunday.

theme. Be sure to remind the congregation that joy does not always mean feeling happy, and be sensitive to those struggling to find joy in times of depression or grief.

Epiphany: Led by Joy
Matthew 2:1–12

When they had heard the king, they set out; and there, ahead of them, went the star they had seen at its rising, until it stopped over the place where the child was. When they saw that the star had stopped, they were overwhelmed with joy. (Matthew 2:9–10)

This morning's Gospel lesson introduces us to the wise men. On occasion I have also heard the joke that had they instead been the wise *women*, they would have stopped and asked for directions, arrived on time, helped deliver the baby, brought practical gifts, made a casserole, and there would indeed be peace on earth. But these astrologers followed a star that eventually led them to Jesus. The star was God's sign for them, and it lit their road all the way to Bethlehem. Of course, don't forget they were waylaid first, and had a meeting with King Herod.

This is where we see that the story isn't really just about three kings journeying from afar. It's about two kings—King Herod and Jesus, the infant king. The three wise men no doubt realized that they had two options: (1) do what they were "supposed to do," follow King Herod's request, and stay in the good graces of a powerful politician; (2) take a risk, follow the way God put before them, and encounter God's very self.

We know that we too are often presented with a similar choice. On one hand we can follow the Herods of the world; those things that would love to knock Jesus off and claim their hold on us as king. Sure, we easily can rattle off greed, war, bigotry, and hatred as Herods. What about selfishness with our resources, or laziness, or lack of interest in our quest to learn more about God? Or apathy toward those in need or experiencing pain? Could those be Herods? What about an unwillingness to get involved or to make a commitment? What about our schedules and calendars and pressures to keep up with everyone else, lest we fall behind? Could those be Herods, something that tries to claim kingship in our life and maybe keeps us from following God with joy? What about holding a grudge or not realizing our part of the blame in a disagreement? Can these things get in the way of our relationship with God? If so, then it might be a Herod, and it will be up to you to decide if you follow it—or not.

On the other hand, we can follow the light of the infant king. We can seek out the newborn king and not just pay him homage, but have an experience where we are overcome with joy and fall on our knees to worship him. What are those things that light our way and lead us to Jesus? What is it about God that excites you—makes you feel alive—and how can you pursue it?

Think about what brings you joy. God leads us by attending to our deepest joy, and we discover who we are in that joy. We discover our own joys, and the possibility that vocation is not just desire or hunger, but joy. My desire for each of us is that we journey and follow the light of the joy that leads us to Jesus. But if you are wondering what in the world that light or sign to follow might look like, here is something more to glean from our text: God led the wise men using what was, for them, an ordinary object: a star. Remember, they were astrologers after all. Our path to joy may not seem revolutionary. God may use something completely ordinary to reveal a new path.

First Sunday after Epiphany: Baptized in Love
Luke 3:15–17, 21–22

John answered all of them by saying, "I baptize you with water; but one who is more powerful than I is coming; I am not worthy to untie the thong of his sandals. He will baptize you with the Holy Spirit and fire." (Luke 3:16)

Last week, we looked at the ways we are called and led in joy, and how God attends to us in that joy in a particular way—to awaken us to God's presence and gifts in our lives and work. The Luke passage this morning signals another aspect of this calling through the story of Jesus' baptism, which happens prior to the beginning of his public ministry according to this account. We are reminded in these texts of the connection between birth and baptism, that is, love, as the Isaiah text tells us of one who created us, formed us, called us, made us his own.

Birth and baptism seem to go hand in hand, as both are a window into eternity, both central to who we are and to whom we belong. Birth is flesh and blood and water and spirit. Birth is pervasive, but still complicated. So, of course, Jesus would use this as an image of God's kingdom, and tie it to baptism and to our own identity.

I'm reminded of the story of Nicodemus in the Gospel of John. Nicodemus is one of the religious elite, and someone who thinks he has earned the keys to the kingdom. Jesus tells him, "Very truly, I tell you, no one can see the kingdom of God without being born from above." Nicodemus is sidelined by this statement, responding, "How can anyone be born after having grown old? Can one enter a second time into the mother's womb and be born?"

Both being born into the world and being born of the kingdom inevitably include some kind of trauma—whether through the water, rivers, or fires, but always, in the end, transformation. Moving from one state to another, we become more fully who we are made to be. Baptism is a sign not only of our identity as God's child, but of persistence and resistance, of the breath of incarnation. God knows and names us in love, and shapes us in that love. This is the real sign, the real miracle that should impress us in that moment of baptism, the sign that God chooses us, God chooses us over and over and over. In that choosing, God calls us beloved and calls us to live in the joy of that belovedness, empowered to share God's love in our everyday lives.

Second Sunday after Epiphany: Called to Delight
John 2:1–11

[The steward said to the bridegroom]: "Everyone serves the good wine first, and then the inferior wine after the guests have become drunk. But you have kept the good wine until now." Jesus did this, the first of his signs, in Cana of Galilee, and revealed his glory; and his disciples believed in him. (John 2:10–11)

One Sunday morning, I go to two churches. The first, I enter expecting to participate in Communion but I see the table up front is empty. No chalice. No bread. Later, the guest preacher mentions skipping Communion because they anticipated low attendance for this particular Sunday. I'm terribly disappointed. At the second church, I am relieved to see the table set, and also struck by the beauty of the Communion table, covered in gold-colored plates and trays, candles, and a small loaf of bread. I get an up-close view during the children's sermon because I have to make sure one of the children that belongs to me doesn't attempt the magic trick of pulling out the sheet from underneath the table elements.

The table is so neat, polished, organized—pretty and in order. I flash back to earlier that morning with the kids around the table for breakfast. The youngest is covered in Nutella and yogurt. Cheerios underfoot covering the carpet. Little pools of milk all over the table from eating cereal. Plastic animals and car tracks making lines of milk and fruit. Too many utensils on the table and under chairs. Ellis, the boxer dog, frantically eating as much as possible on the floor and up on the table.

The images create a cognitive dissonance as I wonder which is a better expression of celebration? In today's Gospel reading, we read of the first act of Jesus' public ministry according to John's account: turning water to wine. In some ways, this might seem strange, but if we take the incarnation seriously, once the Word became flesh, the rest of the Gospel shows us what grace tastes like, looks like, smells like, sounds like, feels like. Then it makes sense to begin with this miracle. It is not simply about turning water to wine, but the miracle of abundance, of extravagant celebration, and of delighting in God's presence.

In this, we see how God persistently calls us to feast and delight in God's presence. Jesus models this for us in his own ministry, taking time to celebrate, to feast, to rest in God's abundance. In a world that is regularly full of news of a kind of scarcity of human compassion and goodness, the call to orient ourselves toward God's sometimes surprising abundance, which seemingly comes out of nowhere, is challenging and transformative. Standing before all these tables, God confronts me with that miraculous grace. I hear Jesus' words, "Take, eat, do this remembering me." They are words of another sign of the promise that God remembers me too. God is putting me back together with this simple meal. God's continuous presence and inspiration is meant as daily bread for our daily living as we work toward God's kingdom.

Third Sunday after Epiphany: Blessed for Good
Nehemiah 8:1–3, 5–6, 8–10; Luke 4:14–21

"This day is holy to the LORD your God; do not mourn or weep." For all the people wept when they heard the words of the law. Then he said to them, "Go your way, eat the fat and drink sweet wine and send portions of them to those for whom nothing is prepared, for this day is holy to our LORD; and do not be grieved, for the joy of the LORD is your strength." (Nehemiah 8:9b–10)

Over the last few weeks we've explored the beginnings of Jesus' public ministry in the different accounts—his baptism, turning water to wine—and the possibility of mapping that joy and abundance onto our own daily living. This week we read the opening scene of the ministry of Jesus in Luke's account, and it is a bit more somber and serious as he returns to Galilee and his hometown to teach in the synagogues.

The prophetic words he offers to the people are words of celebration and hope: "He has sent me to proclaim release to the captives and recovery of sight to the blind, to let the oppressed go free, to proclaim the year of the Lord's favor." Yet the people of Jesus' hometown who hear these words reject them, and they reject Jesus. I wonder what goes through their minds here—not only the question, "Isn't this Joseph's son?" as in *what kind of authority does he think he possesses that he can say these words about our reality?* They take offense because Jesus dares suggest this good news was for everyone.

It is a sharp contrast with the response of the people in the Nehemiah passage—who respond to a reading of the law with mourning and guilt. Nehemiah tells them not to mourn but to celebrate—and to share their celebration with those who don't have meat and wine of their own to enjoy. The people do this, discovering that life with God is something to find joy in—something to be spread to all.

So this is an invitation to choose how we will respond. Will we respond with despair or with hope? By adopting Jesus' spirit and living his imperatives we may discover his wisdom that it isn't just about us. These prophetic words about the jubilee year aren't only about God's daily blessed provision for us but about what it means that we are God's provision for the world. Jesus talks a lot about this promise of God's kingdom, that is, a community, a phenomenon, a reality rooted in the persistent grace of God, no matter what is going on in the world. God meant for us to see God's kingdom all around us, and more than that, to *be* God's kingdom as much as we could bear it in the here and now.

With God's kingdom in our possession, what more could we ever need or want in our lives? This is what God offers us, gives us each day to grasp, to cling to, to trust in every moment. In the end, this is all we need to survive, to live, to love, to be in this life.

Epiphany Series 2: The Art of Hearing

Four Parts: Fourth Sunday after Epiphany through Seventh Sunday after Epiphany

Discovering the power of God's voice through stories from Luke's Gospel.

MIHEE KIM-KORT

Series Overview

As God's creation, all our senses are useful when they are activated for God's purposes. This series focuses on the practice of hearing and being heard by attending to Jesus' words in these stories of Luke's Gospel. Yet clearly it is more than his words; his posture, his orientation, and his relationships speak volumes. What this models for us is not only the power of God's voice and presence, but also our ability to hear and respond, whether with our voices or with our lives. This series shows us what it means to hear, to listen, to attend to God's spirit in every situation, as God promises to provide the Holy Spirit to us. But like any other craft or art form, the art of hearing requires practice, discipline, and intentionality.

Tips and Ideas for This Series

Experiment with sound during this series. Various genres of music are one avenue to pursue, but also nonmusical sounds. Use nature sounds like ocean waves and nighttime crickets as well as urban noises like

	Sermon Title	Focus Scripture	Theme
Fourth Sunday after Epiphany	Hard of Hearing	Luke 4:21–30	God's voice shapes us.
Fifth Sunday after Epiphany	Hearing Is Believing	Luke 5:1–11	God's voice directs us.
Sixth Sunday after Epiphany	Hearing and Healing	Luke 6:17–26	God's voice heals us.
Seventh Sunday after Epiphany	Hearing One Another	Luke 6:27–38	God's voice calls us to reconciliation.

the sound of city streets. Allow time for silence in worship as well, to listen for God and to all the little noises we may often overlook—the ticking of a clock, the whispering of a child, the beating of our own hearts.

Fourth Sunday after Epiphany: Hard of Hearing
Luke 4:21–30

Then he began to say to them, "Today this scripture has been fulfilled in your hearing." All spoke well of him and were amazed at the gracious words that came from his mouth. They said, "Is not this Joseph's son?" (Luke 4:21–22)

The college edition of *This American Life* called "How I Got into College" tells the surprising story about an admissions officer who received an email from one parent inquiring about their engineering program for his son. The email reads: "My second grader has decided on a career in electrical engineering. He is leaning towards MIT, but I do not find them helpful and would prefer a Southern culture." The second and third acts are about Emir Kamenica, a Bosnian-born professor at the University of Chicago, and how he came to America as a refugee through a series of "accidents" and good fortunes. It's a story he loves to tell and includes a particular high school teacher who changed the course of his trajectory, so that he became a student at a prestigious private school, eventually at Harvard, and then a young, brilliant scholar of economics. The twist is that the way he tells the story is different from the way his teacher, Ms. Ames, tells it. She knew he was destined for great things. He thought he got out alive by the skin of his teeth. But she says, "It's as if the more he told the story, the more grateful he became."

It's easy to get lost and overwhelmed by all the voices around us, and especially the ones that try to shape our perspectives on our own stories—both helpful and destructive. But there's no way to avoid the inevitability that there always going to be difficult voices around us—those that we disagree with, those that are frustrating, those that convict us and force us to see differently.

What do we do in this day and age as we seek to hear the voice of Jesus? How will we respond? The people who heard Jesus speak these scandalous words about who would be welcome into God's family—that is, Gentiles, outsiders—were incensed because they did not hear what they expected to hear from one of their own. They heard a different story that did not match up with what they assumed about God, and especially upsetting because it was from one who was a prophet of God, who happened to be from their hometown. This is a familiar scenario even today—people are sometimes hard of hearing when it comes to the challenge and provocation of the gospel when it comes to the boundaries we put up around our identities, communities, and the stories we tell about ourselves.

God's voice shapes us. But when we get in our own way, we miss what is right in front of us. Jesus said, "Today this scripture has been fulfilled in your hearing," and it is significant that he emphasized hearing rather than seeing. We became God's creation by God's voice, which means we are God's handiwork, God's art. It's in our flesh and blood, in our cells, in our skin, which means in a way that we are all artists, we're all meant to be creators of beauty and goodness, and God longs for us to know ourselves and God in this way.

Fifth Sunday after Epiphany: Hearing Is Believing
Luke 5:1–11

Simon answered, "Master, we have worked all night long but have caught nothing. Yet if you say so, I will let down the nets." (Luke 5:5)

I grew up in Colorado Springs, Colorado, home to Pikes Peak, a majestic mountain just a little more than 14,000 feet high. This mountain is the backdrop to every memory. It is impossible to have a terrible view of it, wherever you are in the city. My high school cafeteria had one huge wall of windows that perfectly framed it, as did my church. Pikes Peak—always to the west—was my compass. So I always knew where I was, even if I was lost—whether I was in a car, walking, running, or on a bike—as long as I could see Pikes Peak.

In church, despite the beautiful view of the peak, my compass was harder to identify. It was a Presbyterian church made up mostly of Korean immigrants, including my family. This church became an extended family to us, full of people who were like aunts and uncles, cousins and grandparents. I loved going to church for this reason, but I didn't realize until I was in high school that my faith wasn't really my own; it was my parents'. While hearing the voices of many people I loved, I wasn't hearing God's voice. I really discovered God's presence, God's voice for myself only when a high school friend named Keeley gave me my first "quiet time" book.

It was the first time I had ever read the Bible without a teacher, and prayed with my own voice, and asked questions, and journaled, and engaged God's voice. I learned how to love God with my heart, my soul, my spirit, and my strength—not mediated by my parents' voice or authority or my pastor's or my teacher's or my youth leader's, but mediated by God's spirit. For the first time, I found my compass in God's voice.

In today's Scripture, crowds are swarming around Jesus, desperate to hear his teaching. Before he even opens his mouth, they are confident he will deliver a word from God. Simon Peter and his fellow fishermen are not feeling so confident. They are washing out their nets after a fruitless night of fishing. We can imagine they are just ready to go home and rest, not knowing what else to do after failing so miserably and potentially jeopardizing their week's income. They are ready to pack it in, but Jesus' voice interrupts them. First, he asks a favor: "Row me out a little ways, would you, so I can have some space to preach?" Peter and his partner oblige.

We don't know what Jesus taught the crowd that day, or if Peter and his buddy even paid much attention, tired as they were. But despite their feelings of exhaustion and failure, they were open to Jesus' guidance when he made a second request: to throw out their nets and give it one more try. Of course, Jesus' voice did not steer them wrong but resulted in a bountiful catch of fish. Shocked and humbled, their ears were now wide open to hear the next ask Jesus would make of them: to leave their nets and follow him.

It's sometimes the failures, the aimlessness, the empty nets that open us up to hearing God's voice, making it our compass to show us who we are and why we're here and what we're called to create. God's voice directs us, guiding us where we are to go in the world, once we respond with the words: "Yet if you say so, I will."

Sixth Sunday after Epiphany: Hearing and Healing
Luke 6:17–26

He came down with them and stood on a level place, with a great crowd of his disciples and a great multitude of people from all Judea, Jerusalem, and the coast of Tyre and Sidon. They had come to hear him and to be healed of their diseases; and those who were troubled with unclean spirits were cured. And all in the crowd were trying to touch him, for power came out from him and healed all of them. (Luke 6:17–19)

One of my favorite things to do with my kids is reading to them at bedtime. We're working through the *Chronicles of Narnia* and recently finished *Prince Caspian*. In this volume, the Pevensie children return to Narnia one year after their previous adventure and find that 1,300 years have passed there. War has come to Narnia once again, and the children join forces with Prince Caspian to restore peace to the land.

There's a point early in the book when the Pevensies are making their way through the thick forests of Narnia, sleeping outdoors along the way. This is what it says:

> Lucy woke out of the deepest sleep you can imagine, with the feeling that the voice she liked best in the world had been calling her name. She thought at first it was her father's voice, but that did not seem quite right. Then she thought it was Peter's voice, but that did not seem to fit either. She did not want to get up; not because she was still tired—on the contrary she was wonderfully rested and all the aches had gone from her bones—but because she felt so extremely happy and comfortable.[1]

This scene captures what a voice that you love does to you when you hear it. Think for a moment about the voice you like best in the whole world calling your name. How does it make you feel? What does it make you want to do? God's voice is like that. It makes us alive. God's voice formed and shaped us, but it does something to us; it continues to give us what we need to be alive.

This is what drew people to Jesus in today's Gospel reading. They came "to hear and be healed." Some came with diseases, some with "unclean spirits," everyone with some sort of brokenness, some sort of need. They were seeking the voice of God to give them life. Some were seeking bodily restoration, some love and affirmation, worth and value, freedom from all the other voices telling them they were unclean, unwell, unworthy. And they found it in Jesus. They heard his voice, they crowded in to touch him. The power of God was in his voice and in his touch. "Power came out from him, and he healed all of them." All the broken people there. *All* the broken parts within each person. All of them—healed by the presence of God in Christ.

Seventh Sunday after Epiphany: Hearing One Another
Luke 6:27–38

"But I say to you that listen, Love your enemies, do good to those who hate you, bless those who curse you, pray for those who abuse you." (Luke 6:27–28)

We all have voices. We all have literal voices—some are high pitched, some are gravelly, some are soft, and more—but we also each have a *voice*, as in a perspective, an experience, a story. And these voices matter.

Our children Desmond and Anna gibber and jabber all day long. Desmond has a lot to say, but he usually hangs back and observes

---

1. C. S. Lewis, *Prince Caspian* (New York: HarperCollins, 2002), 144.

in quiet, and won't speak unprompted unless he has something that gets him excited. When the twins started kindergarten, Desmond struggled with differentiating between certain sounds—"p" and "b" sounded similar, the "th" and "f" sounds were difficult for him, and this impacted his literacy and even his developing numeracy. In the beginning he would often get frustrated because he couldn't help but compare himself to Anna or his other friends.

We've had many conversations about the need to be patient and to keep practicing, because we all have unique voices and stories to cultivate, and that takes time. What matters is not what our voices sound like but what we do with those voices: speaking out, praying, blessing others, especially our enemies.

StoryCorps is a podcast that reminds the nation that every voice counts and every story matters. Since 2003, it has given a quarter of a million Americans the chance to record interviews about their lives, to pass wisdom from one generation to the next, and to leave a legacy for the future. These powerful stories illustrate our shared humanity and show that what we have in common is much more than what divides us.

There's one particularly intense story about two men: Greg Gibson and Wayne Lo. Lo is in prison serving two life sentences without the possibility of parole, for killing two people and wounding four others in 1992 on the campus of Simon's Rock College in Massachusetts. Gibson's son Galen was one of the victims killed in that shooting. He said he wasn't looking to forgive Lo or to find closure, but just to look him in the eye and talk. So he went to visit Lo in prison, and it was the first time they had ever spoken to each other.[2]

Most of us would consider the person who killed our child an "enemy," and yet this is who Jesus tells us to love, to bless, to pray for. I doubt Gibson went to the prison with the goal of loving or blessing Lo. But he took one small step toward reconciliation—toward bridging the gap between ourselves and others. He had a conversation. He spoke, and he listened.

This work of reconciliation is ongoing—it's not once and done, a one-off thing in the life we're living here on earth. It's messy and complicated. It's never linear. Sometimes it's two steps forward and one step back, and yes, sometimes you do let the sun go down on your anger, but then you get up the next morning, and reset and reboot and try again. The miracle of our life together is that even while we may seem foreign and strange to one another, we are called together by the voice of God to hear one another's stories. We hear the voice of God in one another as we come together in conversation and experience the love that will not let us go—that love that is powerful enough to make enemies into friends.

2. Greg Gibson, "StoryCorps 518: The Conversation," interview by Michael Garofalo, *Story-Corps*, December 12, 2017, https://storycorps.org/podcast/storycorps-518-the-conversation.

Lenten Series: Character and Calling

Seven Parts: First Sunday in Lent
through Easter Sunday

A Lenten journey with Paul to discover the essentials of Christian character.

MAGREY R. DeVEGA

Series Overview   Here's an interesting thought experiment. If the apostle Paul were around today, what do you think he would give up for Lent? Chances are pretty good he would do more than give up chocolate, caffeine, or social media. Based on his epistles that guide us through this Lenten cycle, he might say that it's not about what you *give up* for Lent that prepares you for the cross. It's about what you *take up*. Each

	Sermon Title	Focus Scripture	Theme
Lent 1	Belief	Rom. 10:8b–13	Belief is the foundation of Christian character.
Lent 2	Discipline	Phil. 3:17–4:1	Character is formed by imitating the example of Christ.
Lent 3	Holiness	1 Cor. 10:1–13	Character resists temptation and maintains purity.
Lent 4	Reconciliation	2 Cor. 5:16–21	Through Christ we have peace with God and can be at peace with others.
Lent 5	Faith	Phil. 3:4b–14	Faith enables us to push on, despite doubt and lack of evidence
Lent 6 (Palm Sunday)	Humility	Phil. 2:5–11	Christ calls us to obedience to the cross.
Easter Sunday	Victory	1 Cor. 15:19–26	God has overcome death and gives us victory.

of these texts explores a different component of Christian character that, when considered through the eyes of the cross, calls us to deeper obedience to Christ and fuller trust in Christ.

Tips and Ideas for This Series

Lent invites people to look below the surface of the masks and images they project for others to see, and to allow the Spirit to renew their character and their commitment to God's call. For a strong visual, consider revealing or adding a portion of an image each week to suggest these character traits coming together to form a faithful life. The resulting image might be a cross or a person in prayer.

Lent 1: Belief
Romans 10:8b–13

If you confess with your lips that Jesus is Lord and believe in your heart that God raised him from the dead, you will be saved. For one believes with the heart and so is justified, and one confesses with the mouth and so is saved. (Romans 10:9–10)

It should not surprise us that this Lenten journey with Paul begins with Romans. Of his many letters, Romans contains the most complete, most comprehensive articulation of Christian convictions. The lectionary's choice to begin Lent in Romans is a reminder to us that before we go any further on this journey to the cross, before we look at what a Christian does, we must remember what a Christian *believes*.

This book, after all, was formative to many significant influences throughout Christian history. Augustine heard a voice from a group of playing children next door telling him to "Pick up and read," only to discover an open Bible, turned to Romans. John Chrysostom had someone read the entire book of Romans to him two times every week. After a long period of struggling to find inner peace and the assurance of his own salvation, Martin Luther read Romans 1:17: "The just shall live by faith." He then experienced a peace with God and a confidence that his sins were forgiven. And John Wesley's hearing of Luther's commentary on Romans while attending a worship service on Aldersgate Street gave him a heartwarming assurance of God's free gift of grace for him.

For Paul, belief in Jesus was foundational. All other aspects of the spiritual life—character, charity, acts of piety and justice, community, and many others—are mere fruits of the basic convictions one has about God's grace and the assurances that come from it.

This sermon, then, might reiterate the basic message of the gospel:

we have been saved by God's grace alone, and our only response is to believe. That act of belief is not itself a work necessary for salvation, for believing is possible only because of God's grace at work in us. For us to begin the Lenten journey to the cross, we must believe in what the cross has done for us.

At the same time, we recognize that for many people, the journey of discipleship does not begin with belief, but with practice. Sometimes, as the saying goes, we have to practice it, not because we believe it, but *until* we believe it.

The end of the text reminds us that the product of belief is Christian unity. There is no longer Jew or Greek, for Jesus is the same Lord over all who believe. This conclusion to the text is an important reminder to us at a time when strong religious convictions can often divide us from other believers, and divide those of us inside the church from those outside the church, particularly when overlaid with cultural, political, and ideological divisions. But belief in Christ ought to unite us, not divide us, for we can affirm that despite whatever other peripheral differences we may have with each other, we have a common core of beliefs that hold us together. The goodness of God, the saving work of Jesus, and the authority of Scripture are just a few of those beliefs that can unite us. Ultimately, it is belief in the lordship of Jesus that rises above all our divisions.

Lent 2: Discipline
Philippians 3:17–4:1

Brothers and sisters, join in imitating me, and observe those who live according to the example you have in us. (Philippians 3:17)

Think about some of the more significant mentors, teachers, and spiritual influences in your life. It is likely that their impact on you was not just from what they said, but how they lived. They likely modeled for you the qualities and ideals that agreed with their words. I think of a Sunday school teacher who taught me about God's love for me through her gentle, loving demeanor. I think of a high school teacher who taught me humility through his acts of servanthood, empathy, and compassion. I think of a senior pastor whose sermons about justice and equality were backed up with letters to government officials and participation in nonviolent protest marches.

We might think that Paul's command to the Philippian church to "imitate" him was arrogant and presumptuous, that he was attempting to set himself on some kind of idealized pedestal. But Paul was not telling disciples to follow him, but directing people to follow Jesus, in the same way he was seeking to follow Jesus himself. In Paul's mind, to imitate him was to imitate Christ, not in a way that equated Paul and Christ, but to remind disciples of this important truth: To be a follower of Jesus means to follow the example of others, and to be an example for others.

This requires discipline, a quality that is at the heart of the Lenten journey. Discipline through imitation first involves a relationship between the disciple and the person doing the discipling. Who are the people in your life whom you would regard as spiritual mentors? What gives them the credibility to disciple you, and the authenticity for you to believe them? What nurtures the trust that you have in them? What motivates you to heed their guidance and their example?

Discipline also requires that you disciple others. It is not enough for you to mature in your faith if you do not in turn lead others in their discipleship. To be blessed without being a blessing for others is the difference between a vessel and a funnel. We are not intended to be mere recipients of God's grace. We are called to be dispensaries of God's grace, so that others can experience God's love through us. So that others can imitate us.

Finally, discipline requires "standing firm" (Phil. 4:1). That word for *stand* occurs many times throughout Paul's letters, each time connoting a toughness and fortitude through first grounding in God's ways. We are to stand in God's grace (Rom. 5:2), in the gospel (1 Cor. 10:12), and in God's will (Col. 4:12), so that we may stand firm against evil (Eph. 6:11).

Discipline requires imitation and conviction, to both follow and stand. In that way, God can "transform the body of our humiliation that it may be conformed to the body of his glory" (Phil. 3:21).

Lent 3: Holiness
1 Corinthians 10:1–13

We must not indulge in sexual immorality as some of them did, and twenty-three thousand fell in a single day. We must not put Christ to the test, as some of them did, and were destroyed by serpents. (1 Corinthians 10:8–9)

Any survey of Paul's Epistles must include his letters to Corinth, sometimes referred to as "the America of ancient Greece." It was an intercultural mix of ethnicities and backgrounds, in which ideas were strenuously debated in public forums. Some of the greatest Greek philosophers—Plato, Aristotle, and Socrates—had students that lived in the city.

Of all the churches that Paul birthed and nurtured, the Corinthian church became the most conflicted in the New Testament, despite his devoting more than a year of his life trying to make things work. The Corinthians were prone to infighting over many issues, from how members of the church should eat meat to how women should conduct themselves in worship and in public. There were arguments over which Christians were the most valuable in the church, and over the purpose of spiritual gifts. There were heavy disagreements over the matter of sexual purity and morality, in a city where such morals were ignored. And there were even disagreements over which teacher they were followers of: Paul, or Peter, or Apollos.

You can imagine that as Paul is writing this letter, he is hearing all the debates that these church members are having with one another. This is a church that is about to fracture at the seams, threatening to undo months of hard work, in a city that could not afford to lose an important witness for Jesus Christ.

It might not be a stretch for a preacher to make many connections to the polarized character of the body of Christ today. In a wider culture divided by political and ideological issues, and a church fractured along multiple theological fault lines, the fractured condition of the Corinthians is alive and well today.

Paul offers a few pathways to healing these divisions. First, he reminds them of their common heritage. They are all descendants of the same spiritual ancestors, whose faithfulness was nourished through the same spiritual "food," "drink," and "rock." Second, he tells them that they can all share a lesson from the mistakes of their ancestors. He tells them that the ancient Israelites were prone to idolatry (the worship of a false god) and complaining (a failure to trust in the true God). The preacher might identify evidence in both the congregation and the culture of ways that the temptations of idolatry and complaining are evident.

Ultimately, Paul offers the Corinthians a uniting call to holiness. He identifies sexual immorality as the source of profound downfall for the ancient Israelites, and equates the succumbing to such temptation as "putting Christ to the test." He then offers them hope, reminding them that regardless of the temptation they might face to compromise their personal and relational holiness, God will be faithful to give them what they need to overcome it.

Regardless of the differences that Christians might have with each other, they can share a united goal to live in personal and interpersonal holiness with each other. That mutual desire to love one another can indeed heal many wounds.

Lent 4: Reconciliation
2 Corinthians 5:16–21

So if anyone is in Christ, there is a new creation: everything old has passed away; see, everything has become new! All this is from God, who reconciled us to himself through Christ, and has given us the ministry of reconciliation; that is, in Christ God was reconciling the world to himself, not counting their trespasses against them, and entrusting the message of reconciliation to us. (2 Corinthians 5:17–19)

The text begins with a compelling verse: "From now on, therefore, we regard no one from a human point of view." In contrast to the way human merit is typically measured, Paul invites the church to consider a deeper criterion, namely, the orientation of one's heart toward God.

The preacher might explore this contrast by making connections with contemporary culture. Consider the ways that the world of advertising and marketing defines success and beauty. Or the preferential treatment our culture offers the powerful at the expense of the poor, outcast, and marginalized. Or our intrinsic infatuation with celebrities.

Instead, Paul says that from now on, those standards must be superseded by a focus on the transformation that is possible through the work of Jesus Christ. "Everything old has passed away; see, everything has become new!" What might life be like for us to shift away from the more superficial standards of merit, and toward a celebration of resurrection in those who have discovered new life, hope, and possibility? Might the former addict celebrating twenty-five years of sobriety be celebrated more than the actor making 25 million dollars per film? Might the former hedge-fund manager who walked away from a seven-digit salary to take the helm of a nonprofit be as praised as the reality television star? Might the teacher who works overtime to tutor at-risk youth be as notable as the Washington, DC, power broker?

For Paul, this is what transformation from "old" to "new" looks like: a radical alteration of priorities and perspectives to be more in line with the way and will of God—a reconciliation of our hearts and minds with the heart and mind of God.

All of this is possible because of what God has done for us in Jesus Christ. God no longer counts our trespasses against us (v. 19) and now entrusts us with the task of calling others to reconciliation with God. We are, in Paul's terminology, "ambassadors for Christ," who bear witness to the redemptive, transformative possibilities in others by sharing what God has done and is doing in ourselves.

What might it mean to be this kind of ambassador? The preacher might consider what modern-day ambassadors do, even in the context of the modern political world. An ambassador is different from the national leader who governs the country, but is entrusted with the full authority to speak and act on its behalf. An ambassador for Jesus, then, is not to be equated with God, but does have the capability to represent God's heart and embody God's love before others. An ambassador chooses to live in a foreign country, just as Christians are called to live as "aliens and strangers" in a world that feels antithetical to the message of Jesus. And an ambassador builds relationships with foreign leaders and citizens, all for forging new understandings and pathways to peace. As ambassadors, we are called to be in relationship with others, so that the love of God might be fully revealed in us, shared with others, and set the foundation for peace. We are reconciled to God, and are called to reconcile others to God in Christ. That is the ministry of reconciliation.

Lent 5: Faith
Philippians 3:4b–14

I want to know Christ and the power of his resurrection and the sharing of his sufferings by becoming like him in his death, if somehow I may attain the resurrection from the dead. Not that I have already obtained this or have already reached the goal; but I press on to make it my own, because Christ Jesus has made me his own. (Philippians 3:10–12)

In the opening verses of the passage, Paul checks off all the typical boxes one would use to fill out an impressive resume. He affirms the prestige of his lineage, pedigree, nationality, occupation, and character. To hear him describe himself, we might imagine that he would be a sure bet to appear on *Time* magazine's list of "Most Influential People" or to be a *People* magazine "Celebrity of the Year." But in quintessential fashion, Paul's argument zigs where we expect it to zag. He reverses cultural expectations by interpreting his noteworthy background as a liability, rather than an achievement: "Yet whatever gains I had, these I have come to regard as loss because of Christ."

We can hear in this verse echoes of Jesus in the Gospels, who told the disciples that to be first, they needed to be last, and that they needed to lose their lives to gain them. Paul is upending conventional wisdom to point to one of the chief principles of living in God's kingdom: it is not about us, and all about Christ.

He takes this idea one step further in his powerfully transparent admission in verses 10–11: "I want to know Christ and the power of his resurrection and the sharing of his sufferings by becoming like him in his death, if somehow I may attain the resurrection from the dead."

It is hard to imagine the apostle Paul saying these things. The greatest missionary the church would ever know is admitting that he does not have a complete grasp of the mysteries of Christ. He does not say, "I know all about Christ," or "I have full and utter confidence in everything there is to understand about the Christian faith." In saying, "I want to know Christ and the power of his resurrection," he is not only admitting his limitations; he is appealing to God's grace to overcome them.

This is a liberating and empowering word for a preacher to offer everyone in the congregation, regardless of the stage of their spiritual maturity. For the newcomer to the faith, it is a reminder that God's grace has saved them, no matter how noteworthy or sinful their lives have been prior. For the longtime follower of Christ, it is a reminder that if Paul himself had room to grow in his faith, so does everyone. It is not only permissible but healthy to admit one's shortcomings.

By doing so, we remember how little we can depend on our own merits and accomplishments to mature in our discipleship, and how much we need God's grace and power to take the next step. It is why Paul can end this passage with the beautifully visceral and muscular reminder to press forward: "This one thing I do: forgetting what lies behind and straining forward to what lies ahead, I press on toward the goal for the prize of the heavenly call of God in Christ Jesus."

Lent 6 (Palm Sunday): Humility
Philippians 2:5–11

He humbled himself
and became obedient to the point of death—
even death on a cross. (Philippians 2:8)

As we enter the passion and drama of Holy Week, we fix our attention on the events leading up to the death of Jesus, his imminent self-giving sacrifice on the cross. We remember not only his words, actions, and interactions; this text from Philippians invites us to remember his mind-set, his deep-down motivation for why he did what he did. And it is a reminder for us to follow his example.

Philippians 2 contains what is widely considered to be one of the very first hymns in Christian history. It is a hymn about how Jesus Christ fully emptied himself, assumed the fullness of the human condition, and demonstrated a remarkable obedience that produced salvation for all.

Paul quotes this hymn to make an important point: To be like Jesus, we need to have the mind of Jesus, which never seeks its own ambition and always seeks to be a servant. In a world filled with upward, dog-eat-dog mobility, in which we climb up the ladder on the backs of those who are weaker, Paul reminds the Philippians that greatness is defined by a downward mobility that seeks to serve others.

To be like Jesus is to assume a mind-set of humility.

Fully understanding what humility means is critical to interpreting this text. Some may have a distorted view of what it means to be humble. If boasting is seeing oneself as "everything," it is tempting to equate humility with seeing oneself as "nothing." But being humble does not mean minimizing one's own talents and abilities or thinking that everyone else is better than you. Humility is not to be equated with low self-esteem or poor self-worth.

Instead, consider the etymology of *humility*. It comes from the Latin word *humus*, which literally means "dirt." To be humble means to see oneself as grounded, drawn from the earth, connected to all of life, no better and no worse than the rest of all creation.

To be humble means that you are linked to every other living creature on earth, and you are as dependent on others as they are on you. You cannot claim to be better than anyone else because you depend on others, and you are no worse than anyone else because others depend on you.

Here is another way of looking at it: You are never as bad as you think you are, and you are never as good as other people say you are. The converse is true as well: You are never as good as you think you are, and you are never as bad as others say you are. In other words, the appropriate balance between ego and self-abasement is always remembering that your value is neither found in what you think of yourself nor dependent on the affirmation that people give you. True humility is the gift of seeing yourself the way God sees you, and seeing yourself as part of an interconnected dependence on the lives of people with you and around you.

Easter Sunday: Victory
1 Corinthians 15:19–26

But in fact Christ has been raised from the dead, the first fruits of those who have died. . . . The last enemy to be destroyed is death. (1 Corinthians 15:20, 26)

There is a Greek legend told of Sisyphus, a mortal who fell out of favor with Zeus, king of the gods. Zeus sentenced him to spending the rest of his life in the underworld, with one and only one task to accomplish—to push a gigantic rock up and over a hill.

During his first attempt, he started at the base of the mountain, trying with all his might to move it up the steep slope. He succeeded at getting it near the top, almost over the hill, but he was fatigued and the weight of the rock and the pull of gravity caused the rock to tumble back to the base of the hill.

Over and over again, Sisyphus tried to push the rock over the hill, each time coming close to getting it to the top. But every time, the same thing occurred, and the rock came tumbling back down. As legend has it, he is still pushing to this day.

The story is an apt opening for Easter morning, in which a connection can be made to the women concerned about how they will roll away the stone sealing Jesus' tomb. And it is also a fitting metaphor for the human condition, in which we are prone to feel overcome by forces and influences beyond our power to defeat them.

But the text from 1 Corinthians proclaims the good news of Easter: Christ has been raised, and the final enemy—death—has been destroyed. In Christ, we can have a victory that could not be won on our own.

Theologian Alister McGrath recounts a story of a man who served in the army during World War II.[1] He was captured and imprisoned as a POW in a Japanese prison camp. Day after day, the man wondered whether he was going to die or live to see another day. He wondered what has happening to his fallen comrades, whether they were still alive, whether they were even there in the same prison camp. And he wondered how the war was going on out in the rest of the world. Were they winning? Were they being beaten back? What was happening?

Then the man received word. One of the other prisoners was listening to a short-wave radio one day when the word was broadcast. The Japanese had just surrendered. The Allied forces had won. Victory has just been guaranteed. Having heard the news, he sat there in disbelief. Then he rejoiced.

Then the man realized that nothing about his situation had really changed. It would eventually take weeks for the prisoners to be found in their prison camp in Singapore and eventually released. In the meantime, they were still there, living with rationed food, in inhumane conditions, in the presence of their tormentors and their captors.

1. Alister McGrath, *What Was God Doing on the Cross?* (Grand Rapids: Zondervan. 1992).

But even though their day-to-day problems had not changed, there was something about the guarantee of victory that changed their perspective and their outlook. They knew that even though their situation seemed the same, in the grand scheme of things victory was assured, and they were not going to be in this condition forever.

Soon the attitude of the prisoners changed. They were still prisoners, but they acted free. They celebrated, they sang songs. They laughed and they cried together. For they knew that their victory was assured.

Easter Series:
Living with the End in Mind

Seven Parts: Second Sunday of Easter through
Pentecost Sunday

*Revelation's guide to embodying our faith as a resurrection
people.*

MAGREY R. DeVEGA

Series Overview The book of Revelation contains some of the most cryptic language
and most fanciful imagery in the entire Bible. It has been used to
try to forecast the events of the end times, as well as to call hopeless
Christians to fortitude and endurance. Its lectionary placement in

	Sermon Title	Focus Scripture	Theme
Easter 2	Beginning with the End	Rev. 1:4–8	Revelation calls us to hope and endurance for today.
Easter 3	A Vision of Worship	Rev. 5:11–14	Through worship, we embody and enact eternity.
Easter 4	A Vision of the Church	Rev. 7:9–17	Revelation offers an ideal picture of the church that we can work to become today.
Easter 5	A God of New Beginnings	Rev. 21:1–6	Resurrection is not just an event in the past, but an ongoing work of God.
Easter 6	Heaven Here and Now	Rev. 21:10, 22–22:5	Heaven is not just a hope for tomorrow; it is a promise to be claimed now.
Easter 7	Come, Lord Jesus!	Rev. 22:12–14, 16–17, 20–21	No matter what we go through in life, hope in Christ is at hand.
Pentecost Sunday	Now Is the Time	Acts 2:1–21	The Holy Spirit empowers us to live out the resurrection today.

the season of Easter is notable, as it draws us to another contemporary application of this book: as a guide to experiencing the resurrected life. John's vision allows us to see the world, the church, and the Christian life in the way God envisions it: not for how it is, but for how it can be. And each week, through the power of the one who makes all things new, we are called to make those possibilities a resurrection reality.

Tips and Ideas for This Series

Revelation was originally circulated as a letter to churches, intended to be read aloud in gathered community. To give the congregation the full flavor of how these texts might have been first experienced, each text might be memorized and rendered by a storyteller. Graphics and social-media promotion might also be filled with the kinds of vivid imagery that are evident in the texts.

Given the misconceptions, mystery, and confusion that often surround the book of Revelation, consider offering a Bible study during this season to explore the book more fully, or even a one-night "Revelation 101" class.

Easter 2: Beginning with the End
Revelation 1:4–8

"I am the Alpha and the Omega," says the Lord God, who is and who was and who is to come, the Almighty. (Revelation 1:8)

Revelation is most popularly interpreted to be a literal prediction of the future and the events that will unfold at the end of time. That interpretation is a view advanced by the nineteenth-century preacher John Nelson Darby, who developed the notion of dispensationalism as a way of predicting the actual second coming of Jesus.

A major critique of this interpretation is that it becomes far too easy to be apathetic and lazy in the face of world crises. If one believes that international tensions and hostilities between countries are signs of the end times, as "wars and rumors of wars," then what is the motivation for the church to work for peace? If we believe that mounting crises in the environment, global poverty, AIDS, and suffering of all kinds are simply part of the end game of human history, then why try to deal with them?

But God has not called the church to be sideline spectators of global chaos. Instead, we are called to be agents of healing, hope, and justice, over against the forces of evil and destruction.

So, rather than look at Revelation predictively, a better option is to view it contextually. What was the message of Revelation to the early church community that first heard John's vision?

We remember that the community to which Revelation was written was under intense persecution by the Roman Empire. People died because of their profession of faith in Christ; so Christians often had to meet in fearful seclusion.

The book of Revelation is filled with veiled language acknowledging the terror of the empire; it names Caesar, the Roman military, and the government establishment with colorful, dreamlike, terrifying language. Over and against this vivid imagery, a simple theme runs throughout the book to the Christian church: Don't give up. Hope is coming. Victory will be yours in the end. Have patience. Endure suffering. Persevere.

Read in that light, the book of Revelation becomes less a book about the end of time and more a word of encouragement for us today.

In a time when demonic forces of violence, injustice, and oppression assault us from all sides, in a time when we are tempted to mute our convictions about peace and forgiveness, and stifle our prophetic message of justice and social change, the book of Revelation calls the church to hang in there, not give up, and not stop being a witness for Jesus, because God will see us through to the end.

Revelation also reminds us that as God always sides with the oppressed, so should we. It contains a challenging question for today's Christians: with whom do you identify more, the persecuted church or the Roman persecutors? Are you in a position of privilege, prestige, and self-made power, or are you in the position of self-sacrificial, self-giving love? Are you on the side of the love of power, or on the side of powerless love?

Regardless of how and when Jesus comes back, we are left a mission that constitutes our daily purpose and consumes our daily energies: to side with God's activity in the work of the kingdom, reaching out to those desperate, desolate, and deserted.

Easter 3: A Vision of Worship
Revelation 5:11–14

Then I looked, and I heard the voice of many angels surrounding the throne and the living creatures and the elders; they numbered myriads of myriads and thousands of thousands, singing with full voice, "Worthy is the Lamb that was slaughtered to receive power and wealth and wisdom and might and honor and glory and blessing!" (Revelation 5:11–12)

The focal point of this text from Revelation is a throne. We do not know anything about it at first, as John does not reveal much right away. Instead of telling us what is on that throne, John prefers to tell us what is around it. First, there are angels: otherworldly beings that suggest that there is something supernatural, something extraordinary, about to be revealed here.

John also tells us that all the living creatures are there. Dogs, elephants, hyenas, praying mantises, muskrats, and turtles. All of them. Whatever this scene is, it apparently has captured the attention of all creation. But in case we think this is all too weird to believe, John tells us that there are also human beings here. Just regular, ordinary, common Joes and Janes. Not just one or two, but a legion of them—"thousands upon thousands," according to Revelation 5.

What John is painting here is a picture of concentric circles. There are angels in the inner ring, then an outer ring of animals and living creatures. And an external ring of a massive crowd of people. And it all centers on a focal point.

Finally, John reveals that in the center is a Lamb sitting on the throne. It is an unmistakable reference to Jesus, the slaughtered Lamb who has now ascended as ruler of all living things. Every creature—in the upper decks of heaven, observing creation from the balcony seats, all the way down into the lowest depths of the oceans, where life should not survive but somehow finds a way—is united in proclamation. There is no corner or nook or cranny that does not contain some part of creation that is in universal agreement that there is one and only one who sits on that throne.

Now what does this scene mean? What did it mean to those who originally heard it, and what does it mean to us? John's portrait proclaims this fundamental truth: you are not the one who sits on that throne.

It is our human tendency to put ourselves there. We like to think that we are the center of the universe. There might be days when we think that the only problems that matter are the ones affecting us, the ones we are dealing with. We get so wrapped up in our own issues that we think we are the only ones who matter.

But John tells us squarely in Revelation 5 that whenever we fall for those ideas, we fall for the lie that suggests that we are the ones who are sitting on that throne. That all the company of heaven bows at our feet, and all the living creatures listen to our commands, and all the people in our lives and in our world bend to our whims and our discretions.

Instead, it is all about the one who gave his life for us. This entire vision is not just about the end of time; it is about keeping our priorities straight in the present. Life is not about pleasing oneself. It is about living a worshipful life that is pleasing to and honoring God.

Easter 4: A Vision of the Church
Revelation 7:9–17

After this I looked, and there was a great multitude that no one could count, from every nation, from all tribes and peoples and languages, standing before the throne and before the Lamb, robed in white, with palm branches in their hands. (Revelation 7:9)

What a great image. It is a gathering of people who have come to worship. It is a church service, if you will, when all the believers have entered the presence of the Lamb of God, seated on the throne. It is a community defined by three primary characteristics.

First, the passage says there is a great multitude, a big crowd, more people than anyone can count. And they are diverse, from all walks of life, from all nations, speaking all languages. This vision of the church is one where all people, regardless of race, gender, sexuality, age, socioeconomic status, and background are included in this grand cosmic party. It is a community of diversity.

Second, we are told that they are all robed in white. There are not some dressed in fine linens and royal jewels, nor some dressed in rags or strips of cloth. Despite their diversity, there is equality. This community of the future is one in which all stand before the throne of grace as equally redeemed by God. A community of equality.

Third, we are told that they hold in their hands palm branches. It is an unmistakable reference to the palm branches of the triumphal entry of Jesus. This community of the future is single-minded in its purpose: to give praise to God, the true source of their victory, the object of their worship. This community of the future, this community of the end of time, is one of diversity, equality, and praise.

Our instincts would interpret this as a vision for the future. But the early Christians who first heard these words would have understood them to be less about the future, and more about the possibilities of the present. Like a football coach giving a fiery pep talk to a team down at halftime, John is coaching the early Christians to imagine a future in which persecution from Rome is defeated, and victory in God is secured. And then he tells them to go out and make that future vision a reality.

So what is the playbook for the church today? What is the game plan God has given us to make that future vision a reality now?

First, John calls us to become a church of diversity. A church that reaches out to people who have long felt shunned by the church because they were thought to be the "wrong" kind of people. The future prompts us to believe that we can become a body of Christ more numerous than the eye can see, from all walks of life, from all ends of the earth.

Second, John tells the church to be a community of equality. In a country where power hierarchies stoke desires for upward mobility, we must be a church that proclaims that all are equal. We are all children of God. We are all connected to one another, regardless of our past, regardless of our material, physical, or intellectual merit. In a world that preaches "moving to the top" and "getting ahead," we need to preach downward mobility: being servants to one another, considering each other as equals, treating others as we would want to be treated ourselves. There is no one who deserves to be shunned from the church. And there is no one who deserves to be second-rate in the church.

Third, we must strive to be a community of praise today. A church that is clear about its priorities. Not becoming more club-like, but more Christlike; not becoming more self-centered, but more Christ-centered; a church that directs the world toward the glory of the risen Jesus.

John tells the church to go out into the world, into the face of persecution, where the odds are stacked against you, and make it happen.

Easter 5: A God of New Beginnings
Revelation 21:1–6

And the one who was seated on the throne said, "See, I am making all things new." Also he said, "Write this, for these words are trustworthy and true." (Revelation 21:5)

John reminds the early Christians that "'the home of God is among mortals. He will dwell with them; they will be his peoples'" (Rev. 21:3). It is a statement that resembles the way the Gospel of John describes Jesus, who was the Word who became flesh and dwelled among us. In both Revelation and the Gospel, God is intimately connected to humanity, not transcendent, distant, and apathetic. What that means is that none of us is spiritually orphaned. God has claimed us, and we belong to God. It is an idea reinforced throughout the Bible in the linguistic formula of covenant: God will be our God, and we will be God's people. Despite possible evidence to the contrary all around us, we are not alone in dealing with our sufferings. God is with us, and has chosen to be in a special relationship with God's people. The preacher may wish to remind the congregation that no matter what they go through in life, they can remember that they belong to God, and God will not let them go.

But there is a second emphasis in God's character in this passage. Not only is God intimately connected to us; God is making all things new. In a way, this is a concept that comes full circle in the Scriptures. For if the very first thing we learn about God in the Bible is that God created all things, it is also the very last thing we learn about God, here in the book of Revelation.

The passage does not say that God has made everything new. It does not say that God will make everything new. It says God *is making* all things new. God has already started transforming our lives, God is currently transforming our lives, and God will not stop transforming the pain, heartache, and dark places of our lives until the moment when the transformation reaches ultimate completion in glory.

This is a God of tenacity, purpose, and diligence. It is the God that Paul described to the Philippians: "the one who began a good work among you will bring it to completion" (Phil. 1:6).

The passage concludes with an emphatic command: "Write this, for these words are trustworthy and true." In a time when skepticism prevails and we are reluctant to trust our human institutions of power, politics, economics, and military strength, John reminds us of God's promises. They are not only true; they are trustworthy. They can be trusted, not because of the preponderance of evidence around us, but because of the faithfulness of God. We can believe these words, even though it still appears that darkness prevails, because God will always deliver on the promises that God has made.

These two basic promises—that we are God's people, and that God is still working in our lives—can give us a profound sense of hope amid our pain, and comfort amid our suffering.

Easter 6: Heaven Here and Now
Revelation 21:10, 22–22:5

I saw no temple in the city, for its temple is the Lord God the Almighty and the Lamb. And the city has no need of sun or moon to shine on it, for the glory of God is its light, and its lamp is the Lamb. (Revelation 21:22–23)

The popular way to interpret Revelation 21:22–22:5 is to see it as a prediction of heaven, conceiving it as a physical place literally depicted by the images in this passage. But the deeper meaning of this passage is in the way it proclaims the ultimate triumph of God in our everyday lives, here and now. It does so through two central metaphors: the light and the tree.

First, it offers a vivid portrayal of the culmination of God's kingdom, in which there is no need for natural or manufactured light. It is an echo of the many instances in the Bible where God's glory is referred to as the light of the world. The prophets say, "Arise, shine, for your light has come!" and "The people in darkness have seen a great light." John's Gospel opens by proclaiming that in Jesus "was life, and the life was the light of all people." It is God's glory alone that offers the world the only light that it needs to overcome all darkness.

These words contrast with the opening of Genesis, in which God separates the darkness and the light, to create day and night. Here in Revelation, God not only separates out the darkness, but conquers it, obliterates it, so that "there will be no night there."

Given the brokenness of the world today, it might be easier to imagine God's activity in Genesis than in Revelation. We might much more readily believe a strategy in which God separates out the darkness, keeps it at bay, holds it in check. That, after all, seems like the best we can do against the seemingly indomitable forces of injustice, oppression, sin, and suffering.

But that is not what John's vision claims. God's aim is to render darkness impotent, in light of the glory of God. This can be a profound word of hope for everyone in the world who feels as if the darkness around them is insurmountable, and that the night draws longer and longer upon them. God's glory revealed in Jesus can provide comfort, strength, and encouragement to believe in brighter days ahead and to work to make that vision a reality.

But the vision continues, shifting metaphors from the light toward the image of a tree. Again, the tree of life in Revelation echoes the book of Genesis, in which the tree of the knowledge of good and evil becomes the impetus for humanity's downfall. Here in Revelation, the tree is a symbol of ultimate redemption. All that humanity has lost in its downward spiral of sin is reclaimed and transformed by the power of God's grace and power. "Nothing accursed will be found there anymore," verse 3 proclaims.

The preacher might build the sermon on these two chief metaphors, light and tree, and offer the congregation the possibility that heaven is not just a place we can anticipate in the future, but a reality we can experience here and now, as the light of God and the fruit of God's goodness vanquish our darkness and fill our spirits today.

Easter 7: Come, Lord Jesus!
Revelation 22:12–14, 16–17, 20–21

"See, I am coming soon; my reward is with me, to repay according to everyone's work. I am the Alpha and the Omega, the first and the last, the beginning and the end." . . . The Spirit and the bride say, "Come." And let everyone who hears say, "Come." And let everyone who is thirsty come. Let anyone who wishes take the water of life as a gift. (Revelation 22:12–13,17)

This text from Revelation is the closing to the entire Bible. These final words offer the lasting, lingering impression within our hearts and minds, prompting us to consider the scope of the whole biblical narrative. "I am the Alpha and the Omega, the first and the last, the beginning and the end," Jesus says.

What is it that we have seen and heard from the beginning of Genesis, and all throughout the Bible? In Genesis and Exodus, we see a God who is able to create order out of chaos, life out of lifelessness, and hope out of despair. In the time of the Israelites, we have seen a God who is faithful to the covenant, dealing justly and graciously with God's people. In the exile, we see a God who does not forget the downtrodden, and leads them home. In the Gospels, we see the fullest expression of God's love, revealed in the words, way, and Spirit of Jesus. And in the epistles, we see a God of relentless grace, who broadens the expanse of the kingdom beyond boundaries and divisions.

In other words, at just the right time, and in just the right way, God consistently breaks through the brokenness and disorder of the human condition and brings us hope and possibility.

These last words in Revelation, then, are more than a conclusion. They are a recap of the Bible's most central theme, and a promise to those who choose to live out its truths moving forward. Stay faithful to the way, and even when all seems lost, the hope of Christ comes to you.

In these seven verses, the words *come* and *coming*, which appear six times, are the key rhetorical element. The image of Jesus coming again soon, amid conditions of hopelessness and despair, conjures archetypal ideas of the cavalry sweeping in to save the day, or the mighty hero coming in to save the people, or the closer coming in to finish the game.

But it is more than that. The truth in this text is not just the assurance that Jesus will come in to save the day, but it is that we must *never stop believing* that there is hope in Christ, and we must *never behave* in a way that contradicts that hope. "See, I am coming soon; my reward is with me, *to repay according to everyone's work.*" This hope that we claim in Christ is an active hope, not a passive one. We who are on the battlefields of hardship and heartache must continue in the struggle, never giving in to apathy, and we must endure to the end. We must *work*. In the immortal saying of Martin Luther King Jr: "The arc of the universe is long, but it bends toward justice."

"Blessed are those who wash their robes, so that they will have the right to the tree of life and may enter the city by the gates" (Rev. 22:14). In other words, keep washing, keep purifying, stay on the right path. Even when our lives have been soiled and torn by the effects of injustice, we must walk the path of integrity, and stay true to the cleansing waters of our baptismal calling, and resist evil, injustice, and oppression.

Yes, the good news is that the cavalry is coming. But we must not lapse into apathy, and we must remain steadfast until the end.

Pentecost Sunday: Now Is the Time
Acts 2:1–21

And at this sound, the crowd gathered and was bewildered, because each one heard them speaking in the native language of each. Amazed and astonished, they asked, "Are not all these speaking Galileans?" . . . All were amazed and perplexed, saying to one another, "What does this mean?" (Act 2:6–7, 12)

In May 2018, a brief audio clip of a computer-generated voice went viral on social media. People were divided over what word the voice was uttering, and were generally in two camps: "Laurel" or "Yanny," two very different words. Audiologists, who study the science and mechanics of hearing, pointed out that what a person heard depended on the specific audio frequency their ears were most attuned to hearing. For those of us who heard "Laurel," it was unfathomable how others could hear "Yanny." And vice versa.

The very idea that different people could come to two different conclusions about the same objective experience is bewildering. In those moments, everything we assumed about our ability to stake a claim on truth is challenged. This is disorienting.

When the Spirit of Pentecost touched the earth and birthed the church, it was similarly disorienting: wind and fire and a cacophony of voices from all the corners of the known world. In an instant, all those prior demographic, ethnic, and ideological boxes, like Medes, Elamites, Persians—Yanny-ites and Laurel-ites—were torn down, and people were able to see the experience empathetically, through the lens, perspective, and language of a person who was different from them.

At the end of the event, the people admitted their disorientation, and they asked, "What does this mean?"

Pentecost Sunday gives us the opportunity not only to remember the birth of the church but to affirm its witness to unity amid our global diversity and its call to empathy in our differences with one another.

The preacher may choose to identify a list of ways that the congregation or the community at large is polarized into entrenched camps of different perspectives on particular issues. The preacher can then remind them that the Spirit comes to break us out of those boxes not only to understand each other better, but to unite together in Christ to love God and one another. How might racial tensions be eased by a call to empathy? How might environmental stewardship be addressed beyond binary choices of pro-earth or pro-business? How might the growing gap between rich and poor become more than an either/or choice of "giving a man a fish" and "teaching a man to fish"? How might Pentecost break through the tired boxes of our political parties and partisan bickering?

In many ways, people around the world might ask the same questions as the people of the first Pentecost: What does this mean? What does it mean to see the old tribes that define us suddenly dissolve? What does it mean for the dogma that we thought was universal suddenly to be challenged by other possibilities? What does it mean for our boxes of assumptions to be blown apart, and the walls that divided us suddenly come down?

Such breakthroughs would be difficult, disorienting, and even painful. But such an alternative view of community is inherent to the church, since its inception. At the end of chapter 2, after the drama of Pentecost had settled, and Peter preached a sermon that called people to commitment to Jesus, the result was a unified church, in which polarization gave way to mission: "All the believers were together and had everything in common."

Summer Series 1: Called In

Seven Parts: Proper 6 through Proper 12

How God can use our mistakes, weaknesses, and experiences to help us grow.

JASPER PETERS

Series Overview Proverbs 3 asks us not to despise the Lord's discipline, as it is a sign of love for us. We find these signs of God's love everywhere. Sometimes we find them in moments that call us out in terms of our actions or behaviors. We also find them in moments that call us in—inviting us

	Sermon Title	Focus Scripture	Theme
Proper 6	Called to Repentance	2 Sam. 11:26–12:10, 13–15	How does God help us to see ourselves when we have made a big mistake?
Proper 7	Called to Self-Care	1 Kgs. 19:1–4 (5–7), 8–15a	We are never left alone, even when all seems lost.
Proper 8	Called to Connection	2 Kgs. 2:1–2, 6–14	Mentors are essential to our growth, especially in matters of faith.
Proper 9	Called to Comfort	Isa. 66:10–14	Maternal figures call us in, offer us comfort, and remind us of our worth.
Proper 10	Called to Humility	Amos 7:7–17	When we can't trust our instincts, how does God let us know right from wrong?
Proper 11	Called to Transformation	Col. 1:15–28	Can enemies become friends? How God can transform our worst inclinations into tools of blessing.
Proper 12	Called to Belonging	Col. 2:6–15 (16–19)	The past can haunt us. How God erases our transgressions and makes room for us to be a new creation.

back into right relationship. This series explores the ways in which God continues to call us in to community, and to divine relationship. Sometimes being called in means being called away from areas where we have clearly done wrong, caused harm, or fallen short. In other moments, God may simply be working to refine us further, encouraging us to continue on a path toward faithful maturity. In every instance, however, God is inviting us into something better, fuller, and more holy.

Tips and Ideas for This Series

Begin by explaining the difference between calling someone out (forcefully challenging someone's words or actions) and calling someone in (inviting someone, through conversation and relationship, to consider a better way). There is an abundance of room for personalization and examples from your community to illustrate this principle as it relates to each weekly theme. Songs like "Consider the Ravens" by Dustin Kersrue and "God Our Mother" by The Liturgists would support well the themes of Proper 7 and 9, respectively. Create a plumb line using a weight and a string for Proper 10. You may consider creating enough for your entire congregation using fishing line and lead fishing weights.

Proper 6: Called to Repentance
2 Samuel 11:26–12:10, 13–15

Then David's anger was greatly kindled against the man. He said to Nathan, "As the LORD lives, the man who has done this deserves to die." . . . Nathan said to David, "You are the man!" (2 Samuel 12:5, 7a)

In the fall of 2017, a decade-old phrase gained widespread attention across the internet. Women who have experienced sexual harassment and assault began to share their stories with heart-wrenching honesty. These statements are bound together by the simple yet powerful words: #metoo. As much as the #metoo movement is about women's stories and experiences, it may also be seen as an examination of the ways in which men have wrongly wielded power and violence against women. Over and over, women used powerful narratives to expose truths that are close to home. One aim of this movement is to call abusers to account.

In today's Scripture, God's displeasure is clearly stated, and we see the prophet Nathan dispatched to call David to account. As the congregation examines David's sinful actions, the preacher would be wise to thoughtfully consider the ways in which this contemporary movement might come to bear on their community.

Though the king cannot see the fault within himself, the prophetic advisor uses a powerful narrative to expose a truth that is close to home. Self-examination and awareness are born as a result of consistent work and discipline. Discipleship and Christian maturity can be understood not by lack of harm done, but by the ability to repent when harm is done. It requires a trust that, in Christ, transgression is a precursor to transformation, not to condemnation.

Nathan's goal was not simply to call David *out*, but to call him *in*, to invite him to repent and reenter right relationship. It was not God's will that David be dismissed but, rather, that his restoration might be deeply connected to understanding the harm he had caused. Those in recovery communities are eventually encouraged to "[make] a list of all persons [they] had harmed, and became willing to make amends to them all." If David's royal power had acted as an intoxicant, Nathan's call to account was the welcome, yet painful, call to sobriety.

For the king, making amends was a complex matter: was his debt to the now-dead Uriah, to his widow Bathsheba, to the people of Israel, or to God? Though one might assume an exclusively divine focus (as asserted in Ps. 51:4, said to be written out of David's repentance), a deeper examination of the Scripture creates a deep link between the harm incurred by David's human victims and God's displeasure. Precisely because David hurt people, he has simultaneously disappointed God.

Much like David, when we are in the position to repent and seek out restored relationship, we must first assume and admit responsibility for the harm. In some cases, a simple acknowledgment is enough to start down the path of healing. In other cases, it is not possible to heal the wounds of the past. In the case of a death, where communicating is not possible, redemption comes through a commitment not to repeat the same mistakes. "The sacrifice acceptable to God is a broken spirit; a broken and contrite heart, O God, you will not despise" (Ps. 51:17).

Proper 7: Called to Self-Care
1 Kings 19:1–4 (5–7), 8–15a

The angel of the LORD came a second time, touched him, and said, "Get up and eat, otherwise the journey will be too much for you." (1 Kings 19:7)

"Hell is other people." This was famously declared in the play *No Exit*, by French existentialist philosopher Jean-Paul Sartre. His characters discover that torture can be experienced not only through overt punishment, but also through consistent exposure to the irksome habits of those around you. Perhaps this sentiment is familiar to the prophet Elijah as he flees into the wilderness. Though the journey is precipitated by death threats, he quickly exposes a distaste for the flaws of his compatriots. Though the entire nation of Israel has been called to obedience to the Lord's decrees, Elijah is convinced that he alone stands faithful.

Elijah seems to find his destination unintentionally, yet the location has significance. Beer-sheba might be translated as "oath." It is said to be where Abraham and Abimelech ended their conflict and made a new covenant of peace (Gen. 21:31). If this place is full of God's providence, then we might see Elijah's journey beyond it as a physical representation of the abandonment that he feels; the peaceful promises of God have been left behind. Precisely in the moment Elijah chooses to run away, God chooses to call him in, drawing him in from physical and emotional isolation.

It is here, in this place set apart, that Elijah admits to himself and to God that he would rather be dead than continue to feel alone. Though the preacher may be tempted to engage God's presence and direction a few verses later, she would be remiss not to consider the weight felt by a person considering suicide. Even if Elijah's statement is hyperbolic, these moments of despair, waiting on the presence of the Lord, create an opportunity to name the real mental-health concerns that exist within every faith community. To name the reality that even a prophet of the Lord might experience seasons of despair and hopelessness may create an opportunity for the listeners honestly to face their own struggles.

After the prophet succumbs to sleep, an angelic presence directly addresses Elijah. Though he would welcome it, he does not receive divine wisdom, nor an answer to satisfy his deepest questions. Instead, a simple directive: "Get up and eat." This is followed by another round of eating and sleeping. We must wonder how long it has been since the prophet has eaten or slept before this time. How often are we surprised by the simplicity of God's providence? Though we might desire answers from the Divine to life's most difficult questions, what may really be needed is the caring presentation of our most basic needs. The importance of self-care must be emphasized in this moment. Doubt, confusion, and frustration may be due in part to a lack of self-care.

Eventually God becomes fully present to the prophet, not through impressive, awesome means, but instead through silence. In this moment, God calls Elijah in, not with a booming voice, but with quiet presence. In the presence of the Lord, Elijah does not hold back. He enumerates the accomplishments of his faithful service, then ends with his most honest statement, "I alone am left, and they are seeking my life, to take it away." At face value, God has fully failed to address Elijah's questions. However, an alternative view might suggest that in the moments of the prophet's greatest needs, God meets him with food, rest, and the joyous blessing of God's own presence. The text would suggest that these simple things are enough.

Proper 8: Called to Connection
2 Kings 2:1–2, 6–14

When they had crossed, Elijah said to Elisha, "Tell me what I may do for you, before I am taken from you." Elisha said, "Please let me inherit a double share of your spirit." He responded, "You have asked a hard thing; yet, if you see me as I am being taken from you, it will be granted you; if not, it will not." (2 Kings 2:9–10)

Serena Williams is arguably the best tennis player of all time. Some would even say she is the best athlete in the world. She began winning titles at age seventeen, and more than two decades later she continues to dominate in her sport. Her accomplishments speak for themselves, and her plaudits are well deserved. It is also worth noting that her path would be markedly different without the influence of her father, Richard. When his daughters were only three years old, he introduced them to the sport they would go on to help define. It would be incorrect to credit Richard with all his daughters' accomplishments, yet their success and his training are intertwined. This can be said of every effective mentor relationship.

We may see this passage as a story about the end of Elijah's ministry, or perhaps as the beginning of Elisha's. In reality, it is an exploration of the complexities that exist when other people speak into our lives, helping us to develop our God-given gifts and graces. Mentors call us in, asking us to focus our efforts and attention, helping to prepare us for the work that lies ahead.

In the passage, the tangible expression of prophetic identity is the mantle. We first see Elijah's mantle as a barrier between him and the terrible power of the divine presence (1 Kgs. 19:13). This simple garment comes to represent his relationship with the Divine, as well as his prophetic authority. Though this week's text shows the role of the mantle at the end of the relationship between Elijah and his long-term student apprentice, Elisha, the diligent preacher will acknowledge that the mantle was central to their meeting as well. Their journey together began when Elijah threw his mantle over Elisha, initiating a shared path and authority.

Yet, here at the culmination of one journey and the consecration of another, we see the mentee make a significant request of the prophet preparing for departure. Elisha says, "Please let me inherit a double share of your spirit." The request might incorrectly be seen as impertinent or as an attempt to diminish Elijah's ministry; it could perhaps be linked to the "greater things" Jesus foresaw for his disciples (John 14:12). In reality, his request is actually rooted in the inheritance regulations found in Deuteronomy 21:17. By this decree, the firstborn son is entitled to receive a double portion of the inheritance, as he will be responsible for carrying on the work and efforts of his father. In the case of Elisha, his request makes clear his understanding of the relationship with Elijah, indicating that for Elisha it is closest to that of a son and his father. In anticipation of the prophetic graces that will be bestowed, the mantle becomes an outward and visible sign, passing from one to the other. We cannot be sure whether Elijah bidding his mentee to keep watching him as he departs (v. 10) has a physical or spiritual urgency (which might mean, differently put, keep your eyes on what is most important). It is clear, however, that Elisha is able to do what is expected of him. The mantle of Elijah falls back to earth, reminiscent of the Holy Spirit descending (Matt. 3:16; Acts 2:3–4). He receives it with grace and begins moving forward as one who has both inherited and developed prophetic authority.

Proper 9: Called to Comfort
Isaiah 66:10–14

Rejoice with Jerusalem, and be glad for her, all you who love her; rejoice with her in joy, all you who mourn over her—that you may nurse and be satisfied from her consoling breast; that you may drink deeply with delight from her glorious bosom. (Isaiah 66:10–11)

Some are surprised to learn that elephants live in a matriarchy. Females provide both critical leadership to the group and consistent care to their offspring. Even when they have grown to great stature, they continue to receive care and comfort from their mothers until around age sixteen.

For humans, the importance of maternal care and attention is not dissimilar. Many have the memory of a mother overseeing their play early in life. Whether from a porch, or perhaps a window overlooking the street, mothers allow children to learn and explore, and yet keep a watchful, caring eye on them. When the time is right, a mother might call us in from our play/journey/toil to rest, be refreshed. So too, when we are injured or upset, a mother might call us in so our wounds might be healed, and so we might receive whatever care we require. The writer tells us that God is this type of mother, one who cares deeply, watches closely, and calls us in when the time is right.

It is this image of consistent, providential care that the writer of Isaiah uses to speak to the care and oversight God offers those who are mourning the state of Jerusalem. Both God herself, as well as her Holy City of Jerusalem are described using feminine, maternal, nurturing analogies. After all, for the people who have experienced rejection and devastation, the solution must be one that acknowledges both emotional and material harm. The idea of mourning is not rejected, and those who are in need of comfort are not dismissed out of hand. The writer is aware of all that has transpired, and how tragedy (often rightly) gives way to a sense of defeat. The tool best utilized to counter mourning is the presence of a consoling, comforting, maternal figure. For many, a mother's home is accessible and open in times of crisis, independent of age or perceived independence. Isaiah's God is calling the brokenhearted and discouraged in from the cold, so that their needs might be supplied.

Eschatological imagery is often focused on the material world: a city restored, a kingdom established. The nurturing God of Isaiah would ensure that the renewed physical world will be met with a renewed emotional world as well. All those who have mourned over a broken, desolate Jerusalem will be embraced and brought to an attitude of rejoicing. Isaiah offers this to the recipient of this message: God is invested in restoration and renewal—not only of the Holy City, but of the hearts and souls of those who love God. The writer believes that God's promises are so close to being realized that they are no longer simply aspirational or a matter of hope; they are to be expected.

This confidence is on full display when those who have experienced the hopelessness of exile are told, "You shall see, and your heart shall rejoice; your bodies shall flourish like the grass" (Isa. 66:14). This promise is embodied; the eyes you have now will see this glory, the bodies you have now will flourish as they have never before. Any uncertainty or doubt will be dismissed, and the faithfulness of God to her children will be known by all who look to the Holy City.

Proper 10: Called to Humility
Amos 7:7–17

This is what he showed me: the Lord was standing beside a wall built with a plumb line, with a plumb line in his hand. And the Lord *said to me, "Amos, what do you see?" And I said, "A plumb line." Then the Lord said, "See, I am setting a plumb line in the midst of my people Israel; I will never again pass them by." (Amos 7:7–8)*

When children are small, before they are willing to play with each other, they practice playing alongside one another. They measure and match their movements to those around them, especially older children. This process is a means by which we learn what behaviors will let us thrive in community, and which might lead to our being cast out. Even as we grow older, we all evaluate our thoughts and actions by some external standard. Whether as children or as adults, we encounter trouble when our external standards prove to be less than trustworthy.

This passage uses an amazing analogy of a plumb line, a weight affixed at the bottom of a long string or rope. It serves the function of showing a true vertical, as gravity forces the weight to point directly toward the center of the earth. Simply put, a plumb line gives us an accurate standard against which to measure. This tool can quickly expose a good guess or best effort as being actually faulty or incorrect. A plumb line has fidelity even when all else fails. Verse 7 makes reference not only to a plumb line, but also a wall. The implied truth is simple: walls built without being plumb are not effectively able to support weight. Even if they appear to the naked eye to be strong, they will not be effective and cannot stand the tests of time or pressure.

Amos understands that the Lord is offering up a tool by which the Israelites will be measured. The prophet himself is to be that example, the one who by sharp contrast will show the brokenness that has become prevalent in their society. Rather than God offering holy correction directly to the people, Amos is positioned as the means by which others must be compared and corrected.

Amos, like so many of us, is deeply aware of his shortcomings. His pedigree is not that of a prophet, and others might rightly glance at him and dismiss him. Yet he knows what God has called him to do and to be. It is his role to call in those who have gone astray. Even when the leaders insist that he, Amos, must be mistaken and ought to reconsider his stance, he stands faithfully offering a simple truth, akin to being an indicator of what is up.

Amos even acknowledges that his prophetic voice is inconvenient at best: "You say, 'Do not prophesy against Israel, and do not preach against the house of Isaac.'" In some sense, he had been given permission by the royal authorities to prophesy—as long as it did not directly implicate those in a position of power. And yet, up is up, and down is down. Amos was called not to tell a convenient truth, but rather to offer a simple one: If Israel desires God's favor and presence, there are changes and sacrifices that must be made.

Proper 11: Called to Transformation
Colossians 1:15–28

And you who were once estranged and hostile in mind, doing evil deeds, he has now reconciled in his fleshly body through death, so as to present you holy and blameless and irreproachable before him. (Colossians 1:21–22)

In 1971, Ann Atwater, a black civil rights activist, was appointed to chair a committee on easing tensions around desegregating public schools. Unhelpfully, Claiborne P. Ellis, a Ku Klux Klan member, was assigned to cochair the committee. Ellis is said to have brought a machine gun to their first meeting. In the course of their work together, a gospel choir came to perform. Atwater noticed Ellis clapping on 1 and 3 and chose to help him clap with the beat. From there, it was a steady, yet not simple, journey toward friendship. Ellis ultimately would not only renounce his membership in the KKK, but become a civil rights activist himself. He also called Atwater a dear friend until his death in 2005. It is unlikely, but all too possible, to move from a place of hostility to a place of holy reconciliation.

In this passage, we see the writer making the case for a holy transformation. Whether the connection is the result of the authentic Paul recalling his own experiences, or an intentional invocation of Pauline experiences by a pseudonymous author, we see clear parallels between the proclamations made here and the experiences of Paul before his experience on the road to Damascus. We even see a direct appeal to his own experiences, perhaps included for the benefit of those not moved by previous exhortations: "I, Paul, became a servant of this gospel." Perhaps the goal is to express to the one who might choose self-loathing and disgust, "Even I could become a servant to this message because I have died and risen with Christ."

Paul's story is one of simultaneous qualification and disqualification. His credentials in religious zeal are unmatched (Phil. 3:4–6), yet he must always remember that his past also includes a zealous persecution of the church (Gal. 1:13). Paul cannot claim simply to have been neutral toward the cause of Christ in the world. Rather, he was openly hostile, desiring that the church cease to exist.

While some seem to find a position of peace, unity, and collaboration by default, the author is addressing another kind of experience. This passage is inviting the one who has known hostility in thought and deed to experience the restoration of minds and actions.

Many would claim not to be hostile toward the cause of Christ in the way that Paul once was. Though most Christians may not have open hostilities toward other Christians, we can still recognize the hostility that lives in many of our hearts. Theologian Peter Rollins has claimed, "[I] deny the resurrection of Christ every time I do not serve at the feet of the oppressed, each day that I turn my back on the poor; I deny the resurrection of Christ when I close my ears to the cries of the downtrodden and lend my support to an unjust and corrupt system." How many of us deny Christ's resurrection, not through our failure to adhere to some orthodoxy, but rather in our refusal to live out the call of Jesus that we might be known by our love? In this passage we are invited to see that it is not only the outwardly hostile who are invited to restoration, but even those of us who have quietly, consistently, or even secretly denied Christ's call to peace. We are invited to the restoration available through Christ, even now (Col. 1:22).

Proper 12: Called to Belonging
Colossians 2:6–15 (16–19)

And when you were dead in trespasses and the uncircumcision of your flesh, God made you alive together with him, when he forgave us all our trespasses, erasing the record that stood against us with its legal demands. He set this aside, nailing it to the cross. (Colossians 2:13–14)

In 2014, a European court ruled that Google must comply with requests from individuals to be forgotten. Whether for youthful indiscretions, or for victims of slander and revenge campaigns, the courts ruled that individuals had a right to be forgotten, more specifically, a right to have their names and references to them directly removed from Google's search results. Over the next four years, Google received more than 650,000 requests to be forgotten.[1] Those whose requests are processed are eligible to receive a veritable new (digital) life.

For the Gentile Christians in Colossae, gaining this sort of fresh start may have seemed appealing. Not only were they seeking a new life and identity in Christ, they also sought a sense of belonging

1. https://www.npr.org/sections/thetwo-way/2018/02/28/589411543/google-received-650-000 -right-to-be-forgotten-requests-since-2014.

within the larger community. Yet their cultural practices were out of sync with their Jewish Christian counterparts. The latter held their cultural uniqueness as a means of maintaining their religious identity. The driving force in this passage is the idea that people ought not be judged or defined exclusively by the past, nor by the expectations of other people.

How often do visitors and newcomers to church communities complain about how hard it is to become a part of the community? When they question practices and procedures, they are told that "we've always done it this way!" They are implicitly or explicitly told that they must behave in order that they might someday belong.

This same sense of belonging seems to elude the Gentile Christians. Without adopting the practices of the others, they were consistently reminded of their differences. The adherence to legalism is as dangerous and pervasive now as it was when this letter was written. As always, it threatens to exclude, isolate, or reject those whom Christ has accepted.

Paul attends to the qualification and justification of the Christians in his care. With Christ, in all his sacrifice and glory, these Christians put on a justification that cannot be removed by any critique of qualifications. The justification of the Gentile Christians descends from Christ, not from their Jewish fellows.

Contrary to the fate of Jewish people in the centuries to come, in this space the Jewish Christians held relative privilege over the Gentile Christians. They shared religious and cultural ties to Jesus, Paul, and the other apostles, giving them something of the inside track. Paul recognizes this power and privilege clearly, and simultaneously recognizes the best way to end the subjugation of the Gentiles is to begin to discharge privilege, beginning with his own. He reminds the Jewish and Gentile Christians alike that all must submit to the Christ who is the head, who holds us all together.

Summer Series 2: Final Instructions

Four Parts: Proper 14 through Proper 17

Guidance for enduring in the life of faith, from the book of Hebrews.

JASPER PETERS

Series Overview

Often, parting words serve the function of offering the highest points and ideals we wish to relay to others. Either in summary or by means of a larger conclusion, often the very best and most important parts of a message come as a part of our final instructions. The end of the book of Hebrews works to summarize the most important aspects, not only of the book itself, but of a life of faith. These exhortations, warnings, and guidelines are a helpful overview of the traits of a faithful Christian, and they also serve as an opportunity for self-reflection.

	Sermon Title	Focus Scripture	Theme
Proper 14	Seeking a Homeland	Heb. 11:1–3, 8–16	As followers of Christ, we are strangers in a strange land. How can our hearts lead us to our true home?
Proper 15	Leaning on a Great Cloud	Heb. 11:29–12:2	Our ancestors and all who have come before have set a path for us. How can their example spur us onward?
Proper 16	Unshaken	Heb. 12:18–29	How do we identify the essentials of our life? How do we separate the temporary from the eternal?
Proper 17	Known by Our Love	Heb. 13:1–8, 15–16	We are called by Christ to be known by our love. How can we allow love to define our relationships?

Look for quotes or meaningful messages that have been given to your community as a means of establishing a core identity, particularly if they were given as parting words or "wisdom for the road." Books like *The Last Lecture* can offer a good example, though connections to your own family or community are typically more powerful. Use a map on Proper 14 to show where your family came from (as best you can tell) and a faith-related heirloom such as an old family Bible or a gift received at baptism or confirmation on Proper 15 to show how our faith is bolstered by those who have come before.

Proper 14: Seeking a Homeland
Hebrews 11:1–3, 8–16

By faith Abraham obeyed when he was called to set out for a place that he was to receive as an inheritance; and he set out, not knowing where he was going. . . . For he looked forward to the city that has foundations, whose architect and builder is God. (Hebrews 11:8, 10)

Since 2014, more than 1.5 million Venezuelans have fled their country. Crises ranging from a volatile economy and lack of food and medicine to threats of violence have been enough to force many to abandon the only home they've ever known in order to seek safety and peace in the form of a new home. Even the idea of a new home seems foolish at times. How might a place that one has never seen become a home?

Few of us have ever had to make such a harrowing decision, to weigh a hope for the future against all your past experiences. It is only truly possible if the past is sufficiently painful, or if the future hope, though not guaranteed, offers a possibility of great reward. In the case of the many migrants and refugees in the world today, the possible reward is an existence mostly or wholly exempt from insecurity. In the case of the faithful, our understanding of a reward must shift.

The writer of Hebrews enumerates the accomplishments of the faithful: Abraham's willingness to say yes to God and leave behind his traditions, Sarah's willingness to believe she might bear a child, though many years of infertility had robbed her of that hope.

For some, a life of faith is reward enough. If the Creator invites us to live according to certain standards, there will always be those blessed few who follow without resistance or questioning. Though, for some, faithfulness might be motivation enough all on its own, the writer invites us to see that it is a hope in a future of great reward that has motivated these heroes of faith to pursue God with vigor and consistency. Simply put, their reward was finding the home they'd always known but never possessed.

The psalmist writes, "One thing I asked of the LORD, that will I seek after: to live in the house of the LORD all the days of my life, to behold the beauty of the LORD, and to inquire in his temple" (Ps. 27:4). Such is the heart of the faithful, driven by a desire to dwell in the place that God has prepared, they hold a deep desire for a better country. In reality, it is not an abstract hope for heavenly vistas that motivates faithful actions on their behalf. Rather, it is an innate sense that this place is not our home.

Given this, the faithful are not yet the rulers of a Holy City that has been prepared for us. Instead, we are refugees, asked to identify with the outcast and the exile. Unlike exiles as seen elsewhere in Scripture, who are almost always working to escape from exile, the faithful here are painted as exiles with a mission. To be an exile full of faith is to embrace the inconsistency and unsure nature of this liminal phase. We are not called simply to long for the days that have passed, though they may have been simpler. The greater call is to hunger and thirst for righteousness (Matt. 5:6), remembering that our calling is ahead, not behind (Phil. 3:13).

Proper 15: Leaning on a Great Cloud
Hebrews 11:29–12:2

Yet all these, though they were commended for their faith, did not receive what was promised, since God had provided something better so that they would not, without us, be made perfect. Therefore, since we are surrounded by so great a cloud of witnesses, let us also lay aside every weight and the sin that clings so closely, and let us run with perseverance the race that is set before us. (Hebrews 11:39–12:1)

There are more than ten thousand saints in the Catholic tradition, though the number is debatable, as there is no definitive listing of saints. A handful of these saints are even said to be sensitive to specific plights, like becoming the patron saint of some particular cause. These assembled saints represent an untold number of stories of the faithful. Many cultures of African descent similarly speak about the "ancestors." Whether they are related directly, or simply are those who have contributed to the depth and beauty of the culture at large, the ancestors are those whose lives are honored in the present. Both of these beliefs seem to be somewhat reminiscent of the "cloud of witnesses," so named by the author of Hebrews. The reader is invited to the foundational truth that the vibrancy and vitality of faith today depends directly upon the faith that has been handed down.

This passage begins with an examination of the accomplishments of the faithful over the ages. The writer offers an abundance of evidence to support the central argument of this section of Hebrews: that the life of faith is central to the transformation of the individual and of the world. The proof of this truth is in the narrative of faith, told and retold through the lives of the faithful heroes of the Hebrew Bible.

The use of running imagery is not necessarily unique in the New Testament (Gal. 2:2; 2 Tim. 4:7), yet the metaphor shifts drastically here. Rather than a race seen as a single runner event (as in 1 Cor. 9:24–27), this passage offers up the life of faith as a relay race; we are directly related to and dependent upon those who have come before us. The accomplishments of the ancestors (Heb. 11:33–34) are, in a very real sense, our accomplishments. The challenges of the ancestors (Heb. 11:35–38) have already been overcome, so when we face them again in our time, we should not despair, as victory has already been won for us.

While our contribution to the race is real and not to be undermined, it is also deeply dependent on the perseverance of those who have come before. Moreover, now that the baton has been handed to us, we are invited to see the cloud of witnesses as those who continue to cheer us on, building up the church with testimonies of faithfulness through the ages. Perhaps best of all, these ancestor witnesses are not simply to rest on their laurels. Instead, their perfection depends not only on their own accomplishments, but also on ours. No generation will see the fullness of Christ's glorious return alone—we are inexorably in this together.

Proper 16: Unshaken
Hebrews 12:18–29

At that time his voice shook the earth; but now he has promised, "Yet once more I will shake not only the earth but also the heaven." This phrase, "Yet once more," indicates the removal of what is shaken—that is, created things—so that what cannot be shaken may remain. Therefore, since we are receiving a kingdom that cannot be shaken, let us give thanks, by which we offer to God an acceptable worship with reverence and awe; for indeed our God is a consuming fire. (Hebrews 12:26–29)

In 2017 a strong earthquake struck central Mexico, causing widespread destruction. Yet this earthquake also unearthed an archaeological treasure. When the earthquake shook the city of Cuernavaca, at the base of a newer temple, a more ancient temple was revealed. Artifacts within the newly discovered temple date back nearly a millennium. It is hard to reconcile a force that could both bring destruction and uncover something ancient and sacred. A similar force is described in this passage in Hebrews, one that is able to expose what is temporary and also present what is permanent, all in one moment. Is such a force good or evil, kind or cruel?

Matthew recalls Jesus saying that his followers were like those who built a house upon a rock, compared to those who built upon sand (Matt. 7:24–27). The former are said to be wise, because when the world becomes inhospitable, their houses will continue to stand. The latter are inherently unstable, and sooner or later will fall. This passage in Hebrews recalls this juxtaposition, comparing that which might be shaken by the power of the divine voice against that which is immovable. In both cases, there is an ephemeral nature to the less desirable option. One might envision sand being sifted away, virtually disappearing before your eyes. While we often speak of the God who creates, renews, and transforms, it seems to be another thing entirely to speak of the God who destroys. Yet this language is clear and powerful. This God will bring an end to the inconsequential, leaving behind only that which cannot be shaken. For the writer of this passage, it is a kind of grace that allows the inconsequential to be removed so that the best things may remain and thrive.

For years, residents of the western United States have been accustomed to wildfires threatening land and structures. Each year millions of acres of land are burned, including homes and businesses, devastating the lives of many who are left in the ashes. As a means of trying to limit the damage of these larger fires, smaller, controlled burns are prescribed. By creating a fire under controlled circumstances, experts are able to mitigate future damage. These controlled burns consume the small brush and dry, unhealthy plants. In their wake, the soil is renewed, full of nutrients, and is prepared to foster new life. In a place where some see destruction, others are left to see the blessing of a consuming fire. To speak of a God who is a consuming fire may elicit fears of punishment and condemnation. The true focus of this passage is on the uplifting of that which is unshakable. Though these gifts may not be tangible in this moment (Heb. 12:18), they are the very substance of Christ's kingdom come to earth.

Proper 17: Known by Our Love
Hebrews 13:1–8, 15–16

Let mutual love continue. Do not neglect to show hospitality to strangers, for by doing that some have entertained angels without knowing it. (Hebrews 13:1–2)

Theologian N. T. Wright was asked to imagine offering final instructions to his children in preparation for his death. He says he would tell them, "If you want to know who God is, if you want to know what it means to be human, . . . what love is, . . . what grief is, look at Jesus . . . and go on looking until you're not just a spectator, but you're actually part of the drama which has him as its central character."[1]

As Jesus prepared to meet the cross, he gave a set of parting instructions to his disciples. Some were practical, but only one stands alone as being able to define his followers: "I give you a new commandment, that you love one another. Just as I have loved you, you also should love one another. By this everyone will know that you are my disciples, if you have love for one another" (John 13:34–35).

These words, spoken shortly after displaying servant leadership by washing the feet of his disciples, may strike us as simple enough to accomplish, yet it is a challenge for the ages. It is challenging enough that it is echoed by the writer of Hebrews, who also prepares a set of final instructions. The conclusion of this series coincides with the concluding thoughts of Hebrews. In general, the concern seems to be with maintaining peace in relationships within the Christian community. In regard to friendships, marriage, respect for leadership, even caring for prisoners, the impetus is to "let mutual love continue" to be the defining factor of these relationships.

Maintaining a love for one another becomes the frame for the parting words of Jesus. Perhaps we can admit that personifying love as our defining ethos is far more easily said than done. This passage makes reference to strangers, those dangerously neutral individuals who might become enemies, or perhaps friends. Rather than let suspicion influence how we see those strangers, the author invites us to something even more bold: to show not just a neutral acceptance but a full-throated embrace of strangers, as they may truly be divine representatives (reminiscent of Lot in Gen. 19).

For some, the most challenging aspect rises from the idea of mutual love. Though we desire mutuality, the New Testament makes it clear that the Christian is to offer up this sacrificial hospitality before expecting that it be returned to us. The love we share should not be limited or dependent upon the love we hope or expect to receive in

1. https://www.theworkofthepeople.com/look-at-jesus.

return. We cannot engage in some version of a prisoner's dilemma, offering our cooperation only when our safety and self-interests are secured. Instead, we are called to be the first to give, the first to sacrifice, the first to welcome those in need—not because we demand it be reciprocated, but because by showing our love we honor the mutuality between us and the Christ who has sacrificed for us all.

Fall Series 1: RE:boot

Four Parts: Proper 18 through Proper 21

Life-changing challenges from Paul's letters to Philemon and Timothy.

BRIAN ERICKSON

Series Overview

This time of year is often a time of renewal, especially for those with school-age children. Even for those of us who haven't set foot in a classroom this century, it can be a time for reinvention and renewal, getting back to a routine after a more relaxed summer. In very personal letters to fellow followers of Jesus, Paul outlines some of the most practical transformations that occur in the life of a disciple, ranging from the reconciliation of broken relationships to finding peace in a world bent on possession. Christ is making all things new, even us. As students head back to school, and summer gives way to fall, this series reminds churchgoers of every age and stage that it's never too late to make a new start.

Tips and Ideas for This Series

Starting around Labor Day, this series coincides with fall programming kickoffs and a feeling of "new beginnings" not unlike early January. Consider using "RE:boot" as a theme not just for Sunday

	Sermon Title	Focus Scripture	Theme
Proper 18	RE:concile Relationships	Phlm. 1–21	It's easier to avoid conflict, but we are called to the hard work of relationships.
Proper 19	RE:imagine Regret	1 Tim. 1:12–17	Sharing our mistakes redeems our stories and reveals God's mercy.
Proper 20	RE:frame Prayer	1 Tim. 2:1–7	"Pray for everyone" means *everyone*—and that's the challenge.
Proper 21	RE:think Happiness	1 Tim. 6:6–19	Learning to be content is the ultimate game-changer.

mornings but for events and initiatives to get people plugged back into educational, fellowship, and service opportunities. On a personal level, invite people to set spiritual, relational goals for the whole season or corresponding to each week of the series.

Proper 18: RE:concile Relationships
Philemon 1–21

Maybe this is the reason Onesimus was separated from you for a while so that you might have him back forever—no longer as a slave but more than a slave—that is, as a dearly beloved brother. (Philemon 15–16)

The brief correspondence with Philemon lacks the soaring prose of Paul's other letters, but what it fails to deliver in scriptural one-liners, it more than makes up for with practical wisdom. Paul's letter is a window into what it looks like when the gospel collides with our daily lives and the realities of how we treat one another, how we conduct ourselves in the real world, and how believers hold each other accountable to the high calling of discipleship.

While we remember this letter by Philemon's name, and the bulk of it is addressed directly to the situation between him and Onesimus, Paul also clearly intends for others to overhear what he has to say to Philemon. He begins the letter by naming Apphia, Archippus, and the entire church that meets in Philemon's house. He wants us all to eavesdrop on his wisdom for this very particular circumstance, because he knows this is about more than just the relationship between Onesimus and Philemon. Perhaps Paul does this to increase the pressure on Philemon to do the right thing, but my guess is that this is more about how Paul understands the role of Christian community. We lean on each other, we learn from each other, and we help each other live more fully into the light. New life is a team sport.

Paul makes it clear that he has options as to how he addresses this situation. The easiest approach is to leave things as they are, and Onesimus never return to Philemon. Paul clearly has use for him, and this simpler approach would avoid an awkward and unpredictable reunion. The temptation to avoid conflict and to maintain the false peace of the status quo lures many well-meaning Christians away from the gospel work of reconciliation. Transformation requires truth-telling, even when confronting one another is uncomfortable.

Paul could simply use his apostolic authority to command reconciliation, mediating between the two parties like an ecclesiastical parent. He writes that he has the confidence to do so, implying that he has little doubt his decision would be heeded. But the right action, carried out due to fear or coercion, cannot transform what is broken in this relationship. Paul wants Philemon's kindness to be "voluntary and not something forced" (v. 14). Real reconciliation cannot be rule-following alone, nor can it be commanded. It must involve a choice of the heart.

So Paul makes the most difficult choice, the one that requires the most of everyone involved, "appealing through love." He sends Onesimus back to Philemon, and while we have no record of that conversation, it's worth spending some time in your sermon standing in Onesimus's shoes, an emancipated slave who is being asked to walk back toward the man who claimed to own him. Onesimus has enough faith in Paul and the gospel he preaches to risk everything for the sake of what Christ can do. This is why reconciliation is so much more difficult than forgiveness, because it demands both parties move toward one another in humility and hope.

The Resurrected One does more than empty the tomb on Easter morning. Christ brings life out of death even in the painful and ordinary interactions of his followers. By allowing us to eavesdrop on his instructions to Philemon, Paul calls on each of us to let the gospel reboot our relationships.

Proper 19: RE:imagine Regret
1 Timothy 1:12–17

Christ Jesus came into the world to save sinners—of which I am foremost. But for that very reason I received mercy, so that in me, as the foremost, Jesus Christ might display the utmost patience, making me an example to those who would come to believe in him for eternal life. (1 Timothy 1:15b–16)

John Wesley had his small groups ask each other the same question every time they gathered: "How is it with your soul?" It's not a question you can ask of a stranger, or even a mild acquaintance, without the conversation becoming painfully awkward. And it's telling that most of our churches are no longer the kind of place where that kind of question could be asked and honestly answered. This may be why well-behaved mainline Protestants have largely edited out the practice of testimony, because the rough edges of rebirth no longer fit into our highly polished orders of worship. But the gospel depends on witness, on persons willing to open a window into their own souls, so that the church might know its Savior is still alive and at work.

These days, the storytelling that used to take place in our churches now happens online, where anyone with a phone can apply the Clarendon filter to their otherwise ordinary lives. My own social media feed seems to be composed mostly of two groups: those who share more than the venue can bear, and those who are so selective in what they present to the world that it might as well be a press conference. It is clear that the modern world is as hungry as ever to know how to narrate their own stories, and to find a place to have those stories heard.

Christians particularly struggle with how to be forthright with each other. As a pastor, I am a little jealous of those whose faith hinges on powerful, 180-degree moments, prodigals who can point to the burning bush that spoke their name. Such stories make my own steady drip of grace seem unworthy of the telling. And while we often tell inspirational anecdotes from the pulpit, what most folks need is a place to tell their unfinished stories, a place to speak honestly about how it is with their souls.

Keeping our mistakes and unpolished parts to ourselves breeds regret, which has less to do with what we've done and more to do with how we think about it. Regret keeps us trapped in the past, preventing our stories from moving on. I remember learning that the Gospels were based on the disciples' testimony, meaning that although they had the chance to erase the details of their denial, they featured them instead. Paul, like the other disciples before him, does not edit out his failures when he tells the story of his faith. He understands that his past is more than just a series of missteps; it reflects the depth of God's mercy. Paul does not rehash his history because he still feels guilty, nor does he bring it up because he has experienced the power of self-forgiveness. He tells his story so that no one who hears him will be tempted to put his faith on a pedestal. The ugliness of his past reveals the glory of God's grace.

So, how is it with your soul?

Proper 20: RE:frame Prayer
1 Timothy 2:1–7

First of all, then, I urge that supplications, prayers, intercessions, and thanksgivings be made for everyone. (1 Timothy 1:1)

Paul spends the opening chapter of 1 Timothy describing the narrow way of faithfulness, and the many who have sought to lead and teach God's people but have missed the mark. He names how blessed he is to have been chosen for this work, and that it is only by the grace of God that he can do it. In other words, Paul says to Timothy, the challenge of what you have been called to is great. Having seen Paul set the stage for how critically important what's he's about to say really is, we imagine the sound track swelling as we anticipate the sage wisdom the mentor is about to pass on to the student. With bated breath, we read that Paul simply tells Timothy to pray. For all people.

This is more subversive advice than it appears at first glance. Prayer is perhaps the most well-known spiritual tool—and also the least understood. Just about every Christian you talk to will admit to feelings of guilt about their lack of prayer, and the honest ones will also confess their confusion as to how to pray in the first place. Paul here offers some very practical advice for prayer, though he says nothing about technique or style. This is not so much a prayer "how-to" as it is a prayer "who-for."

To pray for our enemies is a core teaching of Christ, but here Paul makes that idea even more explicit. The scope of our prayer is a barometer for our understanding of God's reach, the breadth and depth of God's saving intentions. The prayer of the faithful is more than just making requests of God. It is learning to think like God, to love like God. Prayer is a paradigm shift in the way we see the world and our place in it, and this is why it is so fundamental to faithful Christian living. Paul's invitation to pray for all people forces us to ask ourselves, "For whom am I *unwilling* to pray?"

Lest we make this too general, Paul specifically calls for prayers for those in power, not exactly the most sympathetic of intercessory targets. While we may like the idea of grace on a macro scale, when we zoom in on specific people, especially those we disagree with on a cellular level, we understand why Jonah took off for Tarshish. Herein lies the implication of God's so loving the world, that we are to lift before God those for whom Christ died, and nothing less will do. Something happens when we pray for all people, and it's not necessarily pleasant. Rather than our prayers projecting our will onto God, prayer becomes a realignment, our hearts once again formed in the image of God, the one "who wants all people to be saved and to come to a knowledge of the truth."

In an era of political rancor and division writ large, perhaps Paul's instructions seem a little naive. We do well to remember that the early church read these words under a cloud of persecution, and to pray for those in power included those who had clearly established themselves as threats to the church and as enemies of Christ. This is no saccharine patriotism, blindly calling polite Christians to support the status quo. This is the most radical kind of subversion, the kind that transforms human hearts, beginning with our own.

Proper 21: RE:think Happiness
1 Timothy 6:6–19

Of course, there is great gain in godliness combined with contentment; for we brought nothing into the world, so that we can take nothing out of it; but if we have food and clothing, we will be content with these. (1 Timothy 6:6–8)

The church has lost much of her authority when it comes to talking about money, due to parishioners' exhaustion with sermons about stewardship, traveling evangelists with personal jets, and the lack of noticeable distinction between the materialism of God's chosen and the rest of the world. Pastors understandably shy away from tackling anything that might resemble a stewardship talk outside the annual campaign, but I'm not convinced we are doing ourselves any favors. This direct and powerful text offers the pastor a chance to confront one of the chief spiritual struggles of our day, without handing out a pledge card. Paul tackles the dangers of materialism, not to induce feelings of guilt or shame among the wealthy (he's not writing to the wealthy), nor is he trying to raise money for his cause. Here is a pastor at work, speaking honestly with another partner in ministry, about what he fears for his people.

At issue here is contentment, the power of being at peace with what we have and who we are. One of the most devastating ways sin manifests itself in our lives is through the desperate attempt to address a spiritual hunger with a material object. Advertising agencies specialize in helping us discover the thing we need that we didn't even know existed. In the United States, we have a thriving self-storage industry dedicated to all our extra stuff, objects that no longer meet an immediate need but that we hold onto just in case. According to most experts, fights about money remain the number one cause of marital strife. And in the most prosperous age in human history, the desire to have more has never been more powerful. It's no wonder the gospel's commands against materialism still fall on deaf ears—because it's a word of confrontation.

But it's also a word of hope, even for those of us with self-storage units. The text asks some challenging questions about where we place our hope—not to condemn those in a certain income bracket, but to liberate all of us shackled by our stuff. Paul and Timothy alike would be taken aback by the wealth of most North American Christians, though materialism has a way of numbing you to what you've already got. It's telling that most of us think of the wealthy as anyone who has more than we currently do, because the need for more can breed only perpetual discontent with what you have, and a persistent focus on what's parked in the neighbor's driveway. We can't experience healing if we are unwilling to let Paul deliver the diagnosis.

While we don't lift it up as a virtue as often as we should, we all notice when we encounter someone who is content. Mission trip participants of all sorts often take up that familiar refrain, that "they had so little but seemed so happy." What this most often results in is an unsatisfying sense of guilt, that the wealthier participant should be happy with what they have.

But at heart, it's an invitation to see happiness in a completely new way. Not that someone can be happy with less, but that what you have has little or no bearing on happiness at all. Perhaps the most challenging reboot of all is learning holy satisfaction—the practice of relentless gratitude coupled with faith in the Provider.

Fall Series 2: Four Prayers That Don't Work

Four Parts: Proper 22 through Proper 25

A series on prayer from the Gospel of Luke, with applications for stewardship.

BRIAN ERICKSON

Series Overview

What do our prayers say about our faith? These four sermons based on texts from the Gospel of Luke each address some fundamental aspect of prayer, empowering us to speak to God more boldly and more honestly. Fear of "praying wrong" keeps some people from praying at all, but Luke shows us that prayer is ultimately a way of practicing dependence on God. Exploration of that dependence lends itself to a stewardship focus within this series.

Tips and Ideas for This Series

This series should not enhance the anxiety some people feel about "how to pray," but provide encouragement for honest, unfiltered conversation with God. Offer plentiful opportunities for prayer during this series, both during the service and outside of it. Options might include guided prayers for existing classes and groups, sign-ups for short-term prayer circles that might evolve into lasting small groups,

	Sermon Title	Focus Scripture	Theme
Proper 22	The Prayer for Enough Faith to Have No Need for Faith	Luke 17:5–10	Discover the power of the faith you have.
Proper 23	The Prayer That You Didn't Pray	Luke 17:11–19	Don't let gratitude go unexpressed.
Proper 24	The Prayer That Quits	Luke 18:1–8	Persist in prayer and God will answer.
Proper 25	The Prayer of Comparison	Luke 18:9–14	When you're feeling insecure, look up, not around.

and times the sanctuary will be open for silent prayer. Make opportunities for giving and stewardship pledges varied as well, so that generosity can flow naturally as a faithful prayer in action.

Proper 22: The Prayer for Enough Faith to Have No Need for Faith
Luke 17:5–10

The apostles said to the Lord, "Increase our faith." The Lord replied, "If you had faith the size of a mustard seed, you could say to this mulberry tree, 'Be uprooted and planted in the sea' and it would obey you." (Luke 17:5–6)

It must be exhausting for the disciples, having to keep up with Jesus. Not only are they perpetually a step behind, but the longer they follow him, the more difficult it gets. Having just cautioned them against sin, Jesus tells his friends that they must forgive those who wrong them until they lose count. It's no wonder that the disciples throw up their hands and offer this desperate prayer, "Increase our faith!"

While we in the church often make faith seem like the best thing going, it is by nature incredibly difficult. It implies a willingness to deal with uncertainty, to depend on what you cannot see, and to trust what you cannot know. And it never feels like enough, which is why it's called "faith." Even two thousand years after the disciples first offered this request of Jesus, it is not uncommon for his followers to want to trade in their current faith for something a little more substantial.

But Jesus will hear none of it. The problem, he declares, is not a lack of faith, it is a lack of understanding about the nature of faith. We often wish to trade in faith for her shinier cousins, like knowledge and confidence, but those more appealing virtues place the control squarely in our own hands, which is not the nature of discipleship. Faith is less shelter and more sending, less calculation and more chaos.

While the amount of our generosity is never a direct reflection of how faithful we are, one of the primary places where faith plays a role is in the stewardship of our resources. Many of us wait until we "feel like giving" or until all the conditions are favorable. We can often mistake reluctance for responsibility, promising ourselves that we will know when it is time to open our hands and hearts to what God is up to. The disciples no doubt thought the same, that their current state of confusion was simply a quantitative issue, that eventually discipleship would come naturally to them.

But faith and ease are not good partners. Faith leads us out into that place where we are more aware than ever of our need, our lack, our dependence, because it is only in that fragile state that we will discover the One who can move mountains. In this way, faith is not so much something that we possess, but something that possesses us, beckoning us into the life that only God can offer.

Whenever my church is engaged in a stewardship campaign, I like to offer my members the chance to tithe to another congregation. I find that one of the most common excuses many people give as to why they don't give is that they don't believe the church needs their money. It's not true, of course, and it's not their real objection. It's simply another way of avoiding any form of discipleship that might cost us something. At the same time, I find myself as a pastor so anxious about the budget that I forget to trust in the One who is the source of all good gifts. In calling the nongivers' bluff, I am also calling my own.

There is plenty of faith in your congregation, enough to get mulberry bushes to heed your commands, enough to move mountains, enough to change the world. God won't give us more faith until we learn how to use what we already have.

Proper 23: The Prayer That You Didn't Pray
Luke 17:11–19

Then Jesus asked, "Were not ten made clean? But the other nine, where are they? Was none of them found to return and give praise to God except this foreigner?" (Luke 17:17–18)

This is not really a fair question, since Jesus knows exactly where the other nine lepers are—they are at the temple, just as they are supposed to be. They're doing what they were told. But here is this Samaritan, this outsider, causing all sorts of a ruckus giving thanks to God.

Jesus says simply, "Your faith has made you well." Which is a bit confusing, since all ten of the lepers were healed. They were all made well, at least in a way, but this is a deeper kind of well-being that the tenth leper has received. Jesus says, "Your faith has saved you." Ten are healed, one is saved. All are healed, and I would think all are thankful, but one is so full of thanks that he can't control himself.

Gratitude is a funny thing. For one thing, it's invisible. I can't tell when you're grateful. Gratitude becomes visible only when we give thanks. I've always been tempted to oversimplify this story and say that surveys show nine out of ten lepers were found ungrateful, but that's not what the story says. I have no doubt they were thankful. How could you not be grateful for getting everything back? Your health, your community, your family?

I have no doubt that they offered sacrifice in the temple, that they told all their friends and family what Jesus had done for them. They were grateful. To be technical about it, there is no etiquette for miraculous healing. Jesus heals another leper earlier in Luke, and we're not told that he ever came back to say, "thank you." In fact, we have very few occurrences in the Gospels of people saying thanks to Jesus. Are they grateful? Absolutely.

But only one gives thanks, and so he's the only one we know was grateful, because gratitude that doesn't translate into thanksgiving is invisible. That's why I don't think we have a gratitude problem in this country—I think we have a thanksgiving problem.

I think most of us have a lot of things we are grateful for. The problem is we don't always show that gratitude. We don't always give thanks where it is due. If you count mealtime prayers, "thank you" might be the most common prayer you pray. But how often do you really mean it? How often do you go out of your way to pour out thanksgivings to God?

There is a numbness that can set in, a lack of feeling, a sort of spiritual leprosy, when you have been in the church for a long time. You don't show up in worship expecting anything to happen anymore. You don't get all worked up about what you read in the Bible this morning. You're grateful, don't get me wrong—praise God from whom all blessings flow—but you're never tacky about it.

Then along comes some Samaritan. Some outsider. Some newbie to the faith, who's just met Jesus and for whom everything is brand-spanking-new. And they're singing the hymns louder than anybody else is, they're volunteering for every committee and service opportunity, they're reading through their Bible like a starving man set loose at a buffet line. They are grateful.

Perhaps what all of us need is a little Samaritan. Maybe it's as simple as never letting our gratitude go unspoken. Maybe what all of us need is a little more reckless thanksgiving, a life full of unnecessary thank-yous, a life of raising our voice to the one risen King.

Proper 24: The Prayer That Quits
Luke 18:1–8

"And will not God grant justice to his chosen ones who cry to him day and night? Will he delay long in helping them?" (Luke 18:7)

One of the most attractive (and frustrating) elements of Jesus' parables is how recognizable his characters are. I find myself often having to apologize for their behavior, wishing that Jesus would cast a more well-behaved lot. But Jesus seeks to reveal the wisdom hidden in everyday life, not the religious nuggets reserved for the pious and polite. It's also striking that, for all the ways we gloss over the difficulties of faith, Jesus never shies away from them. He speaks plainly here about the reality of unanswered prayer, laying the blame not on lack of faith or proper verbiage but on lack of persistence. When our prayer seems ineffective, Jesus encourages us to harass God.

This parable is situated immediately following instructions about the return of Christ, implying that there will not be a gradual buildup, but that it will all go down, as he says elsewhere, like a "thief in the night." Luke has been offering the faithful a word about remaining faithful in the meantime, clinging to Christ when there are no signs and the odds seem stacked against the truth of the gospel. The Gospel writer characterizes the intent of this parable as leading the faithful to "always pray" and "never lose heart." Sometimes faith will look like persistence, like the sheer force of will.

The story Jesus tells is of a woman who is denied justice, likely because the judge who presides over her case neither fears God nor respects people (as he readily attests), but she will not rest. Her request of him is simple, that justice be served. She doesn't ask for special treatment, or some exceptional judgment, but for him to fulfill the work that he has been called to do. In the end, he relents, not because he has a change of heart, but because he realizes that this woman is not going to quit.

We have to be careful, whenever we read a parable, to take from it what Jesus intends, and not overthink it. This is not meant to indicate that God is a spineless magistrate, unwilling to fulfill his heavenly duties. As he does in other places, Jesus shows that even fallible human beings get it right sometimes, under the right circumstances. And if bad judges can deliver justice with enough encouragement, the Righteous One of Israel will most certainly not fail.

My own prayers are too often bound to their results. If I don't receive what I've asked, I wonder if the prayer was even effective. The power of this story is that it's not one of the widow's midnight annoyances that is somehow more productive than the others, it is that she shows herself determined and confident that justice will be done. Her belief is not in her own actions, but in the justice that she seeks.

This story is about the stewardship of prayer, tending to the unspeakable gift God has given us to knock on heaven's door. Jesus wants his followers in a constant state of courageous prayer, not because it is more effective, but because they so fiercely believe in the justice they seek for this broken world, and in the power of God to deliver it.

Proper 25: The Prayer of Comparison
Luke 18:9–14

"God, I thank you that I'm not like everyone else—crooks, evildoers, adulterers—or even like this tax collector. I fast twice a week, I give a tenth of everything I receive." (Luke 18:11–12)

Sermon starter: Generosity requires gratitude, and nothing disrupts gratitude like comparison. We scroll through the social-media feed of our peers, jaws clenched in jealousy, pining for what someone else has, suddenly unable to count a single blessing of our own. And when we are insecure about our faith, we look horizontally rather than vertically. While the gospel repeatedly reminds us that we are all broken, it's tempting for many Christians to measure our righteousness against the lowest common denominator, typically outside the walls of the church. This is likely why churches whose theology is predicated on the sins of the world focus almost exclusively on the sins of those not listed on their church's roll.

Whenever religion becomes a report card, it leads to hypocrisy rather than humility, as is illustrated by Jesus' parable. "Two men went up into the temple to pray," Jesus tells us, and we should take note of how equal they are in that initial description. Before God, their distinctions do not matter, and their accomplishments are inconsequential. They are simply two human beings, coming into the presence of God. One stands on his own, a Pharisee, offering the wrong kind of gratitude. He thanks God for how he is unlike the more public failures he sees all around him. The catch, of course, is that he is as broken as the rest of them, and yet God still seeks him, which ought to be the source of his thanksgiving.

In the opposite corner is a tax collector, a man who has betrayed his own people to make a profit, who clearly believed at some point that money would cure what ails him. But here in the temple, he confesses his brokenness in brutally honest fashion, unable even to lift his head, as he begs for God's mercy. The humbled man, Jesus says, will be exalted.

Comparison seems to be encoded into our nature. If we know we are better off than somebody else, at least we're not in last place. Since the days of Cain and Abel, an inescapable aspect of the human condition has been grading ourselves by looking at someone else's paper. We claw our way to the top of the pile, believing that besting our neighbor might bring us a sense of peace. It shouldn't be surprising that this approach backfires on us, because more often than not, our comparisons with others only confirm our sense of inadequacy.

Luke tells us that Jesus told this parable for the benefit of those "who trusted in themselves that they were righteous and regarded others with contempt" (Luke 18:9). At its heart, spiritual comparison is a form of fear, that we need a backup plan in case God's grace doesn't work out. Like the elder brother in the Prodigal Son parable, the Pharisee has followed every rule—even tithing!—but he's done it all with an eye toward surpassing the public piety of his neighbor rather than setting his heart on God alone. When we pray the prayer, "God, thank you for sparing me and my family from what so-and-so is going through, because I couldn't handle that," we have missed the mark. Or when we secretly sign up our teenager for a mission trip so they would appreciate everything we've bought them over the years. Gratitude that compares our fortune to others, gratitude that measures us against someone else, gratitude that is tied only to what we have and others don't, isn't the kind of gratitude that Christ is calling us to.

The biblical principles of giving are never rooted in earning God's grace or displaying our faith for the world to see. If that were the case, churches would post lists of their top givers to let the rest of the congregation know who really loves Jesus. Instead, the invitation to give is an invitation to trust, an opportunity to humble ourselves before God, step away from the rat race of comparing and competing, and rest in the merciful arms of our Redeemer.

Fall Series 3: It's the End of the World as We Know It (and I Feel Fine)

Four Parts: Proper 26 through Proper 29
(Reign of Christ)

When things seem out of control, we trust the road Christ walks with us.

BRIAN ERICKSON

Series Overview

These are not passages you have cross-stitched on your wall, or emblazoned on your favorite coffee mug. The lectionary texts over the next few weeks, leading up to Reign of Christ Sunday, tackle some of the Bible's most challenging passages, and invite us all to ask where God is when things go wrong. In a world caught up in a negative news cycle, the texts that speak to hopelessness, fear, and even the close of history can teach us much about remaining faithful in difficult times. Can we look to the apocalyptic texts of the early church to learn how to remain hopeful, even when the headlines seem out of control?

Tips and Ideas for This Series

For bulletin and/or screen graphics, consider imagery inspired by dystopian series in literature and film, or recreate the feel of retro black-and-white newspapers featuring the series title as a bold, all-caps headline and the week's sermon title as a subheading beneath it.

	Sermon Title	Focus Scripture	Theme
Proper 26 (All Saints')	The Work of Waiting	Hab. 1:1–4; 2:1–4	God is at work in the dark places, even when we cannot see it.
Proper 27	Skipping to the End	2 Thess. 2:1–5, 13–17	It may feel like the end is near, but we have to keep going.
Proper 28	Full Disclosure	Luke 21:5–19	Christ never promised an easy walk, but one of sacrifice.
Proper 29 (Reign of Christ)	Proving Who You Are	Luke 23:33–43	Challenged to prove ourselves, we find our identity in Christ, our King.

Help the congregation practice claiming hope in the midst of darkness through small acts of response at the end of the service—lighting a candle, writing a note of encouragement, or giving to a special offering.

Proper 26 (All Saints'): The Work of Waiting
Habakkuk 1:1–4; 2:1–4

O Lord, how long shall I cry for help, and you will not listen? Or cry to you "Violence!" and you will not save? Why do you make me see wrongdoing and look at trouble? Destruction and violence are before me; strife and contention arise. (Habakkuk 1:2–3)

While we tend to focus on the passages that comfort and soothe us, the Scriptures are brimming with verses that give voice to the darkest parts of our human experience. Too often in the church, we make it seem as if the life of faith means sidestepping those moments, but the Bible is brutally honest about how difficult life with God can sometimes be. There are passages throughout the Scriptures that witness to unanswered prayer, soul-crushing doubt, and the pain of feeling forgotten. Many congregations mark All Saints' Day this Sunday, and while those remembrances can certainly be sweet, there will likely be a great deal of unresolved grief and anger sitting in the pews as well.

In addition, the news cycle can seem a bit apocalyptic these days, and the more cynical we all become about the world, the more evidence we will find to confirm those suspicions. But sometimes there is good news hidden in the bad news, in learning to speak the language of our faith during broken times. In fact, the very word "apocalypse" simply means "revealing." The gospel reveals a larger narrative, hidden beneath and beyond the brokenness of this world. Faith in Christ is not a fragile worldview that avoids the jagged edges of real life in order to preserve an unsustainable optimism. It is the way of the cross. What God has promised is to be with us through the trials of this life, not to exempt us from them.

The prophet Habakkuk writes during a time in which all that once was has been lost. The religious landscape is eroding, the people have forgotten who they are and Whose they are, and Habakkuk's prayers seem ineffective. He speaks for all those who are grieving a world that seems to be moving in the wrong direction—a world of escalating warfare, indifference to faith, and a God who is far too silent. This is more than bemoaning the loss of the "good old days." This is a man who wonders if his God will ever speak again. Does any of this sound familiar?

The text concludes with the call to wait, which is a tremendous act of faith. Waiting implies that there is something worth waiting for, and while we don't characterize waiting as a virtue, perhaps we should. While we often think of waiting as a passive activity, waiting in Scripture always involves a commitment and conviction, a willingness to stand firm even when the evidence suggests it's not worth it. One of the most important themes of the Bible is learning to trust that God is at work, even when we cannot see it—learning to believe that God is still speaking, even when we cannot hear it. Most of the Bible was penned during times of exile and persecution, and in some ways it is best understood by the brokenhearted and the hopeless. Habakkuk frames for us what we find so often in the Holy Scriptures: a prayer life so intimate that he models for us the full range of human emotion before God. God can handle all of what we are feeling, even when we cannot.

It's only when we are honest about the bad news that we can hear the full power of the gospel, that "there is still a vision for the appointed time," and "it will not be late" (Hab. 2:3), even though it feels long overdue. In the meantime, the work of hope is learning to wait.

Proper 27: Skipping to the End
2 Thessalonians 2:1–5, 13–17

Brothers and sisters, we have a request for you concerning our Lord Jesus Christ's coming and when we are gathered together to be with him. We don't want you to be easily confused in your mind or upset if you hear that the day of the Lord is already here. (2 Thessalonians 2:1–2)

I am guilty of flipping to the final pages of a novel (especially the suspenseful ones), in order to be assured that all will be made well. Otherwise, I'm not sure I want to invest my time in the story. The Thessalonians seem likewise to have jumped the gun just a bit. As some of the oldest texts in the New Testament, the correspondence with the Thessalonian church gives us a peek into what the earliest followers of Christ were struggling with following his resurrection. At issue is Christ's return, which seems imminent, and as one might imagine, this causes a bit of chaos in the community. Rather than a state of panic or fear, however, it seems the Thessalonians have settled into a state of withdrawal from the world. Other voices have added confusion by suggesting that the Day of the Lord has already arrived, some even going so far as to forge letters from Paul to that effect. The expectation of Jesus coming back imminently changes the way they look at daily life. What is the point of going about your daily work if history is coming to a close?

While this might seem strange to us modern folk, our world seems just as obsessed with its demise, as is evidenced by the amount of pseudo-Christian material on the topic, as well as the various groups that have garnered their fifteen seconds of fame by declaring that the end is near. A quick glance at the fiction bestsellers reveal our obsession with dystopian futures, peddling in the idea that civilization as we know it has almost hit its expiration date. At the same time, most mainline Christians avoid talk of the apocalypse, and perhaps cringe just a bit when our distant cousins in the faith seem unable to talk about anything else. But what might Paul's words to the Thessalonian church say to us today, even those of us who aren't up to date on the latest ancient Mayan prophecy?

At its heart, the Christian teachings about the close of history are words of radical hope. While some Christians now obsess about the monsters in Revelation and read the world news for the coming signs of doom, what the New Testament is clear about is that God is uncontested in having the final word. The Christian witness is that the story finally belongs to God, and at the close, all will be made well. Earth will not be destroyed for the sake of heaven, but earth and heaven will be indistinguishable. God will finish what was started at creation, and make all things new. One can understand why the Thessalonians were a little anxious to drop the curtain, because a sprint is always more manageable than a marathon. It's easier to pull off a burst of faith than it is to manage the day-to-day work of ordinary discipleship.

But the work of being a Christ-follower is learning to hold heaven and earth in tension, at least until they collide in history's final act. That means being actively engaged in this world, taking it seriously, while also believing that we are minor characters in a grand drama, and the narrative is going somewhere. How do we live faithfully in the middle of the story, those of us who look with hope to what lies on the last page?

Proper 28: Full Disclosure
Luke 21:5–19

Then [Jesus] said to them, "Nation will rise against nation, and kingdom against kingdom; there will be great earthquakes, and in various places famines and plagues; and there will be dreadful portents and great signs from heaven. But before all this occurs, they will arrest you and persecute you; they will hand you over to synagogues and prisons . . . because of my name." (Luke 21:10–12)

Jesus does a pretty miserable job of leading the new members class. Rather than leading with the promise of heaven or even the fair-trade coffee in the fellowship hall, he launches into just how bad it's going to get for those who choose to follow him. There will be wars, rebellion, famine; even the sky will seem to come apart. The faithful will be taken hostage, abandoned by their families, even executed. This, Jesus says, is what you are signing up for.

These words sound rather odd from the predictable confines of our Sunday morning worship experiences, but we do well to remember that they were true for many of Luke's early readers, as well as some modern Christians in places around the world. In the sanctuary where I preach most Sundays, the dominant architectural feature is a beautiful piece of stained glass, shaped like a rose, adorned with the signs of the twelve apostles. We are very proud of it, and we make sure to put it on every bulletin, every church cookbook, every pamphlet we produce. I am fond of pointing out these days that the bulk of those apostles' symbols are the method by which they were executed. Again, it's a strange way to welcome people to the faith: "So glad to have you, but in full disclosure, this is what you're signing up for." But it's the truth—faith demands your life, even if you don't give it all away at once.

The most compelling evidence of the resurrection is the church itself, that those who proclaimed Christ was alive believed so boldly in what they preached that they were willing to give their lives for it, to stand before the powers that be and trust that, even then, they would know what to say. While our faith may seem far too tame to bear any familial connection to those martyrs of old, we do well to remember that every time we gather for worship, we gather to proclaim a word that was passed on through the courageous faith of others, who clung to their hope under the most extreme circumstances possible.

"Everyone will hate you because of my name," Jesus tells us. Perhaps this is why so many Christians avoid texts like these, because it's hard to relate to those who gave their lives for their faith when our greatest challenge is staying awake for the sermon. But the lesson here is twofold, even for those whose faith seems to require less of us: (1) the world is broken, and what happens here does not always reflect the will or intention of God; and (2) our faith calls us into those broken places, not away from them.

For those of us whose faith will never be immortalized in stained glass, who will never stand before a firing squad for our Savior, and who are sometimes guilty of turning a blind eye to the suffering of this imperfect world, the bill for our discipleship may not come due in one dramatic payment. But make no mistake, we are called to the same courageous hope, paid in infinitesimal daily installments—one foot after another, following where he leads.

Proper 29 (Reign of Christ): Proving Who You Are
Luke 23:33–43

One of the criminals hanging next to Jesus insulted him, "Aren't you the Christ? Save your-self and us!" (Luke 23:39)

Over the last few weeks, we've been talking about how to cling to our faith in difficult times, how to remain hopeful even when the headlines conspire to steal our hope away. It's fitting that we close this series by turning to what is simultaneously the darkest moment in human history, and the one from which we draw our greatest hope.

Today is the culmination of the Christian calendar, the climax to which the entire story builds, the day on which we announce that Christ is Lord of heaven and earth. It's striking then, that the lectionary carries us to a dump on the outskirts of town, where the stench of death hangs heavy and flies buzz around the dying bodies of criminals. But this is exactly where we belong, on this day of all days, because this King we have come to crown is unlike any other, and his throne will be a cross—which helps to explain why most of the people around him cannot see him for who he is.

Jesus' public ministry begins with a declaration from the heavens, God's own voice declaring him beloved at his baptism. But that declaration is immediately tested. He is driven into the wilderness by the Holy Spirit to learn a lesson that will undergird his entire ministry, perhaps the most important lesson of all, if he is to complete his mission. That lesson is learning to recognize the voice of the tempter, because rather than trying to seduce Jesus with any of the lesser temptations that might derail the rest of us, the tempter plays to the doubt that will surround Jesus the rest of his earthly life: "If you are the Son of God, prove it."

That voice does not disappear when Jesus emerges from the wilderness after forty days. Outside Caesarea Philippi, Peter declares Jesus to be the Messiah, the one for whom they have prayed. It is a powerful moment, and Peter's bold confession leads Jesus to name him as the rock upon which the church will be built. But then the conversation turns, as Jesus begins to explain exactly what that means. And when

Peter, the newly designated chief of the apostles, hears talk of suffering and a cross, he tries to talk some sense into Jesus. Surely, this is not what being the Messiah means. If they were surprised by his earlier remarks, the disciples are even more shocked when Jesus so quickly turns on Peter, as if he has seen a ghost. Because Jesus recognizes the devil of the desert.

And here, at the end, what was a whisper in the wilderness becomes a chorus of voices, demanding proof. "He saved others—let him save himself!" What they cannot see is that it is precisely the salvation of others that keeps him from saving himself. "If you really are the Son of God, measure up to our expectations!" The religious leaders, the soldiers, even one of the thieves join in the refrain: "If you are a king, act like it."

But meanwhile, as he did in the wilderness, Jesus plays to an audience of One. As they shout their taunts, he whispers forgiveness. As the breath is choked out of his own lungs, he promises paradise to the broken soul who hangs next to him. This is not the proof anyone was looking for, because this is not the king they were looking for. But make no mistake, this is a coronation.

On this, the climactic close of the Christian year, we are exactly where we belong. In the presence of our Savior, who still marches into the middle of all our misguided expectations, who still offers his life for the sake of those who don't know what they are doing. It's here, at the cross of our King, that we too must challenge all the voices that demand we prove who we are. For the only voice that matters has already spoken. The King of kings has given his life to call us beloved.

May we have the strength to remember it—wherever the road carries us.

Calendar of Sundays

This nine-year calendar enables you to plan for up to three lectionary cycles, as well as to observe some of the variation in the liturgical seasons. Due to the varying dates of Lent, Easter, and Pentecost, the seasons of Epiphany before and Ordinary Time after can vary in length. Therefore, you may see blanks in this calendar, denoting Sundays that are not observed in a particular year. For those Sundays that are observed only one or two of the three cycles included in this calendar, you may see "stand-alone sermon" in place of a series sermon. Stand-alone sermons are also suggested for certain weeks between series to allow for special services, a preacher's vacation, or to address a topic independently of a longer series.

YEAR A

SUNDAY	SERIES	2019–20	2022–23	2025–26
First Sunday of Advent	Waiting Well (Part 1)	Dec. 1	Nov. 27	Nov. 30
Second Sunday of Advent	Waiting Well (Part 2)	Dec. 8	Dec. 4	Dec. 7
Third Sunday of Advent	Waiting Well (Part 3)	Dec. 15	Dec. 11	Dec. 14
Fourth Sunday of Advent	Waiting Well (Part 4)	Dec. 22	Dec. 18	Dec. 21
Christmas Eve	Waiting Well (Part 5)	Dec. 24	Dec. 24	Dec. 24
First Sunday of Christmas	*Stand-alone sermon*	Dec. 29	Dec. 25	Dec. 28
Second Sunday of Christmas (Epiphany Observed)	Gifts That Keep On Giving (Part 1)	Jan. 5	Jan. 1	Jan. 4
First Sunday after Epiphany	Gifts That Keep On Giving (Part 2)	Jan. 12	Jan. 8	Jan. 11
Second Sunday after Epiphany	Gifts That Keep On Giving (Part 3)	Jan. 19	Jan. 15	Jan. 18
Third Sunday after Epiphany	Gifts That Keep On Giving (Part 4)	Jan. 26	Jan. 22	Jan. 25
Fourth Sunday after Epiphany	Gifts That Keep On Giving (Part 5)	Feb. 2	Jan. 29	Feb. 1
Fifth Sunday after Epiphany	Gifts That Keep On Giving (Part 6)	Feb. 9	Feb. 5	Feb. 8
Sixth Sunday after Epiphany	Gifts That Keep On Giving (Part 7)	Feb. 16	Feb. 12	
Transfiguration Sunday (last Sunday before Lent)	Gifts That Keep On Giving (Part 8)	Feb. 23	Feb. 19	Feb. 15
First Sunday in Lent	Heart-to-Heart Talks (Part 1)	Mar. 1	Feb. 26	Feb. 22
Second Sunday in Lent	Heart-to-Heart Talks (Part 2)	Mar. 8	Mar. 5	Mar. 1
Third Sunday in Lent	Heart-to-Heart Talks (Part 3)	Mar. 15	Mar. 12	Mar. 8
Fourth Sunday in Lent	Heart-to-Heart Talks (Part 4)	Mar. 22	Mar. 19	Mar. 15
Fifth Sunday in Lent	Heart-to-Heart Talks (Part 5)	Mar. 29	Mar. 26	Mar. 22
Sixth Sunday in Lent (Palm Sunday)	Heart-to-Heart Talks (Part 6)	Apr. 5	Apr. 2	Mar. 29
Easter Sunday	Heart-to-Heart Talks (Part 7)	Apr. 12	Apr. 9	Apr. 5
Second Sunday of Easter	Building Blocks (Part 1)	Apr. 19	Apr. 16	Apr. 12
Third Sunday of Easter	Building Blocks (Part 2)	Apr. 26	Apr. 23	Apr. 19
Fourth Sunday of Easter	Building Blocks (Part 3)	May 3	Apr. 30	Apr. 26
Fifth Sunday of Easter	Building Blocks (Part 4)	May 10	May 7	May 3
Sixth Sunday of Easter	Building Blocks (Part 5)	May 17	May 14	May 10
Seventh Sunday of Easter	Building Blocks (Part 6)	May 24	May 21	May 17

SUNDAY	SERIES	2019–20	2022–23	2025–26
Pentecost Sunday	Building Blocks (Part 7)	May 31	May 28	May 24
Proper 4	*Stand-alone sermon in 2023 and 2026*		June 4	May 31
Proper 5 (Trinity Sunday in 2020)[1]	Family Reunion (Part 1)	June 7	June 11	June 7
Proper 6	Family Reunion (Part 2)	June 14	June 18	June 14
Proper 7	Family Reunion (Part 3)	June 21	June 25	June 21
Proper 8	Family Reunion (Part 4)	June 28	July 2	June 28
Proper 9	Family Reunion (Part 5)	July 5	July 9	July 5
Proper 10	Family Reunion (Part 6)	July 12	July 16	July 12
Proper 11	Family Reunion (Part 7)	July 19	July 23	July 19
Proper 12	Family Reunion (Part 8)	July 26	July 30	July 26
Proper 13	Family Reunion (Part 9)	Aug. 2	Aug. 6	Aug. 2
Proper 14	Family Reunion (Part 10)	Aug. 9	Aug. 13	Aug. 9
Proper 15	Family Reunion (Part 11)	Aug. 16	Aug. 20	Aug. 16
Proper 16	*Stand-alone sermon*	Aug. 23	Aug. 27	Aug. 23
Proper 17	*Stand-alone sermon*	Aug. 30	Sept. 3	Aug. 30
Proper 18	Learning to Love Our Enemies (Part 1)	Sept. 6	Sept. 10	Sept. 6
Proper 19	Learning to Love Our Enemies (Part 2)	Sept. 13	Sept. 17	Sept. 13
Proper 20	Learning to Love Our Enemies (Part 3)	Sept. 20	Sept. 24	Sept. 20
Proper 21	Learning to Love Our Enemies (Part 4)	Sept. 27	Oct. 1	Sept. 27
Proper 22	Thriving (Part 1)	Oct. 4	Oct. 8	Oct. 4
Proper 23	Thriving (Part 2)	Oct. 11	Oct. 15	Oct. 11
Proper 24	Thriving (Part 3)	Oct. 18	Oct. 22	Oct. 18
Proper 25	Thriving (Part 4)	Oct. 25	Oct. 29	Oct. 25
Proper 26 / All Saints' Observed	Entrusted (Part 1)	Nov. 1	Nov. 5	Nov. 1
Proper 27	Entrusted (Part 2)	Nov. 8	Nov. 12	Nov. 8
Proper 28	Entrusted (Part 3)	Nov. 15	Nov. 19	Nov. 15
Reign of Christ Sunday	Entrusted (Part 4)	Nov. 22	Nov. 26	Nov. 22

1. Trinity Sunday is observed the Sunday following Pentecost and takes the place of the Proper that would fall on that Sunday (which could be Proper 3, 4, 5, or 6). In 2020, this is Proper 5, as reflected in this resource. In 2023 and 2026, Trinity Sunday will take the place of Proper 4 and require some adjustment to this series plan.

YEAR B

SUNDAY	SERIES	2020–21	2023–24	2026–27
First Sunday of Advent	Where We Belong (Part 1)	Nov. 29	Dec. 3	Nov. 29
Second Sunday of Advent	Where We Belong (Part 2)	Dec. 6	Dec. 10	Dec. 6
Third Sunday of Advent	Where We Belong (Part 3)	Dec. 13	Dec. 17	Dec. 13
Fourth Sunday of Advent[2]	Where We Belong (Part 4)	Dec. 20	Dec. 24	Dec. 20
Christmas Eve	Where We Belong (Part 5)	Dec. 24	Dec. 24	Dec. 24
First Sunday of Christmas	Where We Belong (Part 6)	Dec. 27	Dec. 31	Dec. 27
Second Sunday of Christmas	*Stand-alone sermon in 2020 and 2026*	Jan. 3		Jan. 3
First Sunday after Epiphany	Created Anew (Part 1)	Jan. 10	Jan. 7	Jan. 10
Second Sunday after Epiphany	Created Anew (Part 2)	Jan. 17	Jan. 14	Jan. 17
Third Sunday after Epiphany	Created Anew (Part 3)	Jan. 24	Jan. 21	Jan. 24
Fourth Sunday after Epiphany	Created Anew (Part 4)	Jan. 31	Jan. 28	Jan. 31
Fifth Sunday after Epiphany	Created Anew (Part 5)	Feb. 7	Feb. 4	
Transfiguration Sunday (last Sunday before Lent)	Created Anew (Part 6)	Feb. 14	Feb. 11	Feb. 7
First Sunday in Lent	The Power of Sacrifice (Part 1)	Feb. 21	Feb. 18	Feb. 14
Second Sunday in Lent	The Power of Sacrifice (Part 2)	Feb. 28	Feb. 25	Feb. 21
Third Sunday in Lent	The Power of Sacrifice (Part 3)	Mar. 7	Mar. 3	Feb. 28
Fourth Sunday in Lent	The Power of Sacrifice (Part 4)	Mar. 14	Mar. 10	Mar. 7
Fifth Sunday in Lent	The Power of Sacrifice (Part 5)	Mar. 21	Mar. 17	Mar. 14
Sixth Sunday in Lent (Palm Sunday)	The Power of Sacrifice (Part 6)	Mar. 28	Mar. 24	Mar. 21
Easter Sunday	Living in a Postresurrection World (Part 1)	Apr. 4	Mar. 31	Mar. 28
Second Sunday of Easter	Living in a Postresurrection World (Part 2)	Apr. 11	Apr. 7	Apr. 4
Third Sunday of Easter	Living in a Postresurrection World (Part 3)	Apr. 18	Apr. 14	Apr. 11
Fourth Sunday of Easter	Living in a Postresurrection World (Part 4)	Apr. 25	Apr. 21	Apr. 18
Fifth Sunday of Easter	Living in a Postresurrection World (Part 5)	May 2	Apr. 28	Apr. 25
Sixth Sunday of Easter	Living in a Postresurrection World (Part 6)	May 9	May 5	May 2
Seventh Sunday of Easter	Living in a Postresurrection World (Part 7)	May 16	May 12	May 9

2. When the Fourth Sunday of Advent falls on Christmas Eve, use Advent 4 sermon for morning worship and Christmas Eve sermon for evening services, or simply eliminate the Advent 4 sermon.

SUNDAY	SERIES	2020–21	2023–24	2026–27
Pentecost Sunday	Living in a Postresurrection World (Part 8)	May 23	May 19	May 16
Proper 3 or Trinity Sunday	*Stand-alone sermon in 2024 and 2027*	May 30	May 26	May 23
Proper 4	More Than Meets the Eye (Part 1)	June 6	June 2	May 30
Proper 5	More Than Meets the Eye (Part 2)	June 13	June 9	June 6
Proper 6	More Than Meets the Eye (Part 3)	June 20	June 16	June 13
Proper 7	More Than Meets the Eye (Part 4)	June 27	June 23	June 20
Proper 8	*Stand-alone sermon*	July 4	June 30	June 27
Proper 9	Everyday Prophecy (Part 1)	July 11	July 7	July 4
Proper 10	Everyday Prophecy (Part 2)	July 18	July 14	July 11
Proper 11	Everyday Prophecy (Part 3)	July 25	July 21	July 18
Proper 12	Everyday Prophecy (Part 4)	Aug. 1	July 28	July 25
Proper 13	*Stand-alone sermon*	Aug. 8	Aug. 4	Aug. 1
Proper 14	Soul Food (Part 1)	Aug. 15	Aug. 11	Aug. 8
Proper 15	Soul Food (Part 2)	Aug. 22	Aug. 18	Aug. 15
Proper 16	Soul Food (Part 3)	Aug. 29	Aug. 25	Aug. 22
Proper 17	Soul Food (Part 4)	Sept. 5	Sept. 1	Aug. 29
Proper 18	A Good Life (Part 1)	Sept. 12	Sept. 8	Sept. 5
Proper 19	A Good Life (Part 2)	Sept. 19	Sept. 15	Sept. 12
Proper 20	A Good Life (Part 3)	Sept. 26	Sept. 22	Sept. 19
Proper 21	A Good Life (Part 4)	Oct. 3	Sept. 29	Sept. 26
Proper 22	A Good Life (Part 5)	Oct. 10	Oct. 6	Oct. 3
Proper 23	Take Up Your Cross (Part 1)	Oct. 17	Oct. 13	Oct. 10
Proper 24	Take Up Your Cross (Part 2)	Oct. 24	Oct. 20	Oct. 17
Proper 25	Take Up Your Cross (Part 3)	Oct. 31	Oct. 27	Oct. 24
Proper 26 / All Saints' Observed	More Than Enough (Part 1)	Nov. 7	Nov. 3	Oct. 31
Proper 27	More Than Enough (Part 2)	Nov. 14	Nov. 10	Nov. 7
Proper 28	More Than Enough (Part 3)	Nov. 21	Nov. 17	Nov. 14
Reign of Christ Sunday	More Than Enough (Part 4)		Nov. 24	Nov. 21

YEAR C

SUNDAY	SERIES	2021–22	2024–25	2027–28
First Sunday of Advent	Boundless (Part 1)	Nov. 28	Dec. 1	Nov. 28
Second Sunday of Advent	Boundless (Part 2)	Dec. 5	Dec. 8	Dec. 5
Third Sunday of Advent	Boundless (Part 3)	Dec. 12	Dec. 15	Dec. 12
Fourth Sunday of Advent	Boundless (Part 4)	Dec. 19	Dec. 22	Dec. 19
Christmas Eve	Boundless (Part 5)	Dec. 24	Dec. 24	Dec. 24
First Sunday of Christmas	Boundless (Part 6)	Dec. 26	Dec. 29	Dec. 26
Second Sunday of Christmas (Epiphany Observed)	Living with Joy (Part 1)	Jan. 2	Jan. 5	Jan. 2
First Sunday after Epiphany	Living with Joy (Part 2)	Jan. 9	Jan. 12	Jan. 9
Second Sunday after Epiphany	Living with Joy (Part 3)	Jan. 16	Jan. 19	Jan. 16
Third Sunday after Epiphany	Living with Joy (Part 4)	Jan. 23	Jan. 26	Jan. 23
Fourth Sunday after Epiphany	The Art of Hearing (Part 1)	Jan. 30	Feb. 2	Jan. 30
Fifth Sunday after Epiphany	The Art of Hearing (Part 2)	Feb. 6	Feb. 9	Feb. 6
Sixth Sunday after Epiphany	The Art of Hearing (Part 3)	Feb. 13	Feb. 16	Feb. 13
Seventh Sunday after Epiphany	The Art of Hearing (Part 4)	Feb. 20	Feb. 23	Feb. 20
Transfiguration Sunday (last Sunday before Lent)	*Stand-alone sermon*	Feb. 27	Mar. 2	Feb. 27
First Sunday in Lent	Character and Calling (Part 1)	Mar. 6	Mar. 9	Mar. 5
Second Sunday in Lent	Character and Calling (Part 2)	Mar. 13	Mar. 16	Mar. 12
Third Sunday in Lent	Character and Calling (Part 3)	Mar. 20	Mar. 23	Mar. 19
Fourth Sunday in Lent	Character and Calling (Part 4)	Mar. 27	Mar. 30	Mar. 26
Fifth Sunday in Lent	Character and Calling (Part 5)	Apr. 3	Apr. 6	Apr. 2
Sixth Sunday in Lent (Palm Sunday)	Character and Calling (Part 6)	Apr. 10	Apr. 13	Apr. 9
Easter Sunday	Character and Calling (Part 7)	Apr. 17	Apr. 20	Apr. 16
Second Sunday of Easter	Living with the End in Mind (Part 1)	Apr. 24	Apr. 27	Apr. 23
Third Sunday of Easter	Living with the End in Mind (Part 2)	May 1	May 4	Apr. 30
Fourth Sunday of Easter	Living with the End in Mind (Part 3)	May 8	May 11	May 7
Fifth Sunday of Easter	Living with the End in Mind (Part 4)	May 15	May 18	May 14

SUNDAY	SERIES	2021–22	2024–25	2027–28
Sixth Sunday of Easter	Living with the End in Mind (Part 5)	May 22	May 25	May 21
Seventh Sunday of Easter	Living with the End in Mind (Part 6)	May 29	June 1	May 28
Pentecost Sunday	Living with the End in Mind (Part 7)	June 5	June 8	June 4
Proper 5 or Trinity Sunday	*Stand-alone sermon in 2028*			June 11
Proper 6	Called In (Part 1)	June 12	June 15	June 18
Proper 7	Called In (Part 2)	June 19	June 22	June 25
Proper 8	Called In (Part 3)	June 26	June 29	July 2
Proper 9	Called In (Part 4)	July 3	July 6	July 9
Proper 10	Called In (Part 5)	July 10	July 13	July 16
Proper 11	Called In (Part 6)	July 17	July 20	July 23
Proper 12	Called In (Part 7)	July 24	July 27	July 30
Proper 13	*Stand-alone sermon*	July 31	Aug. 3	Aug. 6
Proper 14	Final Instructions (Part 1)	Aug. 7	Aug. 10	Aug. 13
Proper 15	Final Instructions (Part 2)	Aug. 14	Aug. 17	Aug. 20
Proper 16	Final Instructions (Part 3)	Aug. 21	Aug. 24	Aug. 27
Proper 17	Final Instructions (Part 4)	Aug. 28	Aug. 31	Sept. 3
Proper 18	RE:boot (Part 1)	Sept. 4	Sept. 7	Sept. 10
Proper 19	RE:boot (Part 2)	Sept. 11	Sept. 14	Sept. 17
Proper 20	RE:boot (Part 3)	Sept. 18	Sept. 21	Sept. 24
Proper 21	RE:boot (Part 4)	Sept. 25	Sept. 28	Oct. 1
Proper 22	Four Prayers That Don't Work (Part 1)	Oct. 2	Oct. 5	Oct. 8
Proper 23	Four Prayers That Don't Work (Part 2)	Oct. 9	Oct. 12	Oct. 15
Proper 24	Four Prayers That Don't Work (Part 3)	Oct. 16	Oct. 19	Oct. 22
Proper 25	Four Prayers That Don't Work (Part 4)	Oct. 23	Oct. 26	Oct. 29
Proper 26 / All Saints' Observed	It's the End of the World . . . (Part 1)	Oct. 30	Nov. 2	Nov. 5
Proper 27	It's the End of the World . . . (Part 2)	Nov. 6	Nov. 9	Nov. 12
Proper 28	It's the End of the World . . . (Part 3)	Nov. 13	Nov. 16	Nov. 19
Reign of Christ Sunday	It's the End of the World . . . (Part 4)	Nov. 20	Nov. 23	Nov. 26

Contributors

Kyle E. Brooks, ordained in the Church of God in Christ, is a native of Detroit, Michigan, a current PhD candidate at Vanderbilt University, and a visiting assistant professor at Methodist Theological School in Ohio. His work has previously been featured in *Church on Purpose: Reinventing Discipleship, Community, and Justice*.

Amy K. Butler is Senior Minister of The Riverside Church in New York City. Her sermons and essays appear on her blog, www.talkwiththepreacher.org, and on the website of the Associated Baptist Press.

Carol Cavin-Dillon is the Senior Pastor of West End United Methodist Church in Nashville, Tennessee. She has written for *The Abingdon Preaching Annual*, the *Upper Room Disciplines*, Cokesbury's *Adult Bible Study* series, and *Circuit Rider* magazine.

Magrey R. deVega is the Senior Pastor at Hyde Park United Methodist Church in Tampa, Florida. He is the author of several books, including *Songs for the Waiting: Devotions Inspired by the Hymns of Advent*, *Embracing the Uncertain: A Lenten Study for Unsteady Times*, and *One Faithful Promise: The Wesleyan Covenant for Renewal*.

Brian Erickson is Senior Pastor of Trinity United Methodist Church in Birmingham, Alabama, and author of *The Theological Implications of Climate Control: Reflections on the Seasons of Faith*.

Mihee Kim-Kort is an ordained Presbyterian (PCUSA) minister. She most recently authored *Outside the Lines: How Embracing*

Queerness Will Transform Your Faith. Her writing and commentary can also be found at *TIME, BBC World Service, USA Today, Huffington Post, Christian Century, On Being, Sojourners,* and *Faith and Leadership.*

Jasper Peters is the founding pastor of Belong Church, a United Methodist church plant in the heart of Denver, called to inclusivity, diversity, and justice. He writes about science fiction and religion, and the power and potential of the church on the margins.

Tuhina Verma Rasche is an ordained minister of Word and Sacrament in the Evangelical Lutheran Church in America. Her articles have been featured in *Inheritance, Bearings Magazine* with the BTS Center, and a number of publications within the Evangelical Lutheran Church in America on preaching, spirituality, and identity.

Bruce Reyes-Chow is an author, speaker, parent, consultant, coach, and pastor. He speaks and writes on issues of faith, technology, race, parenting, and church culture. Bruce welcomes interaction via @breyeschow on most social networks or at www.reyes-chow.com.

Brandan J. Robertson is the Lead Pastor of Missiongathering Christian Church in San Diego, California. He is the author of or a contributing author to eight books, including *Nomad: A Spirituality for Traveling Light* and *True Inclusion: Creating Communities of Radical Embrace.*

Martha K. Spong is the Executive Director of RevGalBlogPals, an ecumenical ministry creating community and resources for clergywomen. A United Church of Christ pastor, she is a clergy coach, a contributor to The Present Word, and the coauthor of *Denial Is My Spiritual Practice (and Other Failures of Faith).*

Anthony J. Tang is the pastor of Desert Mission United Methodist Church in Scottsdale, Arizona. He has worked as the Director of Connectional Ministries for the Desert Southwest Conference and has served on the Board of Directors for his denomination's General Commission on Archives and History and General Council on Finance and Administration.

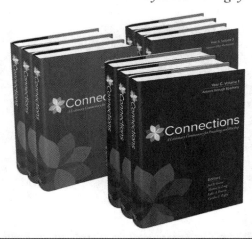